Quotes from Readers

"*Lovely, tender, moving, funny, love stories.*" Linda.

"*Publish and be damned.*" Nigel.

"*You can't do this.*" Dave.

"*Quite funny actually.*" Tom C.

"*Brought back so much. Page turner.*" Alice B.

" *Incredibly detailed and honest. Awesome.*" Cathy Zara

"*I Laughed out loud.*" Catriona.

"*The fluidity, style, grace of your writing. Amazing, wonderful, terrible.*" Prof. Janet Newman.

"*Good luck. Got to go and cook for the masses.*" Patrick.

"*Honestly Michael, I don't know why you want to disinter these half-remembered grievances and ancient slights.*" Tina.

Permissions

Extract from "*Changes In The City*", Communities #5 (1973) used by permission. All back issues are available from www.ic.org/communities.

Extract from "*The Four-Gated City*" reprinted by permission of Harper Collins Publishers Ltd., ©Doris Lessing 1969.

Extract from "*A Voice*" by Tadeusz Rozewicz, used by permission.

Credits

First published in Great Britain in April, 2019
by McConnell & Co.
McConnellChaos@gmail.com.
© Mike Reid 2019

ISBN 978-1-5272-3760-5

Printed and bound by Print2Demand

Design: ©Joan Curtis 2019
Cover Illustration © Clifford Harper 2019

Mix Café

A memoir of Laurieston Hall, 1972-77

To Jude
With love
Mike x

Mike Reid

Foreword

Mix Café is a Memoir about living communally at Laurieston Hall, from 1972-1977. It's a personal statement, as close as I could write it to what seems to me to be the truth, but it is more or less guaranteed to annoy some of my co-communards, who will have entirely different and certainly contradictory personal visions.

As we go to press (2019), Laurieston Hall continues to be home to the Laurieston Hall Community, no longer communal but closer to a co-housing situation. Of the people mentioned here, Alice, Lesley, Richard and Patrick are still residents and they and many others have now lived there for decades.

There are no photos or other visual images here.

A wonderful selection of such images, together with assorted, upbeat reminiscences can be found in "*WOW: A Celebration Of Laurieston Hall*," edited and designed by Tiffy George and published in March 2013. (ISBN 978 0 9575748 0 9).

1

March 1972

Laurieston Hall was this immense, pink-pebble-dashed, Victorian manor house. Early-spring sunlight swirled down the green-slated bell of the tower, cascaded off the roof, splashed past the portico and finished on the lawn with a thirties song and dance number. Clouds of daffodils curtseyed from the long grass. The lime and the ash, the oak and horse-chestnut, gave slight, formal bows. It was warm for March.

The whole scene was pure Walt Disney. I should have known better.

We gathered across the main lawn, by the ash. Stuart with his long straggly beard and pixie hat. Paul, running up from photographing everywhere: the walled garden, its quadrants neatly ploughed, the cottages, stables, laundry, beech mound and so forth. I carried Paul's clipboard of notes. Maureen, five months pregnant, had an armful of daffs and a smile for the camera.

'But it's so *massive*,' says Maureen, 'It's so.' We looked back and thought: Wow!

It had taken two hours to tour the indoors. The celebrated 65 rooms, richly silent. Just our whispers hanging in the air.

'Could have the kids' playroom here.'

'Perfect for a workshop.'

'Maybe make this our main room, for meetings.'

'Be nice to have a proper darkroom.'

Alice, Tina and Gerry had made the same long haul north the previous week. 'Huge,' they'd said, 'You'll have to see for yourselves.'

'First-class condition,' Paul breathed, 'storm guards on the top-floor windows.' Paul the Architect. I liked him a lot. In Spring, '72, we were mentally still in the late sixties, when everyone was beautiful.

'Great for the Regional Arts Centre idea,' Stuart cut in.

'Tongue and groove flooring throughout,' Paul beamed, 'brass door fittings.'

'And the Alt. Tech. Project,' Stuart's voice over. He was another architect, more into grand plans than details. A bit crazy. Nice-crazy.

'What do you think,' I asked the sky.

'Fantastic,' said Paul and Stuart.

I can remember the little shiver, the bubble of a laugh. Could we really live here, in this fairytale palace? The idea was enticing, but scary too.

Paul drove us back along the grand, beech-lined main drive and through the village, leaving behind a big orange sunset. Then across to Carlisle and south down the M6. Next to him, Stuart rehearsed the latest eco-horror stories. The peregrine falcon population had gone negative, or you could walk across Lake Erie. I wished he'd shut up. Stuart's line on the Imminent Total Collapse of Consumer Society - and the implication that we might ourselves avoid the worst - annoyed me. It was silly. If there was no food in the towns, people would come looking. But I was glad Stuart was with us. He fizzed with ideas. I like people who do.

In the back seat, Maureen, whom I hardly knew, slept peacefully, her head resting on my lap. Serene Maureen. Underneath, where we couldn't see it, was a megavolt panic.

At Maureen and Gerry's place in Leeds, we reviewed the competition. Local rumours said a local farmer - Farmer Henty - wanted the stables; Glasgow University, a Research Centre; and some businessman, a caravan site.

Paul, Stuart and Gerry talked house prices, square feet, kilowatts, land prices, acres, miles, population drift and average wind speed. I didn't follow - and I'm the most numerate one.

We totalled up the theoretical cash for the n'th time. The house was up for tender and if we bid, it would be binding. There were four days left. We decided we could manage £25,500, the odd £500 being 'for luck.'

There was a teensy idea getting lost here. The notion that we would property-shop just to give us a focus for deciding things like whether we really wanted to live together and if so how, and to do what, and what for. But this big house was so compelling. We had fallen in love with it. Falling in love: always a recipe for heartache.

Hurried goodbyes, small hugs, and I drove Paul and Stuart back down the M1 to London. I remember finding you at 3.a.m., frazzled by the children, and, on top of that, laid out with a sudden flu. But still awake. I was hyper, myself.

'Amazing, eh?'

'Oh, it's a beautiful place, our Michael.'

'But a long way from our friends. And we're still such an odd group.'

'Smashing for the kids, though.'

'But at least it wouldn't be, you know - just the Four Of Us.'

'And it's only the lowlands,' you croaked to the Roy Orbison tune. With a feeble smile.

'So shall we go ahead?'

We met the next evening in Alice and Paul's open-plan kitchen living room. I was taken with the style of it. Glossy hardboard on the floor. Hand-made kitchen units with rounded corners. Moulded plywood circular table, ditto chairs. Shiny white - Swedish! - teacups that stacked up, just so. Very different from our own shabby-tat, rag-bag lifestyle. I thought it reflected Paul's personal concern with form and function. Much later, I realised it was house-style for Architectural Association alumni that year.

You were still dopey with flu, sprawled across an armchair. The kids were rioting. Paul refereed. Stuart made tea. His wife, Veronica, was away to her family, and hadn't seen the house.

'But is Veronica sure she wants to go ahead?' I pressed him.

'Absolutely,' said Stuart. I believed him. Stuart, with his strong features and drip-dry confidence, could have sold condoms to the Pope.

Alice, in a long dress, dark hair down to her waist, waited by the phone. Something warm and breathless flapped slowly round the room. It was now or never. Gerry rang from Leeds on schedule.

Alice shouts: 'Hi, yes, what have you and Maureen? *Sonya!* Hello? Have you decided? Sorry did you say? *Shut Up, Sonya!* Quite keen? Yes, hello. Yes, well we're all keen too. What? Stuart can go ahead then. Fine. Yes. Love to Maureen.'

We were tired, running on cider and adrenalin, our private thoughts out-shouted by the kids' pandemonium and we had no real understanding of the implications of what we had done. But we had made the basic decision. 'By consensus,' we would say, with vague pride.

After Stuart put in the bid, the waiting was agony. If we lost, it would mean more slogging round the country. But if we won - would the parachutes open? And what if we'd bid much too much? I pictured a bar-room full of lawyers and accountants, opening the sealed bids and cackling when they came to ours. It was a tense two weeks.

Finally, in mid-April, Stuart phoned round: 'We've won.'

The London Lot held a celebration evening at Paul and Alice's, inviting prospective joiners and friends. Paul showed his slides and we passed round the first of the handouts:

Laurieston Hall is a huge, 65-room Victorian manor house in Galloway, South-West Scotland. There is a 1.5 acre walled garden with two long greenhouses, a pond, some lawns and woodland; about 12 acres in all. There are stables, which need repair, and

two cottages. The surrounding countryside - lochs, moorland,
mountains and the sea - is a knockout.

Then came the questions. How did you hear about the house? How many are there of you? What are your aims? How much was it? How could you afford it? How did you all meet? What do you do? Are you all vegetarian? How does the group make decisions? How much land is there, exactly? Won't it be awfully cold?

This was exciting at first, to be the centre of so much attention. Fielding the same questions - the Standard Visitor Questions or SVQ's - will become a little wearing.

The guests drifted away, also Stuart and Veronica. I remember Veronica looking tired, very pale and doubtful. Leaving the Four Of Us. The Originals. Time for Tina and me to go home. Or for Paul to go off with Tina while I stayed with Alice.

We pretty soon have some answers off pat:

The people are Paul and Alice and their two children, Sonya, going on 5 and Polly, just 2. Paul works for Camden Council. Alice has been a lab technician and a secretary.

Mike and Tina have two children, Joel nearly 4 and Sophie, 2½. Mike's a computer consultant, Tina used to be an advertising copywriter ('knockout' was her word).

We got together through Tina and Alice, who met in the Tufnell Park Women's Consciousness-Raising Group. Our first meeting was at Tina and Mike's. Mike had made lamb and apricot on rice but, sadly, Paul had just come out vegetarian.

Stuart knows Paul through the Architectural Association. Veronica's doing an Open University course. No kids.

Gerry teaches sociology at the Jacob Kramer College in Leeds, Maureen's another housebound mum, their children are Zoe, 4 and Jemma, 2 and Maureen's pregnant. We met through friends of friends.

No, Scotland wasn't anyone's first choice. Devon was favourite. But Laurieston came up by a series of fluke connections and it seemed perfect. No: it's supposed not to be cold. Gatehouse, nearby, on the coast, has palm trees growing. It's the Gulf Stream does it. Rains a lot, apparently.

Yes, it's enormous. We're not too sure of the history. Been a house there for centuries, called Clachanpluck. The present building dates from 1897 and was built for a businessman called Laurie, who renamed it - and the village. Been used as a TB hospital during the war and since then as an NHS old people's home. Been empty for 18 months.

We bid £25,500, which'll come from selling our houses. Gerry and Maureen are selling cheap to a friend, but the rest of us will get market prices less the mortgages. It's this property boom. Wonderful thing, capitalism, don'tcha know.

We do have Aims, but they're rather complicated.

'Be nice to know how much you topped the other bids by, wouldn't it?', is the follow-up. 'Oh. it doesn't really matter now, does it,' we lied.

We were committed. Life became frenetic. It was hard to keep in touch. Gerry's job kept him in Leeds, and Mike was commuting to Antwerp - what's a hot-shot common-market consultant doing in a story like this? Weekends, we lugged children, their paraphernalia, books, pamphlets and our weary selves up and down motorways. Our 'wind of change' stank of rubber and petrol.

Before, we had long, jokey, fluid discussions. Alice wanted a Peaceful Garden: Gerry wanted Mahler over loudspeakers. Mike suggested selling up after a year or two and moving to Chile, Allende's Chile it was then. Stuart babbled about creating a Regional Arts Lab and a Free School. And we talked, hesitantly, about adults having a room each. Nobody actually said 'smash the bourgeois nuclear couple' but that notion was out there - and in our minds.

Now, it was all Group Meetings, capital G, capital M, focusing on Housing Association frameworks, budgets and earning our living. Raising the money became a nightmare. Veronica, always on the fringes, faded out altogether. Cornered, Stuart admitted they were splitting up and no, his half of their money wouldn't come through in time. Mike and Tina's house was CPO'd for an extension to the next-door school. And Maureen wanted to stay in Leeds until after the new baby was born, so their money would be late, too.

We needed more people, preferably with money. Enter Dave, Carol and their new baby daughter, Tiffany. Carol was an interior designer, Dave a computer systems analyst (Mike thought they might work together). They were in a street theatre group, and already lived in a collective house, just over the road from Paul and Alice's - to which their money was loaned, but they hoped to get it out. They joined us after another quick meeting and a phone call to Gerry and Maureen (which seems incredible in retrospect - these days, there are probationary periods).

Life was a TV sit-com. Tragedy and belly-laughs predominated over moments of tenderness and insight. All taken at the pace of a moonshot countdown and with the obligatory cliff-hanger every week - will Tina and Mike's house get its full market price? Can Gerry and Maureen get a bridging loan? If we don't raise the cash in time, does Stuart go directly to jail?

Do you remember our trip up to Laurieston that June, when we camped by the pond, and talked about the others?

We liked Gerry best. He was a politico - 'libertarian, I think' - like us, he didn't know what to call himself, exactly. 'Revolutionary' was too pretentious. 'Socialist,' of course, but not in a sectarian way. He was clear and articulate, talked of decentralising society, organising at grass-roots level, of 'not dropping out, but dropping in.' Committed, then, but funny too. Made deadpan quotes from Thurber.

'Yeah, he's the most PLU,' you said. People Like Us. After twelve years together, we often spoke in shorthand. And Maureen was - probably OK. We didn't know much about Maureen except that the children ruled her life. And that she wasn't in a women's group.

But Stuart's hopeless, we agreed. No clue about working with other people (without consulting anyone he'd applied for planning permission for an Art Gallery, Cafe, and Community Centre which, in frenzied calls to the Planning Department, we'd hurriedly scratched, submitting instead a one-line application for residential use). 'And all his hobnobbing with landowners and lawyers and finance companies,' I said. 'And there's his debts,' you said. I stood up and mimicked, him: "I'm" - pause - "anarchist - possibly," - longer pause - "socialist, certainly". You laughed and said, 'Yeah, he hasn't got a clue, politically.'

And Dave and Carol. You were the more caustic: 'Their endless super-8 films! And Carol's not a feminist, you know.'

We had a wood fire going and J&S were asleep in their tent. Little trout splashed on the pond and moorhens were nesting. The big conifers on the hill up to the Kennels cottage took the edge off the breeze and it was too early in the year for midges. Ten o'clock and still light. Paradise. I loved you.

'And at least it won't be just The Four Of Us,' we said again.

'The Fractious Founders,' I offered.

'The Fulsome Foursome,' you countered.

Paul and Alice were kind, reliable, generous and competent and we had started this strange thing with them - 'husband-swapping,' you called it - with some enthusiasm. Gosh, the novelty of it at first! I remember we talked about everything, even the fucking. Paul was 'keen to get it in, but then he stays still and sort of wriggles'. Alice 'doesn't come at all like you do.' It was fun, and exciting, and we were sexual revolutionaries, weren't we? Jealousy wasn't an allowable response and indeed, I don't remember we felt any.

We liked Paul. He'd been to meetings of a Marxist Housing Action group. When we moved, he wanted to set up a Building Project and help people self-build, using recycled materials and solar power. I thought he was pretty Radical. 'Radical' was my word for myself at the time - also 'libertarian socialist,' 'armchair anarchist,' and a 'supporter of women's liberation' - or 'feminist,' except that this word was too newly re-discovered, and no-one was sure whether a man could be one.

We agreed Paul was a little weird. One moment he'd be in a boiler suit, Paul the carpenter, plasterer, plumber, car mechanic. Or in a pinny, making the most delicate omelettes. But the next - 'that's never Paul, is it' - he'd be scissoring hips-first into a party, wearing a long white dress, his mane let down his back, half of bitter taken and beaming, gormlessly handsome, fit to burst his specs across the room. 'Such a gentle guy,' people would remark. I thought so too, until he punched me hard, in the mouth, four years later.

And we liked Alice. Sometimes severe-looking and, you'd point out, a bit Upper Middle (but, common irony, with leftish parents while mine were Tory). This was Alice of the Lycée Francaise. But a Reliable. And with a wonderfully vulgar, cackling laugh. And of course, being in your women's group, politically right-on.

But the idea of living with just the two of them, which we'd talked about the previous Autumn, before The Group came together, was too claustrophobic. We were leery of it. And this making love stuff - we wanted, not sure what, maybe to dilute it, slow it down, maybe stop it altogether.

'The, er, Fumbling *Four*nicators?'

'The Quondam Quartet,' you concluded. You'd always cap me in these exchanges. I could win arguments, which usually did me no good at all.

'And anyway,' we agreed, 'Maybe the people don't matter.' More shorthand. We meant it in the particular. We didn't think we were so special. Free schools, wholefood co-ops, underground magazines, political theatre groups, eco-housing experiments and so forth were mushrooming and we thought communal living - not necessarily rural - was part of this, an idea coming to its time, part of building an Alternative Society. Before long tens, hundreds or even thousands of groups like ours would be springing up. 'We could easily have fifty people here,' I said. 'Or we could move to join another group,' you replied.

'It's still so light,' you observed. I remember looking at you, beautiful droopy-tits (your word), Barkerchops (mine), over the campfire. I remember - indeed I cling to these reference points - feeling happy and relaxed with you. And I am absolutely certain we were, at that moment, not only friends and lovers but comrades, if you like, with shared ideas. So when you wrote recently that you *'followed my lead'* into communal living and multiple relationships, I was both furious and utterly disoriented.

I eventually grew to like Dave a lot. Have hardly spoken to Gerry since that first summer when he left so abruptly.

June and July danced by at the same clip. More motorway excursions, but we never did manage a meeting all of us together. We circulated reams of Personal Statements, Draft Constitutions and Project Plans which have since lain unread, except by this obsessive archivist. And news and gossip. 'Maureen is getting very big.' 'Dave and Carol have decamped to Cheltenham, for Dave to work out his notice.' 'Carol is pregnant again' - so we'll be nine adults with nine children all under five years old. Madness!

At the last minute - imagine a theatrical Phew! - the money came through. Gerry and Maureen borrowed from Maureen's Dad. Paul's father presented Paul and Alice with a big, old Land Rover, surplus from his building firm, and a cheque which evened out the absence of Stuart's money. Mike and Tina's house got close to its valuation. Carol and Dave chipped in £200 to be going on with. The deal went through - after some nail-biting nightmares of solicitor's mistakes on the timing - with Alice, Tina, Maureen and Carol as the registered owners (which upset Stuart). We even had a surplus of capital (which will be the topic of innumerable meetings).

The night before we moved, we went to a farewell party at Dom and Cissy G's. So drove up north with hangovers longer than the M6. You hardly speaking and both Joel and Sophie whinging the whole way. Forward to the revolution! (It occurs to me I'm about-faced these days: trying to set the past to rights).

Finally there we were, "awed and exhausted," you wrote later, "at 8 p.m. on the 29th July 1972, a group of people who hardly knew each other and to whom the local environment, culture, economy, language even, were totally alien."

We slept, camped out in the grand first-floor bedrooms, like explorers in a lost city.

2
March 1977

Imagine five years on.

Laurieston Hall in the Stewartry of Kirkcudbright, S.W. Scotland, is the home of 14 adults, 10 children, and assorted cattle, horses, poultry, pigs, cats and dogs. The surrounding sunsets are a knockout.

The slides Paul took on that first visit show the house empty and clean, the lawns mown and with neatly-clipped edges, the grounds and the drive tidy and the garden, ploughed, bare earth.

By now, the hedge at the road-end has become overgrown. The beech-lined main drive is rough, pitted, gap-toothed. Part of the stables roof has caved in and its yard is full of car wrecks. The back of the house is an obstacle course: mounds of stone, brick, scrap metal, plastic, rusty bicycle frames and other broken machinery. Domestic litter and kids junk is everywhere. Inside the house, although people's individual rooms are worked-on, distinctive and beautiful, the communal spaces are a mess - just barely functional.

But the front of the house has a 'WOW' sign - Julian G. scavenged the letters from the local Woolworths. The walled garden is fabulous and, last summer, brimmed with produce. The greenhouses have been repaired and radiate a dazzling white. Sections of the land are fenced off and cropped or pastured. Neat stacks of logs punctuate a saunter round the grounds.

And here is your actual anarcho-feminist, eco-commune ready for a sunny new day.

Tina leads Beulah from the lush new grass to the milking parlour. Other early risers do Sun Salutation on the front lawn. Lesley lays breakfast for the Big Flame conference visitors. Catriona puts thirty loaves-worth of dough to rise.

Shoes, boots, clogs and bare feet clap the lino. The house is packed. Breakfast is for 110 people, counting the residents.

After breakfast, the house hums. Conference people get into their workshops. Tina finishes up the dairy work, separating the cream for butter, sterilising pails, recording Beulah's yield: three gallons, good for an

Ayrshire (Hega, the Jersey, isn't in milk, having lost her calf prematurely).

Robbie, the new baby, nuzzles at Meg, his mother. Paul, his father, goes off to Lothlorien where he's designed and is helping build their massive communal log-house. Richard feeds the pigs. Alice supervises the making of her classic Laurieston lunch - thick veg soup, puréed through the Mouli and served with a blob of yoghurt, lemon juice and grated cheese. Plus fresh baked rolls, grated carrot and slices of beetroot.

In the pottery, Bridget is open for business. Jay, Linda and Jonathan plant potatoes. Dave and Catriona service the Land Rover. Patrick does whatever beekeepers do. Tim works on the new poultry shed.

Our children, who are in a communal bedroom phase again, have their own leisurely breakfast then wheel away like starlings. They're 'de-schooled,' which should mean they take as full a part as they can in the workaday round, learning as they go.

Sometimes they do, sometimes they don't. Today they play on rafts on the pond.

Coffee time will see a meeting to consider the Education Authority's latest peremptory missive. Our Free School is "not efficient." We are to send the children back to the village school or else. Again, we explore the alternatives. Setting up our own school, formally? A more structured programme of 'lessons', to please the inspectors?

Here is Laurieston thriving, full of life, smiles everywhere. Idyllic.

But that's with the rose-tinted glasses. Behind the smiles there is anger, depression, alienation and loneliness. Alice is into her shell. Carol and Julia have left, to live nearby with their new partners. Mike has been mad for a year. Says he hasn't left, but has been away for months, paying only flying visits home. The smart money says he won't come back. At least while Tina is with Jay.

Mike is holed up in Dumb Tom's cottage, Bentham, near Lancaster.

From his window, he can stare at Ingleborough, which, Sphinx-like, is quite prepared to stare back impassively until the end of the epoch.

Catriona just brought down his entire remaining worldly goods: tenor sax, typewriter, some books, tapes and records but nothing to play them on, case of clothes, walking boots, three boxes of notes. These now fit in the back of a Citroen Ami. Whereas when Mike and Tina moved to LH, their belongings filled a pantechnicon. Mike contemplates taking this as progress.

He's a student in the Peace And Conflict Research Programme of the Politics Department of the University of Lancaster.

The official argument is along the lines that: Planetary Peace is not about to break out in the coming academic year; Peace Research obviously focuses on national and international tensions and conflicts, especially The Cold War (the chilling notion of 'Catastrophe Theory' comes into this somewhere); International problems map onto the interpersonal and vice versa; If we can't get along together, what hope is there?; Collective Living provides some insights here and deserves to be treated as a research area by the P&CRP of the PD of the U of L.

But also: what a neat wheeze, to get a grant for being away from Laurieston Hall, while remaining fixated by it and writing about it, which is what he would be doing anyway.

His two main obsessions are: Whether or not he has left: Whether he and Tina will ever get back together.

Jonathan and Joel are passing through and Joel, now nearly nine, says: 'But Dad, you live here now, you've got your sax here and everything.'

Mike plays with Titles for his Thesis.

'The New Communes: A Participant/Observer (PO) Case Study.' He likes the idea of 'the PO'. Also the Present Author (PA) and Sam are other alter egos which will no doubt feature later in this epic.

Also a runner: 'The Radical Commune: Slow Progress at Laurieston Hall: A Sideways Approach.'

The Radical Commune is where the PA might go next, if it existed. Laurieston Hall Version 2.

He also likes to get silly.

'Anarchism For Fun And Profit.'

'The Alternative Society: Ephemeral, Escapist or Essential? (Sub-title: An Everyday Story Of Hippie Folk.)'

'On going bananas.'

'Feminist Communities, 1972 - 77 - A Male Perspective.'

These prompt Tom C. - Mike's academic supervisor, friend and owner of Dumb Tom's, but no relation to the original dumb one, to say, with some exasperation, 'Michael, I think you should get serious.'

Last night, full moon, there was a Bentham Food Co-op meeting and Tom C. introduces new participant Mike. Your 24-carat alternative lifestyle-person. Mike feels the wave of curiosity to be mixed with a bit of needle. He realises people want to hear Communes Don't Work.

'I gather you don't have communal childcare up there,' says this guy who has lived forever in contented nuclear suburbia.

Mike falls for it. 'Yes we do,' he says,' we just don't have rotas, so visitors can't see it. For example. Joel, my son, was here the other day, travelling around the country with Jonathan.'

And he's off, hurdling the contradictions, won't hear a word against The Group. He's launched on another panegyric when the man catches him with 'Oh, I see, so Why Did You Leave?'

Why Did You Leave? being the biggest SVQ of them all

Collapse of stout party. See Mike wriggle, clench his shoulders, screw his face up and dodge. 'I haven't left,' he says, 'I'm on parole.' Ha Ha. Dear Reader.

Suppose you're in a relationship and some stranger demands to know: 'Is it a success?' or 'Does it work?' or 'Are you totally monogamous?' You might find this a teeny bit intrusive, right? And the questioner - insensitive, or what?

Or if you've had a relationship go shaky and you've been through the multiple double binds (love/ hate, can't stay/ can't go, etc.), then you wouldn't welcome bluff questions like: 'Well, have you left yet or what?' or 'What exactly is going on?'

Indeed, you might need - might even get - some sympathy.

And then again, when you really have split up from someone, then the 'So Why?' isn't usually helpful, even if it's well-meant, is it? It might even be a little upsetting?

I just want you to know that when someone lives in a commune - has many relationships with many people - feels them all go pear-shaped - then leaves all of them - they have much the same response. In spades, redoubled. So you might be circumspect about asking: *'Why Did You Leave?'*

The dedicated student, Mike writes incessantly. He invents statements of the Group Aims, which the P&CRP is very keen to know. Ditto, Group Decision-Making. Plus chronological notes on Group membership, visitors, visitor groups, the Projects; and Relationships, that's a biggie. Footnotes, introspections, cautionary tales. Letters home, to Tina, to The Group, both alternately loving and spiteful. Et cetera, et bloody cetera.

In all of his boxes of notes, Mike has, sadly, no statement of the Group's 'Aims'.

We never had such a thing. On the other hand, we all had quite clear personal needs and desires, which Mike begins to piece together.

The Aims.
The men wanted to give up their day jobs, didn't they? And stop being 'breadwinners.' Paul wrote: 'I think it's important that we all want to live with children - this seems to be a main motive for living together as a community.'

16

And the women, to stop being full-time mothers and housewives; isolated, dependent and tired all the time.

Everyone wanted to 'Make a good place for the children,' 'Live on a lot less money,' 'Share Resources,' 'Pool our skills' and 'Be more creative.'

Beyond these common directions, Alice and Gerry wanted to become gardeners, Dave and Carol were keen to develop the smallholding/ model farm idea and Paul and Stuart would carry on being architects, wouldn't they, but helping people design and build their own homes.

Paul, Dave and Gerry also wanted a 'Building Project' and Gerry wanted to set up a Health Food shop in Castle Douglas. Maureen would have wanted some peace and quiet, wouldn't she just? And Stuart probably wanted us to be a major node on the Intergalactic Alternative Network.

'Alternative' was the 'in' word at the time. Alternative Lifestyles, Alternative Technology, Alternative Communes.

Mike and Gerry were pre-occupied with the 'wider implications of what we are doing' - sanctimonious creeps. But Mike did want to spend more time with his children. Tina had in mind a 'Holiday Project For Under-Privileged Kids' and, Mike's notes say, wanted 'fun, games and jollity.' And 'an alternative Butlins.'

To Tina, Mike writes:
"Dear Group. I love some of you. Are you going to come and visit me? Or are you all tied up with The Hall, and with Jay? I would like the kids here with me for a while, is that OK?"

To The Group, Mike writes:
"Dear Tina. This morning I browsed around Tom C's remarkable library. There is endless stuff on Anarres (a fictional planet), Astrology, The Bagwash sorry Bhagwan Shree Rajneesh (sayings of), Bio-Rhythms (I do try to be open-minded but this does strike me as a particularly unprovable, self-fulfilling, cloying, pseudo-scientific bucket of pigshit), Future Shock, The Goddess, Herbal Tea mixes, Meditation, Mushrooms, Shiatsu, 'Sitting,' Surviving the End Of Growth, Primal Pain (releasing your reservoirs of), Yoga, and Zen (and the arts of dairying, bicycle maintenance and not pushing the river).

"Nothing on Communes and what to do if you, er, aren't getting on with yours.

"So what I do, in fact, is bash the piano a lot.

"I still don't think of myself as having left. I feel sort of squeezed out. I'm just having some time off. I hope you won't take any of the big decisions, like new people joining, without me (I'll come back up for special meetings...)"

The Aims.

The PO identifies three different levels.

First, the few stated aims were individual and personal and often made a virtue of necessity. For example giving up professional jobs implied living more cheaply. And for the women to share in work projects, men would have to do more childcare.

Second, there was always the political dimension. Living more cheaply would imply less consumption, less dependence on The System, less exploitation of the Third World; 'stepping more lightly on the planet.'

And we would be 'Putting Women's Liberation into Practice.' This, if we had to choose, would have been our main mantra. But there were many others. We were flooded with 60s/70s rhetoric. 'Make Work Fun.' 'Productive play, creative work.' 'The personal is political.' We had a slogan for everything.

But 'Self-sufficiency,' interestingly, was never an aim.

Third, there was the meta-political: the notion that we should somehow be exemplars: *'if everyone lived this way'* - we'd have a whole different society. We didn't expect that - how many 65 room mansions are there? - but we did think that a sizeable chunk of our contemporaries would follow us. They never did.

Bastards.

'Pure Bourgeois Escapism,' Len the Leftist would say. We had no shortage of LTLs.

'If your life is a prison,' we would reply, 'why aren't you trying to escape?'

Tina writes to Mike:

"Sometimes I feel bitter and betrayed - I've worked at this commune, worked at multiple relationships, despite pockets of distrust somewhere deep in my guts. I've done it, OK ineffectually, OK misguidedly, but with all my heart, but my total effort is invisible to you. I tried to please you and look at the mess you've got me into. And where are you? I hate you at these moments."

Mike is left disoriented, needing to seriously rearrange his world-view.

'Well, you cunt,' Mike replies - of course it's not right-on to use that word aggressively - 'where are you, if not with yet another man?

How do you make decisions?

The P&CRP people seem especially keen on this one. They don't ask how we survive financially, what we do, what sort of place we live in, nothing even about how we have survived the relationships shenanigans.

But: *How Do You Make Decisions?* as if we are some sort of debating society. 'Leaderless' groups and consensus decision-making map more comfortably onto their world view.

'Well, take conference cooking and bread-making,' says the PO. 'There's a sign-up list to make sure each day of the week is covered. The same applies to dozens of other jobs. Longer-term commitments, like milking, get taken on by people for months at a time. There's not much other organisation.' Somehow this bores them - they want to hear about 'conflict' and 'group dynamics.'

The PO cannot begin to explain how most of the matters which really affect the collective - example, who sleeps with whom; example, whose parents decide to pay for a foreign holiday - are all off-limits to collective decision-making processes.

Mike writes to The Group:
    "Darling, I miss you and think of you every day.
    "It's been five years and sometimes I think that even if we were thriving and developing, it would be time for us to split up and for me to move on. Or at least take a long break. But go where? And do what? Beyond the nuclear family and then beyond communal living, what is there?
    "I can't stay, I can't stand it anymore. The children unhappy and insecure and not learning in a way that will satisfy the Education Police. No collective work-projects, childcare, culture, creativity. Not co-operating on the way we use rooms and possessions and capital. No good times, no meetings, no theory and, most of all, apart from The Couples, our relationships have crumbled as completely as the stables roof.
    Well, you know the catalogue.
    "But I can't go, either. I can't launch myself from this bog, where the big problems slop and lurch like waterlogged tree-trunks.
    "Not knowing whether I'm leaving or staying, I've been vibrating hopelessly, based at Dumb Tom's but shuttling between here and The Hall, Grobdale, and London with my mind god knows where, off somewhere else on a long lead. My life seems such a mess. It's so hard to see my - our - hopes and dreams... um.
    "I could not finish that sentence.
    "I wanted to say how I've been feeling. Still not a total lack of hope, but powerless. I've been crying a lot.For each of you there is... well now, I was going to say, love. Caring, at least. Tina says it's the way I go on that brings you all down, maybe she's right - certainly the reverse is true - and I've been feeling remorseful and guilty and...
    "Angry, basically. Angry with each of you for quite specific reasons (same with the good feelings). Angry with Alice - sweet, vicious Alice - for asking, so coldly: 'Look, are you still using the kitty or what?' Code for: You've left the group. Why don't you simply vanish?

19

"What a lunacy those meetings were, when we talked about Constitutions and perhaps being able to expel someone, when all that's necessary is to freeze them out, ignore their sadness and silences, their pleas and pinned-up proposals, their shouts and tears: witness Stuart, Nicky.

"One longs for the interval of a few years, which might turn all this into warm nostalgia.

"No, I haven't left, by the way. I think I will write each of you an open letter. Don't know what else to do. I'm angry I have all these bad feelings and I think you all do but you're not saying. Angry that none of you are calling meetings (some of you never have). Especially angry that those of you who are 'coping' are, it seems to me, ripping off energy, living selfishly, uncollectively, unconstructively."

No response, of course, to this abuse. Dunno why I keep typing.

Stop Press: Patrick has left to stay at Crabapple pro tem. He doesn't like Tina being with Jay any more than Mike does. Meanwhile Jay, Tina and Jonathan are thinking of upping sticks, too, to go to London.

Jonathan, Mike's best male friend, who has nevertheless pinched Mike's room, leaving Mike's remaining bits and pieces out in the top floor corridor, writes: 'Why not give it a rest.' He means, stop brooding about Laurieston and get a life. Mike would love to, but is unable.

3

Summer 1972

*Laurieston Hall is a gigantic country house in the Stewartry Of
Kirkcudbright, S.W. Scotland. Besides the 65 main rooms, there are
dozens of walk-in cupboards and store-rooms, partitioned off bits
and loos. You could fit the fuselage of a Boeing 747 in the Hall, two
and a half London buses in the kitchen, or your average detached,
4-bed des. res. in Billiard Room. There are four staircases, five
counting the tower. It's quite possible to be lost inside it for weeks,
months or years...*

Waking in a strange room, I'm disoriented - then remember - of course, here
we are, we made it! Twizzling around, I'd disturbed you. Never a wise
move, you're often downright homicidal in the mornings. 'I'll fetch you a
cuppa,' I mutter.

I find my way down to the Old Kitchen, a mere fifty yards from our
bedroom. Only slightly further than the walk from our old house to the local.

Alice is already there. We kiss Good Morning. But she's looking
distracted: 'The Esse didn't stay in overnight.' I volunteer to relight it and
set out into the backyard to scratch together kindling and coal scraps. When
I return, Paul is cradling Polly in one arm, fitting an old-fashioned, round-
pin plug onto his posh kettle and muttering 'the house hadn't been re-wired
for years. It'll cost hundreds'. He's thin-lipped and furious. Not about the
wiring, but the way their removal men had dumped his and Alice's stuff,
any old how, over the floor of the Big Front Room.

'Cheer up Paul.' Pass the cyanide - I don't say that. Instead I rake out
the Esse, light some paper, add kindling, which blazes splendidly and top
it with coal. But too soon. The fire dies. Shit. Stuart turns up.

I say 'I'll just get more paper,' and Stuart says, 'Our top priority must
be a waste-paper store.' *Top* priority, is he serious? Carol appears, toting
Tiffy. Then Dave, rubbing his eyes and wearing the full-length patchwork
dressing gown which Carol made him. They are upset because stuff has
been stolen from their Land Rover the night before they left London.

I try again with the Esse. From a distance, Sonya, presumably lost, is
screaming at glass-shattering pitch and volume. Paul dumps Polly on Alice
and rushes off to soothe her.

Heat at last swells in the Esse. Carol produces bacon and puts some to sizzle in Paul and Alice's cast-iron pan. Paul, returning with Sonya, looks horrified and says to Carol, 'But I thought we'd agreed we wouldn't eat meat? Actually at this stage I don't think we'd agreed anything at all.

'Oh Paul, it's only *bacon*, says Carol, 'and I *am* pregnant.'

'Well, at least I wish you wouldn't use that particular pan,' says Paul, with his eyes closed.

Stuart re-enters: 'The little store beyond the scullery will be best.' 'Best for what?' asks Dave. 'Waste paper store,' says Stuart, impatiently, 'must start as we mean to go on. Recycle paper, metals, glass, plastics. Or maybe not plastics?'

Sonya gives another routine scream, Polly copies, Tiffy echoes. Yells ricochet off the acres of plaster. I pour two cups of tea but, fed up waiting, and grumpy, you turn up, steering Sophie and Joel. Bloody Hell. Communal living, here we come.

The Old Kitchen was, I ask you, 30 feet long by 22 wide by 14 high. The Esse, a two-ton range, was for a long while our only cooker (we'd left previous gas cookers in London - no gas supply here). There was a Hydresse water heater and an enormous hot-water tank, two giant 9' by 6' formica-topped preparation tables and a nine-foot-tall dresser which still left enough room for someone - Stuart demonstrated - to stand upright on top of it. Tina saying 'Christ, Stuart, come down off there, you'll kill yourself.' It was ridiculously big, this kitchen of a monster dolls-house. It was living in Brobdingnag. What are we doing here?

In this room, with its garish Rizla-Red ceiling and lurid, Camping-Gaz-Blue walls - cosy it wasn't - the Commune set up home. We brought in a few token rugs and armchairs and sat down to plan the day. And this became our first piece of communal structure: the Nine O'Clock Meeting.

Then Paul goes shopping in the Ami, doesn't he, taking Sonya and Joel. The rest of us spend the morning passing each other repeatedly with armfuls of possessions, slowly emptying the Big Front room. It's like a jumble sale in reverse.

We take our favourite, special things to our own rooms - hi-fis, records, photo albums, slide collections, un-read books. And electric blankets and paraffin and electric heaters - all ecologically unsound. Music blasted everywhere. My Horace Silver or your Vivaldi vied against Alice's Incredible String Band and Carol and Dave's Bob Dylan.

Paul comes back with round-to-square-pin adapters, Ordnance Survey maps, blackboard paint, chalk, garden fork, hoe, sledgehammer, two steel wedges, milk, a chop for Carol, hand-rolling tobacco for Mike, Tina and

Dave and Mars Bars for himself. Mike volunteers to look after the priced shopping list, thus electing himself Accountant for the next four years, a serious mistake. 'Also,' says Paul, who has seen the bank manager about a joint account for The Group, 'they're asking for a copy of our Rules.'

'Meetings will be held every two hours,' Mike proposes. Alice offers to send off something sensible and thus becomes Chairperson indefinitely.

That afternoon, we explore the grounds.

"A thing that bothered me at first," Tina wrote, "was people forever rushing in saying, 'Have you seen that sky,' or 'There are some amazing reeds down by the lock.' Unreasonably I'd always thought of those things as being unique and private between me and them and maybe other people didn't even notice. Now they were not only noticing but shouting about it. It seemed improper. A bit like seeing your lover making those familiar, special gestures to someone else."

By tea-time, the children are tired, whingy and clingy. I make toast soldiers and boiled eggs but Sophie objects to striped toast - made by putting the bread in a wire netting gadget over the Esse hotplates. Joel's egg is too runny, Sonya's too hard-boiled. Polly screams. Her egg must be made by Paul or Alice.

Ah well. We settle the kids down, spend time with them, then it's bath-time and bed-time. Finally we come back together for our first Laurieston Supper: brown lentils, Patna rice and stir-fried veg, made by Alice. We gabble away about possible projects. A Printing Press, a Community Newspaper, fish farming, adapting the wired radio circuits as an intercom/baby alarm system, a wholemeal bakery (from now on we only eat home-made bread and the kids come to call white sliced, 'party bread'), a minibus service to Castle Douglas and Dumfries, a Cinema Club and others, none of which there would ever be time for.

After supper, we call Gerry and Maureen to tell them we're here, we've made it through the first day. Just about. Exhausted, awed by the scale of the house, we go to bed early.

All that August, the picture is one of incessant movement.

Inside the house, a traffic of beds, mattresses, chests of drawers, tables, cardboard boxes, tea chests. Lost visitors. People trying to remember where they've put down a screwdriver or a book or a child's toy, and having to walk a hundred-yard loop to find it. People with that confusing feeling they've forgotten something more important. And Stuart frantically cataloguing. "2 washing machines, 2 fridges, 3 hoovers, 5 radios, 3 Hi-Fis, 3 TVs, 2 hair dryers, 1 electric blanket, 1 rotary power saw. Citroen Ami, big Land Rover, little Land Rover, Volvo; G&M still to come." What for? I asked him. 'Research,' he explained.

Then there's more exploration of the grounds and outbuildings and, beyond, the woods, Woodhall loch and the Meikle Dornell hill above Craig Farm, with its views. North to the big hills - Corserine and The Merrick - and South to Kirkcudbright and the sea beyond.

In the afternoons - we'd drive out into beautiful Galloway. Yes, drive - bus services being minimal and the Dumfries to Stranraer rail line, axed by Beeching.

Laurieston village itself was hardly more than a populated cross-roads. It had one shop, not stocking the Guardian; no call for it; The Village School, with two teachers and twenty pupils; and The Laurie Arms pub, which drew in people for miles around.

Castle Douglas, which, following the locals, we call 'CD', had a population of 4000. Three main streets, shops, an auction mart, half a dozen small hotels. A cinema with films three nights a week. Motto: 'Forward.' Quite the metropolis.

Twenty-five miles east of CD, Dumfries was a whole big city, with a Cash and Carry warehouse. We giggled at the novelty of shopping for 20-dozen packs of Weetabix, whole cheeses, 7lb. catering size tubs of marge, corn oil by the gallon, boxes of fruit, sacks of veg.

We ranged west beyond Newton Stewart, north to the wild Rhinns of Kells; and south to Kirkcudbright, where the sunsets are so striking they once spawned a whole school of sunset-painters. Beautiful Galloway was just that. Lochs, mountains, the sea, yet off the main tourist track. Perfect. Teatime in The Old Kitchen was always full of people excitedly telling everybody else of their latest discoveries. Brighouse Bay, Rascarrel Bay, and the most beautiful bay on the planet, Carrick. The Jacob Epstein and Henry Moore sculptures on the road from Crocketford to Dunscore. The hidden lochs - Loch Whinyeon, Loch Mannock.

But since we don't want 'work' and 'leisure', do we, those alienating categories of life in cap. soc. - we intend to mix it up, work for fun, play for real, cook for love, wash up for meditation, fuck for Peace - every trip has to have its justification.

So ferrying Joel Sophie and Polly to the playgroup in Crossmichael and fitting in the CD shopping is 'collective childcare'.

Calling on John and Morag A. at Kilquhanity ('Killy') school - 12 miles from us, past Kirkpatrick Durham on the Corsock road, or Ed and Val's smallholding beyond Twynholm, down near Kirkcudbright, or hanging out with Bill and Ben, wild ex-Londoners from the hills is 'making local contacts'.

Going swimming at Carrick, is 'a gardening trip' and involves bringing back a load of seaweed, or pig muck from Ed's. Similarly trips to Brighouse are 'firewood trips' - we scrounged scrap pine slabs from the Kirkcudbright sawmill.

I remember a balmy summer, laced with laughter, hugs, smiles and kisses and the exchanging of little presents. Salad Days. You remember Kids Tea, which was invariably awful. "The children," you wrote later in an article for Spare Rib, "clung to their respective parents like iron filings to a magnet, insisting: "I love *you* and *my* Mummy and *my* sister and *my* granny and *my* (string of distant relations)."

Come to think of it, the adults could be fratchety, too. I recall Paul snarling at Dave: 'I've mentioned it *several* times, the Sabatier knives have to be dried straight away after washing up or they'll rust.'

'I do try to remember,' says Dave, looking, with his sandy hair and big round glasses, like a choirboy caught stealing pennies from the collection, 'but you'll just have to accept me as I am.'

'If we can't even agree about the washing-up…' Paul goes on and rolls his eyes, not intending to look comical.

Ah well, it can't all be perfect. It's the New Commune, taking shape.

Not that we called it that. At first, we fought shy of being called a 'collective', let alone a 'commune.' It seemed like asking for trouble. Even so a Scots national daily, The Record, picked up the story and ran a 'Happy Hippy Hospital' front-page headline.

The editor of the Galloway News, the local paper, promptly rang Stuart, who laughed off the story. And Tina wrote some corrective PR - we were not a 'Hippy Commune', but 'The Laurieston Hall Group'. Responsible, professional families, moving away from the city, healthier for the children, educational and community projects in mind, hardly likely to be flighty and workshy. All very embarrassing. But obligingly enough, the Galloway News front page lead on the 18th August was: "Laurieston Hall Not Hippy Commune." This didn't stop the local lads calling round in the evenings with their carry-outs, hoping to meet some 'huppy women.' And when we called in The Laurie Arms, the tiny, packed bar would go awfully quiet. We'd buy a few bottles of Newcastle Brown and cans of McEwans and slink away.

Evenings, we'd sit about with the visitors - there were nearly always visitors - in the Old Kitchen. The talk would be of practical stuff:

The New Galloway Women's Rural want us to send a speaker.

Paul's parents are coming to visit, where shall we put them?

Up the Back Track there's a dam on the burn and a pipe which feeds down via the Mortuary to the pond. The Mortuary (the hospital's name of course, gruesome or what) was originally a hydro-power plant. Can we re-connect it?

Stuart says we should meet Mrs. Murray Usher, owns half Gatehouse apparently.

Mike has met Farmer Henty, who owns all the surrounding land. 'We met on the drive', says Mike, 'big, stout chap. He says "Ah. Hello. Don't think we've. Name's Christian Henty" and so I say "How d'ye do. Name's Michael Reid."'

Paul tells Stuart he should stop driving the big Landy like a sports car. The roads are rough. It'll burn out the tyres.

Two or three times a week, we communards would withdraw to the Morning Room for a Meeting. It was supposed to be our 'sitting room'. Or 'library' - its built-in shelves were full of our pooled paperbacks, all jumbled together.

We'd make a wood fire, but it never got really warm. It was the only small downstairs room in the main house, but it was miles from the Old Kitchen. Tea and Coffee got cold on the journey.

'So why don't we make a kitchen/ living room on the first floor, then?' - Mike kept asking.

The Meetings would usually be about How Are We Going To Make A Living?

Either way, evenings would often end with just the Four Of Us. Stuart would be out, Dave and Carol away to bed early. They'd only been together for eighteen months - we didn't realise how threatened they felt by our partner-swapping.

Usually, you'd give Paul a peck, and I would Alice, and we'd go off to bed in our nuke fam couples. But sometimes I'd play chess with Alice and after a few polite nothings, you'd go off with Paul. Then Alice and I would cuddle and climb the circular stairs, goosing each other on the way. In my whole life, chess was never more interesting.

I can't recall we ever talked about this, the Four Of Us. It just happened.

Sleeping with Alice meant another panic on waking - another unfamiliar room - the wrong colour of duvet (purple, where ours was blue-green).

After these nights, I'd sidle over to you for a kiss of reassurance, as would Alice to Paul. Then Alice would hug you and I'd hug Paul. Am I making this up?

I never worried then about our relationship, I assumed it would always be there. And I remember pangs that we weren't a family anymore. Communal rhetoric - and practice - was all very well, but I remember wanting us to have breakfast together, just you, me and J & S. Which wasn't practical.

Sometimes we'd walk, though, Joel holding your hand, Sophie up on my shoulders, up the Back Track, along the waterfalls of Kenick Burn and down to the ford. And gossip.

'Paul's such a long streak of misery, sometimes.'

'And so uptight about his stuff.'

'And Alice isn't a bundle of laughs, either'

'Maybe they're not getting on?'

'Paul goes on so about Dave. Behind his back. His wiring job on Tiffy's bedroom.'

'But he's right about that, though. Dave's too speedy.'

'They're always going to clash. Paul's so meticulous and perfectionist. But Dave's a fixer.'

'And Dave can be so dim, considering he's supposed have a first-class degree.'

'Yes, his 'model farm' idea. As if we are still living in Kentish Town. It's loopy.

'And anyway, turn us into a fucking zoo.'

'And Carol doesn't miss a chance to grumble.'

'Mm. Today it was - "Why do we have to have sheets and blankets when duvets seem to be standard issue round here."'

'They don't seem to realise, we've been together for ages, have worked for years and years and bought stuff. '

'Christ, they wouldn't be living here if it wasn't for us.'

'Still, they have a hard time with Tiffy. And Carol's quite heavily pregnant now.'

'And Stuart's still so weird.'

'He doesn't seem to realise we haven't come here to seek out the big land-owners.'

'He's lonely though . But you can't talk to him. I did try, on that London trip we took together, but he feigned sleep the whole way. If he's upset about Veronica, he's not saying.'

'It'll be great when Gerry and Maureen get here.'

We'd walk back via the marsh, perhaps pick a few of those tall, luxurious, frondy rushes, then back up Farmer Henty's field.

Gerry came with Zoe and Jemma for long weekends and he and Maureen finally moved in at the end of August, when Morgan, their new baby, was just six weeks old. We cooed.

It was a big communal event. Everyone helped carry their belongings up to Sunny Room, which we'd decorated for them. Alice and I carried several demi-johns of his home-made wine through to the cellar. Paul served

Laurieston Lunch - on the lawn. Then we strolled around the grounds together. Splashes of red on the maple, by the pond. Van Gogh corn in Henty's cornfield, green shoots under the stubble in his hayfields. Rosebay willow herb along the Long Drive. Rabbits on the skyline. 'It's so beautiful,' everyone keeps saying. Nine adults, eight children. We were thrilled to be, at last - and for the first time - all together. Except Maureen. Maureen wasn't thrilled at all.

We were organised. The Old Kitchen has several blackboards and pinboards. These cover: Announcements, CD Shopping trip plans, CD Shopping lists, Cash and Carry list, Jobs People Are Doing, Paul's list of Urgent House Maintenance Tasks, and all correspondence - both personal and collective. Slogans: "Defeat Gravity: Weigh less heavily on the Third World." "Sisterhood is powerful." "Control Your Own Life." And Messages: "Visitor Rate - 80p. per day," "Last one to bed turn out all lights." And the Kitchen Rota. 'Actually it's not a rota,' we explain to visitors, 'people sign up as they feel like.'

And we are busy. Gerry and Alice work in the garden, planting winter veg. Gerry builds compost boxes. Paul buys an aluminium extension ladder; Mike and Dave spend a few days using it to clear out leaves which are blocking the gutters. Paul surveys the roof timbers for dry rot and woodworm, cutting out and spraying the patches he finds. Carol builds perches in the stables for our first chickens - two dozen, point-of-lay birds, bought from Ed and Val. Dave hammers together a stall for Lucy, our first goat. Tina decorates her and Mike's room in a colour called Passion. Stuart is out.

And sometimes we 'do things as a group' - clearing overhanging shrubs from the beech mound, digging a rubbish pit, Saturday cleaning.

Sonya starts at the village school, taking it in her stride. Tina remembers the other children as clinging close to one or other parent and still playing the 'I Love' game, or claiming: "That's *my* Dads car. *Our* family doesn't do that. *My mum* says I can." But the PO remembers a lot of co-operation over being with the older ones, taking them on trips and making Kids' Tea. And everyone joining in search parties to find where Sophie and Polly, or Joel and Zoe, have wandered off to. Panicking in case they have drowned in the pond, fallen from one of the 40 upper-floor windows, electrocuted themselves or been suffocated by falls of furniture or mattresses. Once it took two hours to find Polly and Sophie - who were silently absorbed in painting Stage Room, upstairs in the West Wing, with marmalade. And laundry: staring doubtfully from the piles of nappies, clothes and bed-linen to the two washing machines, Alice and Paul's beginning to protest, Mike and Tina's downright erratic.

But the Kitchen Sign-up List works incredibly well. Every day, after breakfast, somebody washes up, bakes bread (we all learn how to make batches of a dozen wholemeal loaves at a time), makes lunch, washes up, makes Kids Tea - curiously, the addition of Zoe and Jemma makes the whole thing calmer - more institutional, perhaps - and makes supper for nine, often more. And does all this while everyone else trails in and out for cuppas and chat. And the phone rings. Distant friends, salesmen, 'movement' people - including weirdoes who say 'Hello, you don't know me but I've decided to join you. I'm in Castle Douglas. Can you come and pick me up?' To these, the reply is: 'You should have written first. We're not open to new members, it's too soon. You can stay one night. Try hitching.' On the wall, the Buddhist edict advises: "When cooking, just cook." Some chance.

We play. With friends visiting from London and Leeds, we sit about, swap jokes, laughs, chases, embraces and gossip. Too many friends to list, but the PO will single out John and Wisty H. Because, it turns out later, Gerry takes a walk in the woods with Wisty, to show her the hazel-nut trees.

We play kids games - sardines, and, one moonlit evening, hide and seek out amongst the trees and the fading rhododendrons and azaleas. Gerry reads aloud from his Thurber collection.

You pinned up a spoof of the Galloway News article, featuring "near-bearded Mr Michael Reid, 30, bonny bra-less mother of two Mrs Alice Simpson, 28, petite young brunette Mr Paul Simpson, 31, even petiter, lurex-thigh-booted, red-head Mr Stuart Haden, 29, youthful sociologist Mr Gerry Kennedy, 28, tossing his mane of golden shin-length hair and blushing, balding, ample-thighed Mrs Christina Reid, 30".

And though pleasure trips are a bit frowned on, I remember we snuck out, just the two of us, in the Volvo - I was so fond of that old Volvo - and did the grand tour. North past Woodhall Loch and Loch Ken, where world-record-sized pike lurk, to New Galloway. West to the Black Craig of Dee - you can't help loving the Scottishness of it all. Clatteringshaws where we stop, walk a bit and make exciting but uncomfortable love, alfresco. Minigaff's ancient forest. Then south and east round the Cairnsmore of Fleet, through Creetown to Gatehouse and back across the moors past Grobdale of Balmaghie.

And we have Meetings in Morning Room. Long, stiff, rambling meetings where, at the end the minutes say things like:

"Dave to approach Farmer Henty about stobs for fencing the tennis court. It'll be in his interest too."

"Chickens fine but Carol should have checked with a Meeting before buying them."

"Goat ditto but Dave ditto."

"Aluminium ladder was needed, but Paul ditto. £80 is a lot of money."

"How *are* we going to make a living?"

"Gerry and Tina concerned about the wider issues."

Maureen struggled to join in with all of this. I remember her looking as though she hadn't slept for a week, as she dragged herself and Morgan into a Nine o'clock Meeting, radiating exhaustion and despair. And ambivalence, because communal living wasn't what she wanted.

Gerry made no secret of the fact they weren't getting on. It was too soon for them to have moved - or too late. Their relationship was totally iffy, we realised. What Maureen really wanted was for her and Gerry to have their own little place in the country, where their marriage could be mended.

That one must have been everyone's fantasy at some point. The cottage with roses around the door, kids tucked up in bed, an Aga, gourmet peasant meals for two with home-made wine. In a land where everyone walks naked and the police are mainly called on to help old people cross the street, tra-la.

Sometimes she takes off in their Riley. 'Want company?' I asked her once. 'Not really,' says Maureen.

So we segue through September. With laughs, anger, tears and muddy boots throughout.

4

Spring 1977

At Dumb Toms it's still wild and wintry. Hailstones bounce under the kitchen door. The PO, wearing several sweaters, shuffles notes for his thesis, based on the SVQs.

And What Are Your Aims?
With neither design nor desire, we'd become archetypal, bourgeois nuclear families - precisely the life-style denounced by feminist, marxist, radical psych. writers as oppressive, exploitive, alienating and conducive to schizophrenia (they should see some communes, thinks the PA).

So we'd left behind secure, well-paid, professional lives (and insurance policies, pensions and the like) for a semi-chaos - fluid, disturbing and poor. Experts in big city living, we became bumpkins overnight. Cut off by hundreds of miles from our friends, we became each other's co-workers, co-communards and often, sole company.

We more or less gave up meat-eating and monogamy. We pooled all except a few private possessions. Our lives became public, written up in the tabloids and in 'Movement' magazines.

Living together, sharing everything, isn't easy. And we had no grand social project in mind. No leader, no guru, no Plan To Save The World, no specific political line, no fully-shared projects. As a group, we lacked a common culture. No music of our own. No myth.

We were plagued and blessed with tides of visitors. At least in their eyes, we metamorphosed from solid citizens into 'hippies', 'freaks' or even 'revolutionaries.'

We thought of ourselves as part of a movement, but from the start there were accusations of 'leaving behind the real struggle in the cities.' We tried bleakly to point out that the rural environment is where the class struggle began.

We clung to the notion that, out of all this, we would emerge saner, healthier, more loving. That we'd 'grow', emotionally, spiritually and personally (the PA remains stubbornly five foot six and a bit). We had individual and collective, permanent identity crises. It was alternately exhilarating and frightening.

For some, it was all too much: for others, never quite enough.

Now let's see, what were the Aims?

31

And Is It A Success?

Now this depends.

To the old and new friends, you say: 'Yes, very.' And smile and nod. And they say, 'Oh. Great.'

To the Agressives - the 'join-the-party-sell-the paper' socialists and the 'all men are rapists' les. sep. fems., who want to tell you why you've failed, you say: 'Just brilliant. My whole life is brilliant. *How's yours?'*

It's only to the genuinely curious and thoughtful visitor, who really wants to know, you say: 'Well we've achieved a lot, made our way, been fairly stable - but lots of things are a mess just now - what do you think?' And conversation continues into the night.

I Hear You Have Multiple Relationships?

Dear Alice, I often wish we had talked more about our *affair*, I suppose we should call it.

At first, I didn't *love you* and I wasn't *in love* either. I was much too scared of both. It seemed to me that *loving you* would be being unfaithful to Tina in a way that *just fucking* wasn't. But *making love* with you, besides being great, was also *being communal*. Plus I *fancied you*.

Later, you said you *'loved Paul in a funny kind of way'* and I think that's what I felt about you. Much later again - long after we stopped sleeping together - I realised I just plain *loved you* as ex-lover, friend and communard.

We're all connoisseurs now in these fine gradations, aren't we?

In London, it never felt quite right. Too tacit. I would drive (!) the three-quarters of a mile over to yours and after a brief natter about how things were going, Paul would slip out back to Tina.

But at LH, there we were, co-communards, sexual revolutionaries, ho hum. And, what, half-a-dozen times, it worked, the chess-playing business?

But we were just partner-swapping. We'd not 'dissolved the nuclear couple' – we didn't want to. And the children sure didn't like it. Polly would scream the place down in the mornings, finding me in your bed in Balcony Room.

I wish you weren't so fucking frosty just now. I wish you'd wash up on my beach here at Dumb Toms.

And How Did You Allocate Rooms?

Christ, they come at you sideways, these SVQs. Anyway. The Rooms. Ah. Teeny problem here. Alice, Paul, Tina and Mike had already spoken for four of the main, first-floor bedrooms (Balcony, Roses, Scribble, Passion). Stuart asked for the south-west-facing Sunny Room, but we pointed out that Maureen and Gerry would need it more than he did; he went huffily off to

Tower Room in the West Wing. Latecomers Carol and Dave, choosing from what was left, chose grumpily to go up to the smaller rooms on the top floor.

So at first we had Alice Paul Tina Mike on the first floor, Carol and Dave somewhat separate, Stuart out on a limb. The PO notes that initially, the physical space modelled the social relationships.

'We're the poor relations, alright,' Carol will think for a year or more. Until we all realise that the top floor rooms, with their dormer windows and low, angled ceilings are altogether more interesting, warmer in winter, and generally desirable. Then there's a competition for the top-floor rooms.

And Do You All Sleep With Each Other?
Yep, we confirm. We have a rota. Everybody sleeps with everybody. Visitor's jaw drops. We say: only kidding.

How Did The Rooms Get Their Names?
We should have made this into a figure-it-out-yourself quiz. But since you ask. Some were the original names, taken from the defunct bell-board system for calling servants - Morning Room, Billiard Room. Yes, we are aware that these are ruling class descriptions, thank you, but we've decided to co-opt them. Other bell-board names never stuck: The Big Front Room was never "The Ballroom". "The Dining Room" became Tony's Room then Tony's Old Room then Flight Deck. Some descriptions were the NHS's - Matron's Sitting Room, Nurses Dining Room. Our own additions came from colour of paint (Passion), existing wallpaper (Roses), what the kids did (Scribble), what visitors did (Seaview - Flick A.'s painting of wavelets), wishful thinking (Warm Room, located over the Old Kitchen) and Patrick's attempt at plumbing (Waterfall). Naming and renaming rooms was part of the, er, fun.

But What Are Your Aims?
We had enough individual statements of 'purposes,' 'motives,' 'expectations' and 'principles' to kindle the Esse for months. And slogans: I once counted 168 of them. Some key ones were:
   Freedom for children to relate to adults other than parents
   Share childcare
   Start free school
   Abandon sex-roles
   Women's, men's, parents', children's liberation Now!
   Harmonise action and belief
   Less clash, values vs. lifestyle
Fight sexism, fascism, racism (the latter two are quite tricky in Galloway, where the landowners are charming as only the rich can afford to be - and the only significant ethnic minority is ourselves - the English.)

Fight ageism. We should have some older members.

Involve Local People In Our Projects (and other right-on 'community' ideas).

Increase personal choice
Maximise variety
Waste less
Consume less
Avoid hierarchy
Evolve a 'sensitive life-style structure'
Find spiritual peace
Develop own rituals
Get healthy. Stay healthy.
Become a Red Base (not fully shared, that one - whatever it meant).
Do useful work
Become tribe

You can imagine a circular grid, where each of the above is a spoke in the wheel. The Group is like an amoeba pinned to the middle: stretch it in one direction and it'll yield from another.

So Do You Make All Decisions Collectively?
No. Point-of-lay chickens, Lucy the goat, aluminium ladder, raspberry canes: none of these were collective decisions. Certainly, no-one asked the Accountant.

And Are You Self-Sufficient?
No kidding, people asked us this obviously stupid question right from the start. We had a dozen chickens - and a cockerel, named 'Matron' by Dave, a name that some thought amusing. They clucked attractively round the stables and did indeed lay a few eggs. A rural commune fashion accessory, thought the Accountant.

And following Alice and Gerry's patchy start on the garden, we now had our first home-grown stuff - a few lettuces, lonely carrots, some spinach. And we planted some winter vegetables. But *self-sufficiency*?

And What Are Your Aims?
If you're asked in the middle of clearing up breakfast, you think: to make it through to lunchtime.

But we have this number, don't we.

'Mike,' cooees Patrick, 'seen The Aims recently?'

'The what, ducky?'

'The Aims, darling, this chap wants to see them.'

'Ah! The Aims! Tina,' I yell, 'seen The Aims, dear heart?'

'The what?' says Tina.

And so on. Residents are seen to be urgently searching under cushions, on mantelshelves, beneath armpits, up nostrils. From the hall to the top floor, the chant echoes: 'Aaa…ims! Anyone seen them? Aaa…ims!'.

Well, we think it's hilarious. Gorra laugh, incha?

In fact, it's easy to see why we don't have any clear statement: a pervasive, profoundly anti-intellectual ('radical punk') philosophy which enough people have, either without a university education, but mostly as a revulsion from it, which distrusts words on paper.

After all if there are no aims, how can anyone, including the PO, evaluate what progress has been made?

And Is It A Success?

"Yet More On Our Present Failure," Jonathan wrote in Summer 1976. "We have not moved slowly enough to learn, nor fast enough to stop the stables roof from falling in. We have failed to balance communal childcare against the always urgent demand for productive work. We have not built socialism and on the other hand we have not seen the light although we have experimented with Zazen, Macrobiotics, UFO's, hallucinogens, the Tarot, I Ching, astrology, Carlos Castaneda, R.D.Laing and the Soil Association.

"We are still subject to jealousy, envy, fear, malice, possessiveness, and bouts of wild cornflake-eating. We all have breakfast at different times."

"We find it difficult to talk with each other. One person's meat is another person's poison. We can't tell the difference between a wild fantasy and a rational, honest intention, as in the famous phrase, 'I'm really going to give up smoking.' We consume around the national average of alcohol, tobacco, caffeine, antibiotics. We have little resistance to disease."

"We have not realised our own abilities, to take from each accordingly. Nor our own needs, to give to each accordingly. *We have not made our alternative culture work*."

'Ah Yes, Laurieston Hall, Multiple Relationships, Right?'

Look, I'd spill the beans if I could, tell the whole story, the Compleat Who-Fucks-Whom. It would read a bit like Genesis, but with less begetting.

I'm convinced every sigh and sip, whisper and moan, rush of blood, and coming (or not coming), made a difference. And so did every aspirin, let alone migrating IUD's, heavy periods, floods of spermicidal goo, side-effective pills, dreary durexes (and even so, visits to the VD clinic), pregnancy panics and a couple of abortions.

Conversely - who mistrusts, cuts dead, cold shoulders, can't stand or falsely befriends whom.

I'd tell, but I don't know: nobody knows. If The Personal is Political, it's largely Inscrutable.

All we get to know is the obvious, gossipy 'Have You Heard?' stuff. Jay's up at Grobdale with Alice B. again; Jonathan's with Flick A. - she's thinking of asking to join; Julia and Arthur are moving to Lothlorien, Liz is still totally freaked; Carol's got off with Roger L... and so on.

Relationships are running the show, writing the lines. Like T. Leary's Alien Intelligences, squatting in our Central Nervous Systems. Or, if we're an army of lovers - martial law. Relationships only twice and very tentatively crept on to a meeting agenda.

I Hear Galloway Is Very Beautiful?

We hill-walk a little. Corserine is approached through dank plantations of Sitka - 'agents of capital in our midst,' Jonathan will point out later - along burns foaming with fertiliser.

On the hilltop the only sounds are the wind in the grass, grouse exploding from the heather and, at Mach One and 200 decibels, twenty tons of low-flying jet aimed playfully directly at you by its overgrown school-boy pilot.

There are views all around. To the east is Dumfries - protected if only by the prevailing winds should an accident happen at Chapelcross so-called 'nuclear power' (i.e. weapons plutonium) plant. To the west, an RAF base; and a short distance beyond, Belfast, where again, peace is not expected to break out in the coming academic year. At Mullwharchar to the north, they're planning to dump nuclear waste. South, at Kirkcudbright, you can hardly hear the guns on the tank testing ground as they bang aimlessly into Solway Firth, whose rising level of radio-activity, from Sellafield, remains, we are assured, within safe limits (but coastal farmers with weird sheep and cattle mutations on their hands don't think so).

In reality, Galloway is a war zone. Very beautiful, however.

And How Do You Earn Your Living?

At first, not at all. Day to day, we managed because it snowed money all summer - leftover proceeds from selling our houses, refunds on cancelled insurances, company pension-scheme settlements and the like. Plus we had some dole money coming in at first. We paid all this into the bank, where the account was arranged, despite the manager's anxiety, so that any one of us could sign a cheque. We kept cash in the kitty box in the kitchen, impressing the visitors with our mutual trust.

We argued over what we could spend money on - where were newspapers, tobacco, chocolate, an occasional coffee in The Acropolis café, on the scale of luxuries versus necessities? Everything we spent was written down in the cash book. Trips to the pub went down as 'Personal'. We started keeping 'the accounts'.

And The Capital?
With the dust settled, the picture was: Contributions: Alice and Paul £22152, Tina and Mike £9953, Carol and Dave £226, Maureen and Gerry £1800, Stuart nil, Total £34131. House purchase including fees: £26159. Balance in the building society account: £7972.

Das Kapital.

'Damages,' Tina called it. A couple of times that first Autumn, it was the main item on a meeting agenda. See us, nine tired communards, shivering a little in the Morning Room.

'Is the capital pooled, or what?' is the first and obvious question.

'Well,' says the Accountant, uneasily, 'It's all in the one account. But we haven't got all the capital in yet.' Meaning Stuart hasn't sold his flat and Dave and Carol's previous household, Bickerton Road, still couldn't, it turned out, pay them back what they'd put in.

With these issues unresolved, we plough on, with the tacit assumption that whoever owns the capital, using it is something we all have to agree on. There are three main points of view.

The Idealists think we shouldn't use the capital ourselves, because we'd become even more of a privileged elite. We should lend it to other groups. Or give it away.

Ah, say the Pragmatists, you're forcing your political ideals on us. We should live on it for a year, give ourselves a start. Otherwise, the men, I'm sorry, I mean a lot of us, will have to go out to work and we'll never get anything going here.

No, say the Project People - supporters of specific projects (Building Project, Health Shop in CD, Model Farm, Garden/ Smallholding, Kids Project, Arts Centre - I think that covers everybody) - living on it would soon fritter it away. We should invest it in projects, which will pay it back later.

There are wrinkles which we explore. The idealists agree, with delightful, cock-eyed logic, that it would be OK to buy land, because Land Should Be Free. The Project People point out that Projects Are The Best Way To Involve Local People. The Live-On-It protagonists say that This Is The Best Way To Put Women's Liberation Into Practice.

We will all be by turns Idealists, Pragmatists and Project People. We will have the same meeting over and again, year on year, the talk lurching through this same network of possibilities but passing and re-passing the checkpoints with different actors. Endless plays and counter-plays. And similarly with other perennials.

37

But Dave was pretty consistently Idealist. And why not, thinks the Accountant. After all, it's not his money.

The PO does not recall that anything at all was ever agreed.

I Hear You Have Multiple Relationships?

Such a tedious term, so it is. *Relationship* itself is ambiguous. But - when it's a sexual instance - we don't seem to have anything better. *Scene* sounds too nasty, brutal and short (which may however be the case). *Romance* is past its sell-by date (and almost certainly untrue).

'Why not call them shipwrecks?,' someone suggests, 'or Sargassoes? Albatrosses? Squalls? - something nautical, anyway. Slightly nautical?

House Maintenance Must Take Forever?

Dave and I spend a lot of time 35 feet up, scraping out clogged leaves from the gutters. At first, all very safely. Put up the new ladder vertically, climb, clamp, clear out. Pretty soon we found it was quicker - and more fun - to put up the ladder leaning left a bit, then - while at the top - bounce it over to the right. Paul had hysterics.

And What Are Your Aims, Exactly?

It's that 'exactly', always creases me. 'As a group,' I used to say, 'None. Nada. Niente. Nul Points. We are just four couples and a single bloke, with nine children between us, locked into the Rat Race and wanting out.'

5

Autumn 1972

We'd been earning so much money before, was the problem. In retrospect, Alice was right - we could have gone much more quickly to the current Laurieston economy, based on visitors, gardening, animals and a bit of this and that - shaky though this is.

We knew we could live on less. But how much less? Our middle-class prudence prevailed. The men went off to work, part-time.

Gerry fixed up a day a week teaching at The Jake in Leeds. People would ask the obvious: 'How come it takes him four days?' And you and I would look at each other and say nothing much, knowing that he was having a secret affair with Wisty H. in London. Maureen wasn't supposed to know. But of course, she did.

Paul taught all over the place - London, Cheltenham and Glasgow. Stuart chased around for work locally, but was more often in London. We saw him rarely. He was architecting, we supposed. But not paying in any money. Challenged by the Accountant, he said he was still 'paying off his debts.'

Dave got a job in London, completing a computer system: he, Carol and Tiffy were away for three weeks out of four right through to January.

And I worked part-time for my old employer, management consulting in London and Rotherham.

The men burning up oil tyres and petrol in return for cash. And, quite often, just three women, Alice, Maureen and Tina, home alone with seven kids. Laurieston Hall, the women's liberation, rural, eco-commune. If interested, please apply to our London office.

But when we were all home: collective oomph. People on the move, cleaning windows, mending windows, painting, decorating, cleaning floors, cleaning chimneys (for this, Paul had bought an industrial vacuum cleaner - the 'Dalek' - and we had borrowed chimney brushes from Ken Robson at the pub). Moving furniture about, answering letters, dealing with visitors, chopping wood, making phone calls, washing clothes (both washing machines, stretched beyond their limits, were now breaking down all the time). Sorting mounds of washed clothes (damp, cold and approaching mouldiness - waiting for a dry day or space on the clothes-horse.) Trips out, trips back, loading, unloading. Topping up the Esse and Hydresse. Sawing, drilling. The house resonating with these noises, overlaid with records playing and someone giving their impression of Sheree Baby.

You have to imagine, Dear Reader, that this and much, much more goes on throughout this story. It's a constant backdrop.

Plus there are the children. Imagine children hanging on to your legs or climbing onto your shoulders, every single step of the way.

The PO is going to low-profile the children in this account. Baby chuckles, the full-blast toddler joy of 'catch me, can't catch me,' the wisdom of four year olds (Sophie worked out that 'God isn't a person, it's not a He, God's just everywhere, like a spirit') the canniness of five year olds (Joel telling Lesley he's worried we can't support her, financially) - he'll mostly omit. The children will no doubt tell their own tale later. As for the Groans - Patrick's word - you'll have to interpolate a lot of pleasure and a lot of heartache.

Oomph, but also ambivalence. Alice says making leaf mould is 'vital,' so she and Mike sweep up autumn leaves, in the rain. Or, pissed off that Dave and Carol have bought the chickens then gone to London - Mike nevertheless feeds them, collects the eggs and locks them in at night, which is quite pleasant job. This is learning the hard way what co-operative living is all about. Mike the chicken-minder and leaf-sweeper; Mike the political visionary will have to wait.

Meanwhile paint flakes off the greenhouses, the Land Rover always needs servicing, and dry rot is increasing in the stables. Would there ever be time to do what we really want to do - or even to figure out what that might be?

After an Indian Summer, the nights drew in quickly. On a moonless night, the walk to The Laurie Arms, via the Long Drive, became a matter of exploring forward step by step, head craned back, trying to make out the difference between sky - over the path - and tree tops - over the ditches. Night in the country was, well, seriously dark. Until we thought of carrying torches.

Once at the pub, the stiff silences we'd initially walked into were replaced by a friendly welcome. We had 'caused nae bother' - passed the acid test. And if we came late on a Friday, we couldn't get as far as the bar - just had drinks thrust in our hands. Closing time, at ten-o-clock, was a riot - and then there was the 'carry-oot.' 'We're offtae Jock's bi'. Ya comin?' Sometimes we did.

Or, some nights, we drove to the Palace Cinema in CD, called in the Thistle Inn after and then on the trip home - while trying to avoid it - ran over a pheasant or a rabbit. 'You buy meat?' was the SVQ. 'Course not,' the meat-eaters explain, 'we take two tons of motor car and run it over.'

And we had meetings, meetings, and more meetings. Mostly, uncomfortable and twitchy affairs.

You, me, Dave and occasionally Alice, roll cigarettes and mutter: 'Yes, I know, must try and give it up.' Maureen winds her hair round her fingers. Carol looks drawn. Paul puts pine slabs on the fire - for meetings, we allowed ourselves a wood fire, but only after long conversations about the rate we would burn wood and the rate at which we could replace it.

Use of energy was often the starting point. Electricity. Gerry or Stuart raising the revival of the hydro.

And you say, 'But until we do, maybe we shouldn't buy electrical appliances?'

Dave, realising you're talking about the brand-new, electric hot-plate he's bought, says, 'But we needed it for heating up Tiffy's milk in Carol's Kitchen.'

This blows our sexism detectors off the scale. Alice snaps, 'You shouldn't call it that,' and we get into long squabble about earning money vs. doing childcare. Even today I can't walk into the Top Floor Scullery - which has the hatch onto the roof, and which became Alice's darkroom - without thinking: 'Carol's Kitchen.'

'Sorry,' says Dave.

Short pause.

'Calor Gas would've been better,' says Stuart, 'so we could switch to methane later.'

'Or second-hand anyway,' says the Accountant, 'we shouldn't buy new unless it's unavoidable.'

'Sorry,' says Dave, again. A pause while we realise we have been a bit hard on him.

Brightening up, Dave offers: 'I'm spending a lot of time servicing the Land Rover.' Vehicles were always a safe diversion.

'I wish people,' says Paul - meaning Stuart - 'would remember to check the Big Landy's oil *every trip.* And the Ami. Which needs two new tyres, by the way.'

And the discussion goes: Country roads, gravel chips, awful hard on tyres. Tyres more expensive for foreign cars. Why not sell the Ami and buy a Mini? And bytheway is it really feasible to generate methane and run the cars on that? And when are we going to cut down on all this long-distance commuting and work locally?

Another hiatus.

Then you say, 'We should really talk about the children. I mean, they're still so bewildered.'

41

And Alice suggests: 'Maybe we should have our own playgroup, instead of going to Crossmichael. There are two or three little ones in the village who might come.'

'Well we'd have to clean the place up,' Paul responds, 'the Hall is *filthy*. And the lino will last longer if we keep it clean.'

And the rest of us say, 'Yes. Well. You're right. We should. We will.'

Meetings like these, end in a flak of buzz-words: Shouldn't, Oughtn't, Standards, Hygiene, Efficiency. Projects, Consensus, Obligations, Goodwill. Trust, Principles, Commitment.

And Isolation, Real World and 'Be nice to get a daily paper.'

'I'll pick one up in CD,' says Alice, 'I'm taking the Ami there tomorrow.'

'Like I said, it needs two new tyres,' says Paul.

"Two new tyres, OK," say the minutes.

Dave was particularly manic. One morning, in fifteen minutes flat, he cut down the rhododendron bushes outside the Old Kitchen window, using Paul's rotary saw. At coffee time, Paul - mightily pissed off - says, 'You'll have ruined the saw. It's not designed for rough work, like cutting live wood. In fact, I wish you wouldn't you use my things.'

'And you should have asked people first,' says Mike, looking out of the window at the devastation. 'Yes, says Tina, 'I *liked* those rhododendron bushes.'

'Sorry,' says Dave. 'I thought they kept the light out. I mean I assumed you'd like it if I... And I thought tools were communal. Anyway, I'm not feeling very well. Got a migraine coming on.' And retires to bed. Goody-goody Mike carries his lunch up to him.

But then at tea-time, hearing the arrival of a tractor, which he'd asked to borrow from Farmer Henty, Dave leaps back out of bed, into the tractor saying, 'Might as well finish the job.' With chains, he starts wrenching the rhododendron roots out of the ground. Disapproval ripples over the rest of us:

'Why are we using high-tech when we could use people-power?'

'Why don't you watch the kids instead, and let the women learn how to use a tractor?

And a scowl from me. If you're well enough to play tractors, I thought, you can fetch your own bloody lunch.

'Sorry,' says Dave again.

The upturned rhododendron stumps lay untouched for a couple of years, like severed gorgons' heads.

Just once that Autumn, we had a meeting assisted with a little hashish, courtesy of visitors, and Newcastle Brown, Strongbow cider and few cans of McEwans Export, fetched by Stuart from the Laurie. And the minutes read:

Paul: Shouldn't really buy cans. Until recycle.

Carol: Well what's that can you've got there then.

Paul: Neatsfoot oil, best stuff there is for waterproofing boots.

Tina: Must take an awful lot of neats to make a pint.

Mike: This PeopleCentre idea, having groups of people to stay.

Tina: Want to get going on it, write to women's groups, youth worker contacts in Glasgow.

Stuart: Theatre groups. Artists. Puppets. Film-makers.

Mike: Rest-home for clapped-out revolutionaries.

Tina: Alternative transport caff. Good pull-up for hippies.

Mike: 365 easy miles from Marble Arch.

Carol A proper restaurant, dress up as waiters and waitresses and everything. Or a Tea Shoppe.

Dave: Or a health farm, fleece the rich.

Gerry: An eco-garage at the end of the drive. People drive up with a full tank and we suck out the petrol.

Alice: Convert petrol back into trees?

Gerry: Build a windmill. Savonius rotor. Two halves of an oil drum, offset, S-shape profile.

Dave: Trout farming.

Alice: Fix the greenhouses.

Gerry: Plant fruit trees

Stuart: Get this wholefood shop idea together.

Mike: Bugger wholefood, sell crisps and Coke at youth club, make a fortune (we had revived the village Youth Club, held in the school).

Paul: Youth club pretty boring.

Alice: Maybe have it here.

Stuart: Table tennis. Fits in with the PeopleCentre. Cinema club, too.

Tina: Old people too. Battered wives. Trade unions.

Dave: An Alternative Building Society. What this movement needs. Our social responsibility.

Carol: Recycling. Third world, they recycle everything

Stuart: Methane.

Mike: You Tarzan, methane.

We were pleased with ourselves. The gang's all here (except Maureen - too tired). Alluring Alice. Comely, demurely pregnant Carol with the long black wavy haircut, fringe at the front. Dashing Dave. Gorgeous -wrinkle-

43

free - Gerry. Magnetic Mike. Passionate, practical Paul. Seductive Stuart. Terrific Tina, who doesn't really look at all like Julie Christie.

Maureen was always tired. One morning, when Gerry was away, she didn't show up for breakfast - we assumed she was having a lie-in. And it was lunchtime before someone said: 'Haven't seen Maureen today. Nor Zoe and Jemma and the baby. Has anyone seen Maureen?'

Maureen had fled. Over the next few days, news trickled through:.

'Maureen's apparently just descended on John and Wisty in London. Gerry was there. He's having a scene with Wisty. Almighty row.'

'Maureen's definitely left the group. Split with Gerry. Gone to her family in Poole.'

'Gerry says he's thought about it a lot and he's leaving, too.'

'Gerry's moving in with John and Wisty.'

So that was that. When Gerry came back to pick up his and Maureen's belongings, the rest of us were too busy to help. I remember thinking 'he can load his own bloody wine.' And he did. Every jar.

Gerry left, it was clear to us all, to be with Wisty H. But he told people he'd left because 'the group wasn't committed enough, politically' - then spent years blathering about 'getting back to the land in a political way.'

Meanwhile on a vicious October morning, in a driving horizontal sleet, Alice and I dug 2ft. square holes and planted out the raspberry canes he'd ordered, at our expense. 'Not committed enough,' I thought. Bastard. Gerry wasn't my favourite person anymore.

The Old Kitchen was also our living room, dining room, kids' playroom and office. New Notices began to appear. 'Five Amps Maximum on this socket'. 'Visitors Rate now £1 a day, half for kids.' 'Wood needs sawing.' 'Wood warms you twice.' 'Anarchy Rules, KO.' We installed a carpet, but it covered scarcely a quarter of the floor and the room was still uncomfortable and chaotic.

And always chilly. The Esse and Hydresse warmed it a bit, but both the swing door and the main door were in constant use and both of these lead onto outside doors - which were always being left open. Through either of which, the sodding goat kept appearing. You should write a book, said my mother, and say how funny it was when the goat kept butting its way into the kitchen. Yes Ma. Very funny. Goat in the kitchen.

And insecure. Most callers followed the noise and walked straight in. Fortunately they were friendly, but what if some locals took a dislike? Or the police decided to call, just as, Sod's Law would have it, a Visitor was lighting up a joint?

And so far from our bedrooms. I remember taking the kids to bed along cold, ill-lit corridors - we'd decided on 15 watt bulbs in the corridors, to save on energy - and them not wanting to be left, because they knew we wouldn't be able to hear them later, if they called.

And the floor was always muddy, because no-one wiped their boots. No point, because the floor was always muddy.

And it was murder to cook on the Esse when the people you were cooking for were camped all around and even on top it.

What we should do - I said again - is build cosy, comfortable kitchen and living rooms on the first floor. But to the others it was 'obvious' we had to stay on the ground floor. 'Surely we've come here to be close to the outdoors?' they said. 'Besides, we'd have to carry all the food upstairs.'

And about now, people begin to say: 'Mike. Obsessive. Won't let anything go.'

Gerry and Maureen's defection at first left everyone shaken and bruised. It was a miserable end to the year. Stuart, Carol and Dave were still away a lot. The house felt overwhelmingly lonely and empty. And I'd worry about money - we all worried about money - and begin to wonder if it wasn't all a terrible mistake.

This is a feeling that will keep coming back, once or twice a year.

But we were determined.

We were making our living. Back home, Paul set up a workshop and built a massive workbench. Stuart played badminton and carpet bowls with the locals in the village hall (and was chased home one night for having chatted up a 'married woman'). Dave and Carol sent us London Letters. Mike and Tina gave talks and a slide show to the Women's Rural.

November 5th was clear, still, warm, and lit by a harvest moon. We had invited our local friends and acquaintances to a bonfire by the pond. Rather than fireworks, Paul had made hot air balloons from balsa wood and tissue paper, powered by cotton wool soaked with meths. They soared and flared. Brilliant. Farmer Henty looked distinctly nervous, obviously worried they would set the forests alight.

After that, the sun flew south for the winter. Rain fell or was always in the offing. The roof leaked - Paul patched it. And it froze. Galloway winters may not normally be severe, but this first one was vicious. Pipes burst - Paul or Dave fixed them, then lagged the more exposed bits. But there were miles of piping to go.

There just weren't enough of us. Close to Christmas, we placed an ad in Time Out. It ran under Jobs Offered rather than Accommodation, and didn't mention country idylls at all:

"Hard work; no pay. Laurieston Hall in S.W. Scotland, is the home of seven adults, ages ranging from 24 to 31, and our five young children. We are trying to be ecologically aware, supportive of women's liberation, partly self-sufficient in food... and are seeking new members."

Even so most of the 40 or so replies were hopeless. Men who wanted to Get Out Of Town, eat fresh veg grown by magic, pass the time with a little light art and craft; even some who finished 'P.S. I'm married with two kids.' But Patrick looked promising. We invited him to visit in the New Year.

Meanwhile, Nicky got in touch through the Kilquhanity connection. He'd been a pupil there, travelled, lived in London, done dozens of jobs before becoming roadie for the Incredible String Band (his dog, Leaf, was on one of their record covers). Then he'd run into hard times and finished up back at Killy as cowman, handyman, builder. He called on us a lot, making himself useful. He knew about - oh, everything. Salmon-tickling, paraffin arc lamps, scavenging second-hand timber. And he told Galloway stories. When he asked to join, it was a quick meeting. We'd have him. We still wanted people with capital - but in Nicky's case, we even paid off the £200 or so he owed on his car.

And, quite separately, we received a letter from a couple in Liverpool - but, unusually, written by the woman - Julia. 'Dick and I', she wrote, 'have been trying to find a house/ make a commune/ get a market garden going for about two years now.' By chance, I had a day's work in Liverpool, and arranged to call on them. I remember the day - I slid the Volvo off the road on ice near Gretna, hitched to Carlisle, continued by train, went to my meetings, then went to meet Julia; we sat on the floor and drank tea. Later I reported back: 'Richard was out - but Julia's great. Very clear and together. Very bubbly.' We invited them to visit in the New Year.

'Bubbly, was she?' you said, poking me in the ribs, as we shivered into bed. 'Bet that that means you fancied her.'

'Yes,' I said, 'No. I mean. Anyway she already has another bloke. And Richard, too. He was staying over with his womanfriend. Shades of...'

Mike and Tina and Paul and Alice. Except that that wasn't happening anymore. You'd stopped sleeping with Paul: I'd wondered why, but hadn't asked.

'It's just he's so fussy and finicky,' you mind-read and answered. 'You know. If he's so disgusted with Sophie's pissy bum, I can't imagine what he feels about my smelly body.'

I adored your body, sweat, smells and all. We made love.

'You don't mind, do you?,' you said, after a bit. This was before we each had our own rooms, and I knew you meant: 'If I don't sleep with Paul, then you...'

'Nah,' I say. And I didn't.

Alice and I didn't sleep together anymore. But that didn't stop us sneaking upstairs during the day. Much naughtier. Much more fun. And a couple of times, I'd make love with you later. Communal living: making love with two women in one day. With a smidgen of guilt, because thinking to boast of your sexual exploits is supposed to be a dreadful male, sexist crime - I admit I felt like a helluva fellow.

6
Spring 1977

Why Did You Leave?

Maureen wrote: "I never wanted to go to Laurieston.

"If I was going to try communal living I wanted to be able to plunge in with all my energy. But the two girls, two miscarriages then Morgan, in four and a half years, plus being ill, had left me dried out. I tried to explain this to Gerry, first calmly, then hysterically - but he'd say - 'I don't understand you, it'll solve all your problems, you're mad.'

"So we arrived, Gerry striding ahead, me stumbling behind because I didn't want to lose him.

"I was exhausted, weak, emotionally flat. Gerry had no time for me. And being at Laurieston made the problems worse. I saw everyone else beginning a new life, learning new crafts, making projects, climbing mountains - all things I wanted to do. Instead of endless breast-feeding, nappies. Carrying, calming and rocking Morgan, pacing the bedroom with him at night. I began to feel I didn't have any right to say anything at meetings, because I didn't share the work. I was desperate to get the babies into a routine so that I could cook a meal, wash up, feed the chickens - even though the last thing I wanted to do with baby-free time was housework and chores. I longed for peace and silence.

"Gerry kept telling me - you don't have any cooking or shopping to do, why don't you just enjoy yourself?

"The rest of you urged me to forget Jemma - 'she'll be all right' And I wanted to. (I was 'over-protective.') But the dangers were so great. Once she was nearly run over on the drive. Once she was found pulling at the washing machine lead, in mid-wash, standing in a pool of water. And so on, and so on. And still Gerry said - don't fuss.

"After five weeks of this I was screaming inside. The opposite of the person I thought I was. Couldn't smile, let alone speak. Holding on - nervous breakdowns were luxuries for people who could abandon their responsibilities. And all this in a women's liberation household, wasn't it supposed to be?

"And then Gerry fell in love with Wisty. It was the proverbial last straw. All I could think of was - get away.

"So: no farewells, no explanations - I just couldn't. I'm sorry."

And the rest of us wrote back - no, no, it's us who should be sorry.
And thought: that Gerry: what a bastard.

Why Did You Leave?
Dumb Tom's, April, 1977. Still cold.

I am beginning to understand. That I have, in fact, left. But 're-joining' is obviously on my agenda.

Sophie and Joel are living here with me - family breakfasts at last, except, of course, no you. I miss you. When are you ever going to come and see me?

I just remembered again that you promised, a year ago, that we'd leave together last Autumn. Yes, promised (but failed to cross your heart, hope to die).

But when Autumn came around, you didn't remember. You were 'too worried about the kids.' As if leaving wouldn't have made life 100 times easier. Wonderful thing, selective amnesia. Now that you've got together with Jay, I can see it's just another thing you're going to forget forever. Wonderful thing, selective amnesia.

As the PO, I sift stories from The Diary, Meetings' Minutes, notebooks, project diaries, people's 'Letters To The Group.' Car stories - cars have always been a big issue. Car maintenance and Childcare. Childcare and Energy. Energy and Relationships. Car journeys and Relationships Maintenance.

I'm aware these aren't the most suitable headings for a thesis. What the P&CRP wants to know about is:

Decision-Making

Group Dynamics and Conflict Resolution

Women, Men, Childcare & Work: The Dialectics

A Socialist Critique Of The New Communities ("Duodecimo Editions Of The New Jerusalem," K. Marx)

The Low-Energy-Consumption Eco-Community.

And so forth. Shivering, the PO draws felt-tip lines in different colours between combinations of these and other topics until the wall-chart is more complex than Paris's Metro.

The PA considers the PO has gone doolally. His reporting is unreliable and that this might become a Ph.D. thesis is laughable. Sorry Tom C., sorry Paul S.

Why Did You Leave?
In The Diary, just a month ago, March 1977, before he left for Crabapple, Patrick wrote:

"soph woke me up last night and i started thinking god tina didn't say goodnight i was waiting for her to come to bed she was talking to jay but said she still had mike's letter to finish why didn't she creep in even if i was asleep fuck if she's sleeping with jay oh no...

"so i get up in a daze go to jay's room and she's there so i call her out shaking come out come on and i go into her room and tighten into a ball on the bed oh no i'll kill her.

"why not me she said she would, what does she see in him and i rip a sheet in anger and tremble and she comes and i grab her where were you why you must tell me why.

"and i hit her hard and she screams and jon rushes in and jay's there but i only see tina and i'm crying over her bent body i'm sorry i'm sorry.

"no, she say's, it's me should be sorry i don't know why, i don't remember, it was late, i didn't know what to do"

Meanwhile, I'm still waiting for that letter.

And Sustainable Energy?
That first Winter was cold, I mean cold. Freezing. We went to bed in cold rooms, wearing lots of clothes. It didn't seem special, or all that difficult - it was what being 'ecologically aware' meant. We had a little wood, but kept it for the Morning Room fire.

But I remember a day spent cutting logs and bugger me if Dave and Carol, back from London, didn't calmly take a sack-full up to their room and build a fire!

And Multiple Relationships?
I've suddenly realised that I took you tea in bed all the time. To our bed - or Paul's - or, later, you with Patrick, Georgina V., Alice B., even Jay's room with the 'No Old Movies' sign on the door. But you never brought me a cuppa. Hopeless. One-way energy, our relationship. The other day, here at Dumb Tom's, I made two cups of coffee automatically then threw yours at the wall. Smashed the beaker. Stained the wall a bit. Am hoping Tom won't notice.

7
Winter 1972/73

Stuart had invited some American friends for Hogmanay. Alice and I made cock-a-leekie and cheese straws, which we laid out - on table-cloths, no less - with all the bowls and spoons we could muster. A log fire blazed in the hall, under the holly and Christmas cards. We had whisky, beer and, contributed by one of the Americans, bourbon in a fancy blue bottle. Midnight on the radio: 'And we're together on all wavelengths.' Ho hum.

We falter our way through Auld Lang Syne. Exchange pecks on cheeks. Toast the New Year, the house, our visitors, ourselves. The scene is all rather quiet and decorous.

We had put the word around the village that our house - like everyone else's - would welcome first-footers. But by 12.30 no-one had come calling and most people went off to bed, disappointed. Ah Well. We're still offcomers, of course.

But then Nicky drives Alice, Tina and me to Kilquhanity, where we find a proper Hogmanay party in progress. A hundred people, huge quantities of booze. We dance eightsome reels for an hour or so.

When we get back, around three, we meet a few bewildered locals who, finding the house deathly quiet, are on the point of leaving. No! we say. Don't go! Come in! Happy New Year! We swap whiskies with them, put on some music, stoke the fire. They get on the phone...

By 4.30 a.m. we have 150 people from the village and around. They conjure half bottles from thin air, which then hover magically and slowly across the throng. Paul and Stuart resurface. The din is tremendous. The kids wake and freak (later they'd say, 'Please don't have a Hog'may again'). Everyone is drunk; still the whisky flows - impossible to drink, I pour several glasses away down the loo. The riot goes on past dawn. The locals leave, staggering away down the drive - or slump in heaps, Hieronymus Bosch style, in front of the fire. The Americans sleep through it all in the West Wing. You come up with 'I'm going now' but it doesn't register. I'm being the manically effusive host. You meant you were off to bed with Nicky.

Julia and Richard visited a few days later. Julia, 27, had a uni degree and had done a year's course in Horticulture. Dark-haired and tiny - five feet nothing - she was the one with clear ideas - making the garden really productive, getting a Women's group together, 'creating a real anarchist lifestyle' and 'getting a bit of space from Dick.' They weren't a close couple anymore, and where else could they still live together and share the children if not here? Plus she was due to inherit about £3000 - which would be handy, as we hadn't begun to repay Gerry and Maureen.

Richard, 28, was tall, blonde, wide-shouldered, willowy, slim. He wore floppy home-made pants, embroidered with fishes, and hand-painted, two-tone shoes. He was dreamy and slow, smiled a lot, spoke little. And was a Civil Engineer. Very civil. Called me 'brother' - I liked that.

Their children were Billy, 6, and George, not quite 2.

'Richard's dead good-looking,' you said.

'Yeah. Makes you sick,' I agreed.

'And Billy might be a pal for Joel.'

They wanted to join us and we liked them - but Carol and Dave were away again and hadn't met them. On the phone, we reminded them that 'Gerry and Maureen hadn't met you, when you joined.' So they, too, gave the OK. And if Julia had another lover, Jonathan, who was slowly plodding his way towards us, we ignored that.

Later, when it suits them, Carol and Dave will refer to 'being pressured.'

I was furious with you. Because Christmas had been awful. With you, me and J&S away to my parents, there had been no time for intimacy until we crawled between the overheated nylon sheets. I wanted to talk to you about so many things - The Group, the 'Politics' piece I'd written and not least, about you and me. A recurring pattern in our relationship: me wanting to cement a bottom line, whatever happened. But you wouldn't talk. You fell asleep. You were - this expression arriving conveniently at the time - 'spaced out.'

And now this thing with Nicky. Which you also wouldn't talk about.

A few days later, you went off to sleep with him again. Alone, spread-eagled on our bed, confused about you, me, sex, work, who I was, what I was doing - I couldn't sleep.

At first light, I went for an early-morning stomp, up the Back Track, down the burn towards the loch. I came to the place where old iron girders had rusted to thin tapes, little more than a suggestion of the former footbridge.

Am I going to do this. I inched my way across the twenty-foot drop onto the rocks. Don Genaro came to mind. It was stupid, but I made it.

Elated, I ran, danced, scrambled back along the other side of the burn, up through the silver birch, larches and pines, came out onto the Gatehouse road and sauntered down to the village in immaculate sunshine.

I phoned the office in London from the village call-box. It felt like calling another planet. Told the boss: 'Sorry to spring this on you, but I've decided I'm not coming back to work.'

'Mike, are you all right?.'

'Absolutely.'

Walking back up the drive, I met Paul going out in the Land Rover and gave him the news. Feeling hysterically cheerful, I told him I was: 'not a management consultant anymore'. He looked horrified.

The Group consolidated. Dave, Carol and Tiffany came back from London. They settled properly into their new room - painting it a lurid puce colour called 'Kinky Pink.'

And grew: Richard, Julia, Billy (big grin) and George (wide eyed and affable), moved into rooms on the top floor front.

Stuart had some steady local work; Paul worked just three days a week in Glasgow; Nicky commuted over to Killy. On the whole we were, at last, all home together.

Stuart and Nicky initiated a still-ongoing Laurieston tradition: room shuffling. Nicky moved to Tower Room, Stuart to Sunny Room next to Sonya and Polly. In the Diary, Stuart wrote: 'Sonya woke me at 4 a.m. with her lovely singing.' What a poser.

And Patrick visited. His was the Time Out reply we'd best liked the sound of. Although just 23, he was married, but separated. University degree, teacher training - this was all hidden. With his long, wispy beard and long hair he looked warm and gentle - a Christmas-card Christ. Though the eyes were a bit small and too close together. Aggressive, irritable - this was hidden too.

He fed back enthusiasm: "There is a tremendous fusion between you and what you're doing. The whole place is incredible, being made credible." And criticism, which echoed what others had said, and which arose from having visitors all the time. "You aren't very forthcoming, publicly. You hide behind your work roles."

We invented the 'new people must bring in £500' rule about this time. This would have been a year's living money. Patrick went and got a temporary clerical job in London to save his entrance ticket. And though it took us a couple of weeks, we wrote and said, yes, come and join us.

In February, Carol's baby was born. She and Dave went proudly down to the village, where the local registrar lived, to register him as 'Tam.'

'How could anyone call a boy that,' was the word in the pub, 'I mean, not Thomas, but just *Tam*?'

'I felt horrible when you went off and slept with Nicky,' I said when, at last you agreed to talk about it.

'I thought it was supposed to be OK.'

To Sleep With Other People. But, no, not in my mind it wasn't. I mean, the Paul and Alice thing we had more or less negotiated. Neither of us had a blank cheque .

'Well I was shocked. You running off like a teenager.'

'Sorry. I was pissed. I mean, New Year's Eve.'

'Well OK, but Nicky?'

I had this notion that an 'open relationship' - we never called ours that, but Other People would have - would only work if we felt good about each other's partners. If I could feel close to the other man. It had always proved difficult enough with Paul. But Nicky? I liked having him around, respected his practical knowledge and skills. But he was NOCD, intellectually, wouldn't you say? It was perfectly obvious you were sleeping with him 'cos he was tall, dark and handsome-ish. A sex-object, in fact. Tut-tut from the feminist in me.

'Sometimes I think you want it to be OK for you, but not for me.'

'But I'm not sleeping with anyone else.'

'What about Alice?'

'Well, I think that's finished.'

'Well I'm sorry. And I'm. I mean, I don't quite know how to stop it.' This got neatly around the fact that you didn't particularly want to stop it, not just yet.

We were all together, but there was, quite suddenly, another immediate backdrop to communal living. People being ill all the time - did we pass infections around?.

"Nearly everyone boiled-eyed and legless with this so-called cold" says Julia, writing in the Diary. And shortly after, Tina wrote:

"Alice is in bed on account of she vomits when vertical. Carol has a sore throat and chest. Dave and I are weak but still up and doing. Paul is feeling sick but ditto. Tiffany has a cold and an eye infection. Polly has a bad cold and keeps retiring to bed. Billy has stopped vomiting. Nicky has a swollen, injured hand and Richard a poisoned and swollen lip - both spent yesterday in bed. Stuart's back is still bad, from the time he fell over drunk at the Village Hall party, two months ago."

The PA was not affected, and sometimes thought this was all psycho-somatic, stress-related malingering. Not the most charitable fellow, the PA.

Even so, with everyone around, ill or not, we could at last 'make some decisions.' The minutes book records three defining meetings.

One is on where to live in this tremendous emporium.

In the Old Kitchen, Paul had built a gracefully-curved plate-rack out of plywood and dowelling - it looked like a cubist piano - and new work surfaces. We imported still more armchairs, little tables, novels and Carol and Dave's hi-fi. But it still wasn't comfortable. We agreed we needed a new living space and met - in Dave and Carol's room - to decide where. Julia minuted:

Mike starts on about somewhere on the first floor.

'Play another record, Mike.'

So Mike suggests Big Front Room - at least it's sunny.

'No plumbing,' Paul objects.

'But you're a builder,' says Mike.

Paul thinks it comes down to Billiard Room.

Dave, Carol and Stuart are happy with Billiard Room Tina thinks OK if we can heat it. Stuart and Nicky say OK. Richard and Patrick say nothing.

Mike says it's the biggest, coldest, darkest room in the house.

'Consensus - Billiard Room.'

I was angry with this and felt isolated and beaten. I saw what had happened as a bandwagon - dissenting thoughts lost in the crosswinds - reason lost in favour of conformity with an imaginary group solidarity. It's majority rule, I thought. So much for 'consensus'.

Especially, I was shocked that you hadn't agreed with me - or, worse, that you had thought it was better to 'keep the group happy.'

Because Billiard Room was such a stupid choice. It protrudes north from the house; is even bigger than the Old Kitchen; has three outside walls and its own roof. It's unheatable, and was never going to be homely.

I suppose I should have accepted the majority view gracefully and tried to make it work. Instead I was scornful and disparaging - all that did was slow down the work and upset everyone. (So when everybody finally moved out of Billiard Room, last Autumn - coinciding with the commune falling apart - I felt some schadenfreude).

The Second Big Meeting concerned the PeopleCentre. That is, offering the house for conferences/ workshops/ holidays to women's groups, youth groups, arts groups, trade unions, radical professionals, gay/ lesbian groups, politicos. We go through all the arguments again.

'We'll need all the room we've got for new members'

'We could have twice as many members and still have room.'

'It'll make life here a hassle - what we're trying to get away from.'

'It'll bring us into closer contact with The Movement. Visitors stimulate us.'

'We can't afford the time.'

'It'll pay us for our time.'

'We'll be just like servants.'

'I *like* cooking for lots of people.'

'Having visitors all the time tends to overwhelm us.'

'Yes, but life without them is a bit claustrophobic. And we can have 'visitor-free' times in between events...

'Some visitors won't fit in with our lifestyle.' (This refers to chips-with-everything diets, men having to sign up for cooking and childcare, our lack of central-heating, and so forth.)

'Well, we'll work on that...'

'Anyway whoever heard of groups like these going away together?'

'Well. Er. We'll just have to start a trend. Run our own events.'

And so on. The minutes point gingerly to a typical Laurieston inconclusive 'consensus.' Several for, and no-one, in the end, against. A neat meeting.

So when Nicky heard of an army surplus auction in Sterling, it seemed like a good idea to buy some more bedding, for the PeopleCentre. Alice and Nicky went.

'Alice and Nicky?' I asked you.

'Mmm,' you said, 'Well I'm not sleeping with him anymore, but I think Alice is.'

Heigh Ho.

'Didn't you buy anything, then?' we asked when they came home with the car empty.

But they had - mattresses; sheets; blankets; pillowslips; pillows; formica-top, square metal tables; tools Nicky couldn't resist. So much stuff, they'd had to hire a furniture van to ship it down to us.

'Hey,' we chorused, 'how much have you spent?'

'£450.'

'Jesus.' 'God.' 'But we didn't agree.'

'We hardly know where next month's money is coming from,' says the dumbstruck Accountant (though he was a PeopleCentre Project main fan.)

We were shocked. But soon accepted the sense of it. And the stuff arrived just in time for our first 'try-out' group booking - students from the Jake in Leeds, brought by a previous colleague of Gerry's, Dave W.

The third, most important, meeting was about sharing money.

We were still working to the notion that we'd take equal responsibility for earning money - Stuart and Nicky were expected to contribute one share each, the couples two shares. We kept track of everyone's contributions into the Group account.

Planning was still individual, too. Mike, having given up his job, said he wanted to live on his capital for a while (curious - hadn't he previously been an idealist, 'mustn't live on it' person?) And Carol and Dave were aiming to live on their Bickerton Road money, if it ever came through.

Then suddenly - nine months into communal living - we just agreed to forget all of this and genuinely pool all income and expenses completely. It was like we got married. In retrospect, we should have had a celebration. It was one of the easiest decisions we ever made.

And became our most solid and enduring collective practice. Even though we hadn't agreed on how to earn and spend our money.

I thought it felt right; it gave substance to that abstract notion, 'trust' that was called for so often; and it was also a political commitment. Dave blathered on about how it was a 'practical necessity' - a form of words I took exception to, and argued with him about.

But the decision stayed - right up to now. I'm living on my student grant, which, OK, I haven't 'paid in.' But I still think of it as Laurieston's money, and I'm doing Laurieston work. For my Commune.

That March it stayed cold, and snowed. Dave and Paul built sledges, Nicky borrowed skis and we used Farmer Henty's back field as a nursery slope. The Ami and Landy had to be push-started - the pushers slipping on packed ice. People started wearing two of everything - trousers, sweaters, woolly hats, pairs of socks - and that was just indoors. Nicky fixed the washing machines and plumbed them in to the newly-named Laundry Room. And work started on Billiard Room.

Our lives become crowded with neighbours. Chuck and Jill - he an American horror-movie scriptwriter, she an English Aristo - came and stayed with their children in one of the cottages. We started decorating the other. We'd decided, after the briefest of discussions - 'surely we can't be landlords' vs. 'we need the money' - to rent out the cottages for summer holiday lets.

Alice and Paul, then me and Tina were invited out by more new friends, Rosemary and Tony G. We invited them back to our collective supper, but it didn't work, the couples-to-couples thing.

In April, at long last, it thawed. The gardeners bought a Versatiller. Julia and Richard built the first propagation beds in the main greenhouse. We collected yet more pig-muck from Val and Ed's. Tina started an OU course in Sociology, Alice a course in farming, both of them travelling to Dumfries. Life zoomed on.

8
Spring 1977

At Dumb Toms, days are scrawny and featherless. No word from you, no word from anyone except Catriona.

Why Did You Leave?
This third time, the trigger was your phone call, confirming what I didn't want to hear. That, after visiting your mum, you'd be spending a week hanging out with Jay before coming home.

In Mix Café the sink was chin-high with supper washing up, the floor shin-deep with uncollected washing, old wellies, useless glass jars, unanswered letters and dogshit. Sunny Room, through the connecting door, looked like a waxworks after closing time. Tam flickered a light switch and at least got a response: 'Stop that, Tam.'

Linda asked thin air: 'Who's cut the rope off the drying rack?' 'Or nicked my bootlaces,' Patrick added.

Someone put on the McGarrigle Sisters' mournful ditty, 'Heart Like a Wheel'. Whispered conversations started - below my slowly diminishing hearing threshold. This deafness is no joke. I was shivering and crying, maggots of jealousy and terror chomping their way out of my stomach, bats fluttering around my brain. You really were, now, a couple with Jay. Who, of all people, was such a closed-off, emotional miser. And, why the hell can't we keep dogs out of the kitchen? And what am I doing here?

I stood up and shouted, 'It's dead here, we're all dead.' Lesley threw a cup of cold coffee over me, I was briefly glad of that.

So with no farewells, except for Catriona, whom I asked to tell Patrick to watch for Sophie until your return - it was into the Ami and a moonlight flit, 120 miles down here to Dumb Tom's. And this was to be the final time, although I didn't realise or accept this for months. Tom C. was waiting at midnight with a cup of tea and a 'why did you leave?' I needed a way of side-stepping this.

'Non-attachment therapy,' I told Tom. 'Avoiding possessions. Usefulness comes from what is not there.'

'You'd better sit down,' says Tom.

Pinned to his notice-board was a badge which I have taken to wearing: 'Reality is for people who can't handle drugs.'

9
Spring 1973

In Winter the Rhinns of Kells recede, snow-capped, their full 25 miles north. Lone crows, sometimes a buzzard, fly precessive loops up the valley. The burn is a black cascade.

But in Spring, the hills close back in, the burn sparkles, there are a hundred shades of green, all vibrant; and the countryside looks business-like.

Still a city person, I was dazzled by this Spring - the first I'd really watched through since childhood. The snowdrops, crocuses, daffodils, narcissi, primroses, bluebells and early blossoms. Bees touring and sipping. Lambs kicking and scratching themselves like dogs, in hallucinatory green daylight. The pied wagtail. On the back stream, dippers. Dozens of other wild flowers for which I have a mental catalogue of names, but which I can only patchily fit to the right plants.

We celebrated the 'Spring Equinox' - we had just discovered the year has 'equinoxes' and 'solstices' - with a Daffodil Tea, in fancy dress. Bye-bye, illnesses of Winter. Except that Paul's face swelled to football size with some mysterious infection, and Dave still had his migraines.

Then we're off in all directions, at a brisk pace.

Billy and Joel join Sonya at school. School and pub hours become the main influence on our lives of the official clock. Nicky scavenges, bringing home wood, building materials, abandoned but possibly repairable machinery. Julia joins the local branch of the Soil Association. Stuart was still working and even began to pay in his wages. Everyone gardened, but Julia and Richard did most of the work. Alice wanted to be involved, but had quarrelled with Julia over what needed doing.

Nicky, Stuart, Dave, and a gang of visitors, reconnected the springs on the hill to feed the main water tank, reducing our need for metered mains water. Paul rushed everywhere, building, fixing. Dave too (while Carol watched Tam). We urged them to slow down.

And I spent time indoors. I didn't want to, but there was paperwork to do and somehow I'd got the job. Doing the accounts, dealing with cottage bookings, writing to hundreds of people and groups about the event we were planning for the summer.

We lived together better. Didn't argue anymore about meat-eating (but we stopped buying meat). The essential cleaning just got done, as did the dishes. And the who-is-cooking list stayed full for several days ahead, most times. Too full, said Richard. 'It would be nice to have some days when meals didn't appear automatically - days when it would be bread and cheese or egg on toast. Something simple...'

Not that these disputes were ever really resolved - they just got lost amongst new ones.

Car journeys, for example. We made too many of them and the minimum round trip, to CD or the playgroup, was about 15 miles. We had four working vehicles - the big Land Rover, the Ami, Nicky's car and the little Land Rover. Richard and Julia had a written-off VW.

We have meeting after meeting about cars, don't we just.

"Sunday evening. Julia taking minutes. Vehicles, use of.
    "Nicky took Land Rover when needed by Richard.
    "Dave will lay up Little Rover and save the insurance.
    "Nicky should sell his when tax and insurance used up.
    "Nicky not want to because insecure.
    "Nidder nidder about cars.
    "Stuart wants a motorbike. Not helpful.
    "Children should walk to school, we shouldn't leave it so late.
    "What are we here for?"
    "Oh fuck it all."

Bridget, Tim and burly two-year-old Angus, who had written to us and were committed to self-sufficiency/ alternative technology, parked their caravan down by the pond. Bridget went to work as a telephonist (a handy small-town skill at the time). We began an uneasy co-existence, never tackling the issue, of a nuclear couple in the middle of our commune.

Meetings might start with Carol crocheting, Nicky carving wood, Julia darning, Tina sewing, Patrick apparently reading, Alice making tea, Dave checking his (home-made from old telephones) baby alarm, Richard looking bored with it all. But he or Nicky would roll a herbal ciggy. Paul would often be away working and Stuart, theatrically late.

We might start with 'We really must get around to registering as a Housing Association,' or 'How *are* we going to make a living?' But then fantasy would ride into town.

'I'd like to have around fifty people living here.'

'Aren't we trying to become a Loving Group? An echo from the sixties.

We should found an Alternative building society. Publish our own newsletter - Twin Oaks in the States and Findhorn here do it, why not us? Set up a community press.

'Fish farming would be easy,' says Dave. But Dave, we'd learned from the goats experience, sometimes sounded like an expert when he wasn't.

A travelling circus...

Put a windmill on the roof. Solar heating, too. Buy more land (we were hardly using what we'd got). Build Laurieston New Town, ready for when they extend the motorway through to Stranraer, ha ha. Design and build a marina at Kirkcudbright, was Stuart's plan. We asked: 'Are you serious?'

Which would lead on to the 'Why are we here?' ritual and the 'No dope in meetings' closing resolution.

It was room-swap time again.

When Julia and Richard joined, they'd taken a room each. Hello, we wondered. Soon they were fighting. 'You're a horrible man,' Julia yelled, throwing a jar of pickles at him - which missed by just a whisker.

Richard levitated to the top of the tower and immersed himself in a private dream-world. In the Diary, he wrote gibberish, in his neat, round handwriting:

"well well well/ I've been hearing the most amazing things on
the trans attic link up/ quite a little world on
its own and apart from that a person from the electric city
making flagships to sail in those raging torrents of red/ almost
exactly as a mirror there is my boxer oxo/ are the signals
really real or is it the game of the white knight?/ While I'm
here I might as well mention that the princess disappeared
ages ago and I don't suppose will ever come back, and again I
want, don't get, sayin' nothin'."

Rough Translation: the princess is Alice, boxer oxo might be his lover Kate B., no idea for the rest, but I suppose it must refer to Jonathan and Julia.

Julia had moved into the west, top-floor room which I had called my 'workroom' (and which is now 'Catriona's room') So I opted for the room on the first-floor front which later became the Library. In the course of moving my stuff I decided, rather nervously, to make it 'my room' - that is, to put a bed in it. And Paul put a bed into Roses Room, his workroom. So suddenly, apart from Dave and Carol, every adult had their own room. Were we were going our own ways? Uncoupling? I was full of apprehension, wasn't sure I wanted to do it.

I wanted you close to me, not just as lover but as friend. I wanted to talk about all this with you, but you were 'travelling through space in an isolated capsule.' You were frightened, lost, a bit mad. I tried to help, but I couldn't (= you wouldn't let me). So we didn't talk generally about The Group, the way things were going. This was when you wrote in the Diary:

People freaked in, people freaked out

When my house is empty
quiet (not silence) can come
The doors will stand open
Sun can come in
The distance from sounds
will make itself heard.

A cat can sit sunning
in the open frontal lobe.

If he's quick, a sparrow
can make his way in
Peck the specks that spoil
the spickness and the spanness.

Room after room will declare itself
Empty but for its own dust.

I always wanted a quiet house."

Anyway, you said, recently, "we never used to work together and maybe that's why our relationship thrived, for so long." Thus again undermining the whole basis of my life these last 17 years. You are rather good at this.

Alice never did come and spend a night with me in my room, that bed. It was a mattress resting on a couple of doors and angle iron trestles. Crammed underneath with treasures. Back issues of OZ, IT, Ink, Seven Days, Communes Journal, Hapt, Shrew, Anarchy, Freedom, Agitprop's Red Letter, Black Dwarf, Spare Rib, Undercurrents and more, waiting for all this spare time, surely just around the corner, when I meant to sift it all into the definitive article about the sixties, early seventies, feminism, ecology, revolutionary socialism and communal living...

But sometimes she came in the day. We would argue about this or that, or just chat, looking through the windows, watch the trees ballroom dancing to the breeze, then fuck. Once, from her balcony, I spied Alice weeding in the garden. I ran down to her and popped the 'have you got twenty minutes' question. Private code for - 'you wanna?' Or sometimes I'd sleep with Alice in her room. Paul had occasional lovers...

And we were about to become holiday cottage landlords. Working on the cottages meant balancing on shaky stepladders, scrubbing old whitewash from the ceilings, getting soaked with a thin alkaline slip. Patiently scraping off eighty years' worth of wallpaper. Shovelling and scooping away bucketfuls of sodden paper and plaster chunks. Sanding, re-plastering, repainting. Paul insisted on the professional way: work the paint this way, then that way, finish off with light strokes along the grain. Hours of cleaning up.

Everyone helped - except Rich and Julia, who gardened - planting out cabbages, stringing up runner-bean poles; grabbing the sunshine.

'Look, this isn't fair,' we might begin, over supper.

'Suppose you're right, yeah' they'd reply. But then they'd carry on gardening just the same.

Or sometimes they'd counter with 'Well why don't you come and work in the garden?' Meaning, 'It's not important to let the cottages.' Meaning, 'It's not right, anyway.'

And once again we'd have to go through the arguments. Everyone knows it isn't what we want to do in the long run but we could do with the money and you're going to be living off like everyone else - or have you got a better idea for bringing in money? And we've agreed to do it, we've taken bookings and there's only two weeks left. And there's still a lot to do...

So they promised to help. Julia came and painted. And Richard promised to make a bed-base.

10
Spring 1977

I stroll aimlessly in this part of North Yorkshire, head buzzing with the patchy chronology I'm constructing. Or making up. Using the Diaries, the visitors' books, the minutes books. A heron just flapped by.

I am missing you all. I am feeling the distance. (I am sounding like Alice.)

Maybe I have 'taken leave of my senses?' You would maybe say so. Why don't you write?

So Are You Self- Sufficient?
No, but in that June, Lucy kidded and we tiptoed to her stall, kids and adults, 2 or 3 at a time, aah-ing as you do. It was a Billy kid - so we intended to wean it onto dried milk, fatten it a bit, then, er, well, curry it.

Dave organised milking Lucy and did the morning shift. 'Great way to start the day,' he burbles. I think: if you're into fantasy. An hour's work for a quart of milk.

Later, Dave will admit 'We were just unlucky. We wouldn't buy another goat like Lucy - she was kidded too soon.'

It is not only the Accountant who thinks: 'They saw you coming.'

But Dave goes on to insist how, 'If we had three good milkers, the Goats Project would break even after a year.' We acquiesced. Dave built more stalls, and bought two more goats - Maxi and Pearl.

And Dave will continue to enthuse about how we 'make decisions by consensus.'

Self-sufficient? We didn't even eat the billy kid - it hung, rank and maggoty in the cellar before being thrown out.

And How Do You Make Decisions?
We said we'd chalk up each day, what we planned to do. Richard, Of course, didn't. So we nagged him: 'But we agreed,' and he'd sign up for 2 or 3 days and then stop again.

Thus, Ladeez and Gents, one Bourgeois Individual, can effortlessly subvert the Anarchist Commune.

And do you have Multiple.?
Tina was quite right - ever since meeting her in Liverpool I'd thought Julia

was - well, dead attractive. But here at LH she was struggling with Richard and pre-occupied with Jonathan.

Suddenly, with just me and her working together on the far cottage, we took a break, held hands in the sun, then rushed back into one of the rooms we'd finished and furnished and made love, rather hastily.

I would have liked this to continue. I checked that Tina, Alice and Richard weren't upset. Jonathan was still on his way.

Richard's reply - in his enigmatic drawl - is etched on my psyche: 'I think it's great if anyone can manage to get it together in this place.'

I spent a couple of nights in Julia's bed. But then that was that. Perhaps because she was cross about Chris F., an old friend of mine and Tina's who I'd also made love with, just the once, when she visited.

'Why don't you just fuck with the women here?' Julia demanded.

And Meetings?

Julia is quite right, we do witter on about vehicles. Minutes say:

"Stuart crashed and wrote off the Ami" - he wasn't hurt - "Paul bought another with the insurance."

"Peter," - a visiting 11-year-old - "drove the little Landy into the stables wall and it's wrecked."

"Nicky's car needs tax and insurance."

"The new Ami has blocked fuel line."

The P&CRP people never ask about our eco-footprint. Few do. But we are actually rather proud that we operate with say a third of the per capita national average of vehicles. Ditto, washing machines, fridges, hi-fis and the like.

And Multiple?

Dear Alice, I can't piece together what happened to our relationship. I remember the beginning, that time the Four Of Us went to visit Birchwood, as fantastic. But later you explained: 'I just wanted to get the sex thing over with.' I'm still puzzled by that.

And our early days at LH, it seems to me, were lovely.

But lately? It was you, after all, who first slept with 'somebody new' - I mean, Nicky. Yet you made me feel, in my tiny fling with Chris F., that I'd betrayed you. You stopped coming to see me.

A month or so later, with Paul away a lot in Glasgow, you invented Door Language. Pretty simple. Shut: I'm busy. Ajar: come in. Alice as Queen Bee, waiting for me, Tony or Richard to drone by. I was amused by this - until I kept finding the door shut. (I did also wonder about empowerment and feminism, but knew you'd rubbish anything I might ask.)

Gradually we drifted away from each other, kept out of each other's way. Our arguments in meetings became fewer, that's right isn't it?

11
Summer 1973

Laurieston Hall - wrote Alice - is a huge mansion house in Galloway, the communal home of 13 adults, 9 children, 3 goats, 4 cats, many dreams.

After a year of being "The LH Group," living "in our *collective* home" - we have at last, rather suddenly, come out as a "Commune."

Patrick joins. At 23, he takes the mantle of 'the youngest' from Dave. With Rich, he's equal tallest. He's definitely split with his wife - an element of mystery there. And he came across more 'spiritual' than I remembered. He brought a few books and clothes, and plenty of energy. 'But only £250, when we'd said £500,' muttered the Accountant - who was firmly told to shut up by just about everyone.

Also Tony joins with his son Alistair (always called, Ali) initially as 'three-month visitors.' Tony had this project to build a pedal-powered aeroplane and try for the £10,000 prize offered for a figure-of-eight, one-mile flight. Besides, it turns out, wanting to be out of London, and into a trial separation from his wife. He set to work, with blocks of polystyrene, melinex film and a few bicycle parts. Ali - at eight, the oldest child - wasn't happy and created mayhem. Many times we had to intervene to stop the destruction of furniture or calm the screams of the littler ones.

And the much-heralded Jonathan, Julia's lover, arrived, having walked for two months, from Land's End. We talked about him joining us. He went back to Liverpool to earn some money, leaving this message in the Diary:

"Restharrow, wood vetch, wild thyme, sea lavender, marsh bird's-foot trefoil, skull cap, sea centaury, yellow meadow vetchling, corn spurrey, thrift, common mullein, agrimony, dyers greenweed, beautiful St. John's wort, field woundwort, meadow sweet, valerian, sea plaintain, harebell, english stonecrop, tormentil, ladies bedstraw, heath bedstraw, tufted vetch, meadow cranesbill, herb robert, pearlswort, thyme leaved sandwort, lousewort, eyebright, bladder campion, rockrose, hayrattle, woodsage, babington's orache, dactylorhiza purpurella (purple orchid), yellow flag, yarrow, wild carrot, scarlet pimpernel… all these were by the sea today."

You have to admire a man who knows Babington's Orache when he sees it, don'tcha?

So we're one commune: but with many identities.

Summer starts with 'Dance Weekend.' Picture a score of face-painted, fancy-dressed, mightily-stoned, beautiful-people, boogieing in Big Front room. Or (snap): seven of the same, perched precariously on its mantelpiece. And next day, on the lawn, making a circle and dancing in a light, warm rain (while, from a first-floor window, Tina's mum watches in a mild state of shock). Richard, pants flapping, banging on a coffee-tin drum, leading us in single file round the lawns - up to the pond - into the pond. We ran back, gloriously muddy, piled into the four working bathrooms. I bathed nonchalantly with a woman whose name I didn't catch. Afterwards, tea, bread and jam and chatter.

Dance Weekend was, I think, Kate B.'s production. On the last morning, she and Richard, in mock hospital outfits, brought early morning tea to all the 'patients'. Later, on film, they're seen interfering with each other amidst the lupin crop.

So here is your regular, peace and love, Woodstock nation, liberated hippy commune.

But a few days later, we are eight men clasping eight children as Alice, Carol, Julia and Tina set off in the Ami for the 1973 National Women's conference. Women's meetings had been fairly regular since Julia's arrival. There was one uncertain Men's meeting, maybe two. For some of the men, this apparent closeness and solidarity amongst the women was new and bewildering, even frightening. Other men wondered, well of course we support women's liberation, but we are rather busy and Bristol is a long way away. Even so, here is the radical, feminist, anti-sexist cadre, in motion.

We have more visitor groups. Some of Paul's students visited from Strathclyde University. We thought they were coming to do bits of building work, join in our lives. But really they wanted lectures about ecology and communal living, and to rest and play before their examinations. It wasn't a happy visit. They departed with a large number of our tools. I stopped one, carrying our best new hammer into their minibus.

'Sorry' he lied, 'I thought it was ours.' (There's a guy, currently planning Gay Men's Week '77, who writes "Basically we are planning to rip you off. Straight exploits gay every day." "Why not," I write back, "everyone else has.")

Octopus Club, mostly teachers from Liverpool, came for a holiday - we cleaned and catered. Plus we had people staying in both cottages (but only just - Meeting Minutes, two days before the first cottage guests were due to arrive, say: "Still waiting for Richard to finish cottage bed.").

Meanwhile Paul was designing a house for Chuck and Jill, who had moved on to Lothlorien. Stuart was doing drawings for a caravan site for a local landowner. We sold our first vegetables and eggs. Laurieston Hall as the independent, small business, self-employed, rural commune, making its way?

We celebrated our first year with a garden party. Everyone was there: farmers, farmhands, the minister and his wife, the man from the Pru, the washing machine man and Greta, the landlady from the Laurie Arms. I found all this dreadfully embarrassing. Nick H., a visitor, called it 'a sociological feast.' We had argued endlessly about how the locals perceived us - and how we make our living - and we'd been successful in not being seen as 'rich hippies.'

But was this the image we wanted to convey to the village - a bunch of ordinary, hardworking, middle-class, happy families?

Lastly, in August - and in contrast - we took on another aspect of our fragmented collective identity: Laurieston Hall as the non-sectarian, libertarian/ socialist, personal-is-political revolutionary group. Laurieston as a movement 'base.' Here comes - dah dada dah dah, dada, da dah! - the PeopleCentre.

Dance weekend, Paul's students and Octopus had been cleaning/ catering trial runs. A few of us had been working since Easter, with the help of friends elsewhere - Keith P., Peter H. - to put together a Political Conference.

But 'Conference' wasn't the right word. This was to be a softer, looser, 'tribal gathering', blurring conference with holiday, living together and consciousness-raising.

To set the tone, we'd called the whole thing LARFFS: Laurieston's Alternative Revolutionary Fun-Fair & Seminar. That would be your suggestion (it's strange that I don't remember you being part of it, hardly at all).

Richard and Patrick dressed up weird and sat out in the drive, waiting to greet the visitors. But by 8 p.m. only half a dozen had showed up. I sat and shivered with these in Big Front room. What an anti-climax. People began to drift off to an early bedtime. Disappointment showed all round.

'Come on,' I said to Rose H., 'let's go down the pub.'

Rose had visited a couple of weeks before, with her two children. She was a long-time friend of Alice and Paul's (and her kids, friends with Sonya and Polly). But I'd met her, too - when, back in 1970, I'd painted the W in Agitprop's "Vietnam Burns While Oxbridge Paddles" banner, which was sneaked onto TV by showing it at Mortlake during the boat race.

Paul, who fancied Rose, had high hopes. But she'd brought Catch C., the man she lived with in, the gossip went, a more off than on relationship.

Rose had cooked, cleaned, taken the kids to the seaside. Paul and Catch burst in and out of doors, walked briskly along corridors - Paul trying to get time alone with Rose, Catch trying to prevent it. Great melodrama. On her last day, Rose told me all about it. Then she kissed me. Then she fucked me. Then she got dressed and went back off to bed with Catch. I thought: Goodness Gracious.

Now she was back, without Catch, to spend LARFFS Week with me. (Dear Paul, I know you were upset and cross but what was I supposed to do? And it was nice of you to warn me that Rose was fickle. I should have listened.)

'Does Tina mind?' asked Rose, in the Laurie Arms, sipping orange juice. She had a liver complaint, potentially serious - cancer was mentioned - which added a dramatic urgency.

'No, she likes you,' I said. The whole conversation was nervous. We hardly knew each other. 'But you should ask her yourself.'

I wanted suddenly to see what was happening back at the house, at this event I'd looked forward to for so long.

And at eleven p.m.: a transformation! Dozens of people milling around, more arriving all the time. The house again showing the bustle it would have had in its early days. Greetings, hugs and howd'yedos. Palpable excitement. A buzzing of exclamations at the awesome size of the house. Small parties of visitors wandering lost between the spare bedrooms and the Hall, their paths crossing and re-crossing, making a game of it. In the Old Kitchen, soup, bread and talk of what the Week would hold.

"LARFFS week," wrote one of the visitors, "was frenetic, ambitious, remarkable, impossible to encapsulate."

"Seventy adults in the house and a couple of dozen children. We ate together in the Hall, at tables angled in towards the enormous fireplace. There was an open timetable/ sign-up system for meetings and discussions. We had plenty of these. Plus tête-à- têtes, confrontations, small group discussions, conversations which people passed through as if on a rota, conversations which people dropped into, and stayed...

"Women's and Men's meetings - some suspicion between the two. Culture and Art and Symbols and Everyday Life and Revolution. The people from Living Theatre (London) - Jeremy, Diane, Sylvia, Donald - objecting to the signal boards of the old bell system used for summoning servants. Mike, one of the residents, saying they hadn't got time to do everything and if they didn't like them they could take them down. 'I am not your servant,' roared Sylvia.

"Breathing and chanting workshops and Tai Chi Chuan 'form' on the grass. Meetings about Images Of Utopia; Utopian Change; Non-Violence;

Beyond Reformism; Where Are We Now; Housing; Tenant Co-ops; Squatting. Alternative and straight technology. The press, other media. Work collectives. Community groups.

"And Sexuality And Relationships. 'Do you really think you can make it work?' someone asked Mike. 'Definitely,' says Mike, I love Tina and I love Rose." Rose hugged her knees and didn't say anything.

"Every morning, warm-up, games, massage exercises led by Martin O., a theatre director. But a gloomy one 'These people are surviving multiple relationships,' he says, 'I haven't even got one.'

"Two evenings dancing, once on the lawn to a rock band called Iron Claw which resident Nicky had arranged. All week, tag and frisbee on the lawn. Trust games, where you let yourself fall, eyes closed, stiff, like a plank, surrounded by a small circle of people who catch you and bounce you back up. Another where you have a partner who leads you, blindfolded, towards different things to feel, smell, touch. Mime. One evening, a free music session with recorders, tin whistles, violin, cello, guitars and people clapping and singing. Another night, late, a group of naked people playing table tennis.

"All this and more. Joyful, tearful, thoughtful, comical. Part tightly organised - meals, bed-linen, food - but mostly chaos. The schedule was too full at the beginning and again at the end. Meetings ran in parallel and some grew so big they over-spilled into a second or even a third group. In the middle, a lull. People sitting quiet, resting, playing chess, reading - there was a literature table stacked with pamphlets, duplicated hand-outs, magazines), recuperating, exploring the 'knock-out' countryside."

In this week with Rose H., I was often last to bed, being night-watch-person, putting out lights. I was, in this supposedly self-organising event, the arranger, information point, announcer and catalyst. To bed at 2 a.m. Then up at 7 to milk the goats. I have no idea why I, no goat enthusiast, was doing goat-milking during this week.

Being-in-love-with-Rose was a rather public matter. Would it have been the same without an audience? Don't know. Indeed, without the explanation of LARFFS, would Rose have been able to return so soon? Probably not. But as things were, we were left almost deferentially alone at times to hold hands on the lawn, walk up to the burn, make love and sleep in the afternoons.

And what were you doing? You liked Rose, said you didn't feel jealous. You were supportive. But I remember the look on your face when I mentioned that Rose might sell her flat and come to live here. Aghast, you were.

While absorbed with Rose, I was besotted with LARFFS.

This was my high point of the year. Suddenly it was possible to believe again in 'The Movement' or 'The Alternative.' Intricate and dense networks of communes, tribal connections of friends and lovers, nationally co-ordinated activities, 'The macro and the micro coming together'.

(The PA wonders: Where are you now?)

And - this was strange - since I was fucking someone else I sort of wanted you to, as well. So I was pleased when you spent a night, towards the end of the week, with my old friend Alan C. True, I hadn't been so pleased when you'd fucked with anonymous men at the Open University summer school; I think it was more the anonymity than the fucking which upset me.

I wouldn't mention it except for what it says about us. 'Open marriage,' is that what we had? Still sounds like American Jargon. I remember feeling very confident and loving. And we were talking together again; at least about these romances. Everything from people's world-views to who did what and to whom and how it was.

There was a poster-poem which finished up: 'I keep on wanting everything, and wanting you to want that too.' It's still around. That's still me...

Wanting everything. Revolutionaries Come Out. Be realistic, demand the impossible. And so on. It was all too much. We were setting ourselves up to fail.

LARFFS was a 'good times' week - tons of warmth, emotion, love and intelligence. We learned how the house felt, full of people - and most of us liked it. We gained a new identity - the 'Residents.' (Later, 'Rezzies.')

Passing each other in the corridors, we hugged as old friends do, meeting by coincidence on a street corner in a foreign city. Our 'House Meeting' saw us all present and promptly so, pleased with each other. With no urgent business, it was a moment simply to enjoy being together. The visitors had helped with the cooking, the cleaning, the gardening and even done a little work on the billiard room kitchen. And we'd made some money.

And the visitors thought of us as: "really together."And we had made many, new, informal links between us, our visitors, projects and places. But the final meeting - on What Happens Next - was an inconclusive mess.

In the morning the visitors, including Rose, drifted away, drained, silent, as though they had stayed too long at a party.

The goats got into the garden, again. And Polly and Sophie, cocky three-year olds, took off for a long walk, in a cold drizzle, deaf to all our calls and whistles (we found them eventually in Willowbank cottage, opposite the end of our drive, after they'd meandered across the Main Road to New Galloway).

71

The house exuded gloom. Middle Front room was thick with mud, waste paper and hush.

Nobody cooked, nobody swept up. And Ali, Billy, Sonya and Joel, cross at lack of attention, vandalised a sofa - perhaps reclaiming territory. Tiffany, Tam and George howled and clung. The phone rang unanswered.

Imagine a monumental stack of dishes in Old Kitchen sink One of the cats, slapped off the kitchen table, took a couple of plates with it. And were there really only four bloody cats?

What a bummer. This was a day that shouldn't have bothered turning in. It should have taken itself off sick. A day when we asked ourselves, 'Why are we here?' Which became an incantation. Or an ironic, all-purpose response.

'D'you want a cup of tea?'

'Why are we here?'

'Why are we here' insinuated itself to the top of meeting agendas, only to be ritually deferred and then adjourned. People used it to imply they were aware of the problems; to score communal points. Pushed to answer it individually, we tended to embark on liturgical recaps of our personal histories. 'Well, I wanted to live in the country.'

None of us knew - or could spell out - what we wanted. It was maybe time to find out.

Hence our first 'Laurieston Crisis Week' - a week's-worth of meetings.

Dave R., an old friend of mine and a Management Consultant, had just written us a 'Situation Review.' He said we should "concentrate on developing our strengths rather than on eradicating our weaknesses."

This and other of his prescriptions for action, were, I thought, spot on. But most people didn't like the 'Business Language.' So his Report was ignored.

Instead, we had Nicky touring the company with his questionnaire, a goulash of weird questions, strange notes and random codes. But then he lost the results.

Alice did a more orderly production - and pinned the results to a couple of 6' by 4' notice-boards. It was a lot to take in, in one go.

I responded, topic by topic; Alice replied; and so it fell once again to Alice and me to act out arguments for everyone else's benefit. Our exchanges were clothes-pegged in swatches to Old Kitchen's door. From which the PO can snip the following exchanges:

The Capital
Alice: "The capital. Oh dear, I can hardly bear it."

Mike: "Yeah, like we talk about this every day. In fact, I only remember two or three times since we've been here."

A: "We didn't live off capital last year."

M: "Well, yes we did, ducks. OK, the money is still in the bank. But it's what we didn't spend, but which we should have, for example to maintain the house, that's the problem."

A: "We don't intend to live off capital this year."

M: "And how exactly do we intend not to do this? Are we going to do the PeopleCentre properly, or not? If not, how do we..?"

Making A Living

A: "Dearest Mike, I just met you in the corridor. I was feeling very happy but you came out of your room, tried to avoid a kiss, and said, 'The PeopleCentre - I've given up on it.'"

M: "Dearest Alice, what I meant was, I don't want it to be *my* project - it has to be a collective thing."

Understandably this drew rather hostile comments. In the meeting which followed, I had to explain myself. Of course, I agreed that everyone (well, nearly everyone) had worked really hard on LARFFS. People had taken turns cooking for six times our usual numbers, served food, washed up, cleaned baths and loos - and kept everything else going too (goats, chickens, garden, washing and, er, our children…) They'd tried to help the visitors have a good time (besides, themselves, dancing with them on the lawn). They'd been really supportive. And it had worked OK, practically. And we'd made some money.

'But?'

This was difficult for me. It was something I hadn't noticed during the commotion of the event, amidst the euphoria, but which had come from that dismal morning after. It was simply that Conference and Commune hadn't really met.

Most of my co-communards just weren't into this high-octane, intellectual-plus-physical, alternative political stuff, nor how these issues might map onto our own lives (maybe they already knew all they needed to know).

'I mean, most of you didn't come to any of the meetings and discussions.'

But then, no-one had said they would.

'So, what else was wrong, then?'

'Well, I was left on my own, to run things.'

'I thought you enjoyed that,' said Richard. He had a point.

Alice suggested: 'We could talk about how much support you can expect from people here.'

And I say: "But - who else really wants the PeopleCentre? Apart from Tina, who wants it to include a Kids Project?"

More nidder nidder, as Julia would say. We pass on making any decision. Which leads us on to:

Planning/ Decision-Making, How Do You?
A: "You want a master plan and I don't, so working it out means talking to one another and understanding one another."

M: "How many times, Alice, no! No master plan! But I do think we need clear, written-down Aims and Objectives, that's all. I mean, where are we going?"

And here I added a quote from heavyweight academic, Stafford Beer: "Unless we plan we will get a future which nobody chose and which we probably will not like."

(In fact, we didn't plan. Crisis Weeks have become routine. Every year since, the first week in September is blocked off in the Calendar. Here comes our annual, communal, '19th', nervous breakdown. Traditionally, nothing is ever decided. And Jay just wrote, last February, 'We are all on the outside of nothing.')

Meanwhile, regrouping after the Summer, we were (The PO has now to think alphabetically):

Alice, who, after LARFFS, wrote "It took a lot of energy to cope with the people we had. For example, this guy R. who talked for an hour about himself and what he's doing, his hopes for communal living, his farming experience and his views on Women's Liberation."

Translation: 'I am fed up of my time being stolen by these sad cases we get.' Alternatively 'He was obviously a tedious eedjit, on the make.'

It seems to be that, in any visiting group, the waifs, strays, downright bigoted or quite mentally ill will promptly be sucked in by Alice's aura (or something) And this will - over the years - give her some company and stimulation, while causing her considerable grief.

Carol, who wrote later that she felt herself "caught in innumerable double binds...Wanting to share the responsibility of Tam and Tiffy with adults who had had a bellyful of baby-care. Being edged towards nuclear caring for them, surrounded by moves towards the destruction of the nuclear family. Feeling the physical and emotional demands of two babies close together and feeling guilty about not pulling my weight on the communal front."

Dave, jack-of-all-trades, who, seeing jobs to do everywhere - not least, finishing the billiard room kitchen which he'd supported so strongly - was frustrated by the babes at his feet, or lost or missing tools, or what must have been a spooky communal disapproval for the way he worked. And by being also an intellectual with little or no time to think (but most of us had already been there when our kids were tiny). And by having the Accountant on his back about the goats.

'About Dave,' Paul would ask, 'did you know that he's....?'

And you or I would pull him up and say, primly, 'you must take your criticisms directly to the people they concern.' An encounter-group-style bollocks edict we'd learned over the summer (coinciding conveniently with the meaning 'I'm fed up of hearing you moaning on.')

But privately we agreed with Paul. We said: 'If they weren't living with us they'd have to look after their kids and make a living. Here we help with Tam and Tiffy but all they do is the goats and the chickens. And nick the Group's firewood for their personal fires. And row between themselves.'

Meanwhile your PO, wearing 'St. Michael' underpants, continued to wash machine-loads of Tam's nappies

Julia (aka *Jools*) - now you see her, now you don't. We all made trips to parents. This was another unquestioned institution (*How do make decisions?* Well, by inertia, mainly). We dragged up and down motorways with squalling car-sick kids to keep family ties going. Or Paul, or Carol flew, parent-paid, to Jersey, where Carol's dad was a pharmacist and Paul's, a retired builder.

But Julia - it seemed - took rather more time away than most. To her Problem Family (we are not going there.) But also - since she couldn't stand the disturbance of so many visitors - she ran away for a month to be with Jonathan in Liverpool.

Nicky, who installed a set of brushes, buckets, mops and so on for each area of the house, all colour-coded by area. Your PO was quick to belittle this brilliant idea as 'institutional' and 'coming from Nicky's need for his childhood lifestyle.'

Patrick was the new one, feeling his way. I was really pleased he'd joined us. He did a bit of everything. Once, in the goat yard, I told him that Alice had said she fancied him, which, I hadn't understood, was a confidence I shouldn't have broken. Alice was furious with me for a year. Maybe longer. Maybe still.

Paul was, as ever, wrapped up in his work; about to move from the U. of Strathclyde to the Mackintosh school of art, also in Glasgow, and busy preparing a new course. And he had, apparently, more local work than he could cope with. The PO wondered whether this work could have been shared. Maybe divided so that Paul did the designs and others did the labouring - turning out detailed drawings?

No luck there. Paul will not like this at all, but it seemed to me that he was peripheral to the Commune from this point on. Except, of course, that we relied on his income. I'll say that again, knowing how your eye,

Dear Reader - and mine - runs past the difficult bits. It seemed to me: Paul was peripheral to the Commune. He will hate that.

And *Richard* (called *Dick* just by Julia). I wrote him a note, but didn't send it. "Dear Richard. You agreed to the cottages project, same as the rest of us, and you are going to benefit from the income. When you call those of us who deal with enquiries the 'Office Workers,' this is plain fucking insulting. And by not building the bed-base until 24 hours before it was needed, you made that office-worker role one of nail-biting misery. Then you said we were foolish to worry, which, looking back, was contemptuous. You want to know how it felt? Oppressive, that's how."

But then, Richard wasn't happy, either.

Nor was *Stuart*. His behaviour was strange and disturbing. When he was here.

It's only now that I understand what Stuart must have been going through. Lonely: no lover. And this wretched process where you move away from the 'Group' and then, boy, does the group close you out. Stuart asked for his own area in the house - wanting, I suppose, to live independently?

Tony, about to morph from 'long-stay visitor' into a proper member, had made an impressive start on his flying machine. He came to meetings and chipped in sensibly. I liked him enormously.

Tina. I am not sure how we were getting on. Or how you were. Except that you were planning Women's Week.

And *Moi*. Some have suggested that the PA might be a less than perfect human being. He finds this hard to understand and is awaiting the results of tests.

Summer finished with a small Women's Week. Nine visiting women plus Alice, Carol, Tina and Julia, closeted away in meetings all week. All of the housework/ childcare was left, without consultation, to the men (where before, visitors had always shared all the chores.)

Suddenly we have (women) guests getting full board, cooked meals and childcare, from a struggling rural commune, for £1 a day. The Accountant dared not comment.

This also was when Bill and Ben came looking for a fight. Actually - can this be right? - they came primarily for one Sue G. They were outraged that she'd defected to a gathering of women while living with them at Knockengarroch as their house-keeper. Richard, Tony and Patrick circled them, hoping for no trouble,but showing willing to throw them out if there was.

But your PO, arriving late, feeling a surge of good-neighbourliness, and seeing Bill and Ben were moderate as newts, rushed up and hugged both of them so tight, this prevented any further fighting. And we agreed to go off for a J.

Tony says later: 'He's got some violence in him, that Patrick.'

A young couple, Rosie and Neill, moved in with their baby Emma to the village. Neill was an Art teacher at CD High. Tina and I went to supper. Wow, we know some actual Scots!

Ali joined Bill and Sonya at the village school; Sophie and Polly were back at the playgroup. Work picked up again on the Billiard Room kitchen.

Days were crowded with children, callers, small tasks. The talking had stopped - though we kept up a weekly 'business meeting.'

Paul made another long list of Essential House Maintenance tasks. We couldn't possibly do it all. But Richard, Patrick and I at least cleaned out the house gutters again.

Stuart wrote invitations for an event he called a Festival of Alternative and Radical Technology. Get it?

Julia returned from Liverpool, followed shortly afterwards by Jonathan. We were all simply getting on with living.

12

And Is It A Success?

'Well, if you mean financially,' says The Accountant, 'we've just about made our way.'

Meanwhile he's done the research: In Year 1 (72/73) - hardly.

Income was £5167, nearly all of it from the men's outside work. All of the projects, including visitors, cost us more than they brought in. But we'd lived on £10 a week per adult, £2.50 per child. Less than half our previous living costs - we should have been chuffed about that.

The Accountant pinned these figures up in Crisis Week '73, but there was scarcely a murmur of comment. We are living with people as one economic family – but no-one wants to look at the books. This has been such a strange sleigh-ride.

And in Year 2 (73/74) - hardly.

Income was up, at £5500 - but was less, per person, per week, than in the first year (the Accountant supposes that's progress). More than half the income was Paul's salary. PeopleCentre Visitors and 'Freefall' - the Kids Project, of which, more later - brought in a quarter. The rest was Richard's Liverpool job, Dave's period on the dole, cottage rents and some cash Stuart paid in. We just about kept spending within income.

For the record our total income is about what any one of us professionals would have earned for a full year. Tina, if she'd stayed in advertising, would have been on double that.

But in Year 3 (74/75) - not at all.

We earned £5202; spent £5943; result, a loss of £741. (This ignores holiday air fares, paid by parents, of £546 - more than 10% of all expenditure.)

Paul had again earned half the income. The PeopleCentre (including Freefall), Richard's building Henry's barn, and publishing the Legal Frameworks Handbook another 40%. The remainder was from other bits of outside work. As for garden sales - well, they were pathetic. We do need a way of talking about the garden…

And Do You Have, Er -

Well, yes we do, but that Autumn, no-one seemed happy.

Alice was upset about Paul (but was seeing Tony and Rich).

And occasionally, your PA, who remembers an afternoon with Alice when Dave - it would have to be Dave - barges in past the Please Knock notice and Alice giggled because he'd done the same thing the day before, finding her with Tony.

(Dave had called Alice's crisis-week questionnaire, 'superb.' Meanwhile, on the Kitchen blackboard, Alice had rather publicly liked Dave's muesli mix. And she'd started saying she "really supported the Goats project" because, she felt, "it has political overtones." Sort of a mutual appreciation society happening there, then. Watch this space.)

(Someday, I hope to 'feel' a political overtone myself. From about now, Alice has ceased to think, believe, reason or consider - she only 'feels.')

Richard was living in what looked like a druggie, fantasy world, into which Kate B. was willingly co-opted. All to do, we thought, with his rejection by Julia.

Julia, even with Jonathan here, was depressed and lonely. 'I know it's not right,' she told the PA, referring to Richard/ Alice and Richard/ Kate B., 'but I still get jealous.'

Nicky was seriously depressed. Mainly about Tina, who wouldn't fuck him anymore. Alice and Julia had both dallied briefly with him; he'd got over that. But Tina had been a dithering part-time lover for six months, before she'd stopped.

But also, he'd come out as bisexual. And suddenly there weren't any actual or potential male lovers around anymore. And he'd given up his job at Kilquhanity and set out to be a commercial handy-man. He demanded his own bank account and an 'allowance.' We said, 'You don't understand, Nicky.'

And Mike realises all he has, with Rose, is a long-distance fantasy. People say of him that 'He's living in a world of his own.'

(We hid all this from visitors. We closed ranks. We were opaque. Always, one measure of our collectivity - how little we let outsiders know about what's rattling in our cupboards.)

And Self-Sufficiency?

We have ducks and geese, introduced by Bridget and Tim, multiplying and meandering happily between the stables and the pond. We have chickens, doing well at this point - recovered after Rosie's dog, Flossie, had attacked the flock. Carol and Tim built gates for the stables entrance, to keep foxes and dogs out and the chickens in.

And we have bees, thanks to Nicky. He and I fed the bees sugar to help them through the winter.

That's about it. Self-sufficiency is a dream. We have, for example, no rice, soya or wheat, and no prospect of any.

13

Autumn 1973

Morning Room, 26 September '73. Every half hour, Nicky interrupts the meeting, ferociously hand-axing logs into smaller chips to feed a fine blaze. But the fireplaces were designed for coal. It was cold, cold, cold. We huddled and shivered. Julia wore a woollen skull-cap. Dave, his best white pullover and serious manner.

The question at hand was: 'Can Jonathan join?'

Everyone has tense stomach muscles and shoulders. Because things can never be as simple - as 'one-issue' - as this.

Tina chain-smoked, round-shouldered, in a coat and two pairs of jeans. Paul blinked behind his glasses, in his Guernsey sweater and a new pair of shoes.

It could have been a simple meeting. Straight-forward at least.

Julia could have said she wanted Jonathan to join because she loved him. Richard, that he was upset at the prospect of living beside the pair of them but that he wouldn't say no. The rest of us, that we didn't mind strongly one way or the other, but that the new people/ income argument would have to be sorted out. And that we really need to talk about 1001 other things, without distorting them to fit: 'Can Jonathan join.'

But meetings were hopeless.

'Well, he seems OK to me,' says Paul - Jonathan wasn't present to hear all this - 'but on what basis would he be coming?'

'On what basis' meaning money. The implication being that if we can divert to our financial problems, by now alarming and grim, and solve these, then Jonathan could join without further discussion.

Tension rises. Julia winces. She rarely spoke in meetings; but when she did, she was always clear and to-the-point. And here, she has to be a player.

'Well,' she suggests, 'the same as anyone else.' Neatly implying that the rest of us are already here on the same financial basis. But we all knew that Julia had commandeered the garden, but not worked on visiting groups (so is not a 'money-earner.')

Nicky shivers despite his well-made sports jacket (high class jumble from the local gentry.) Richard, in pink and green shoes, white trousers with embroidered fishes - we realise it's his motif - is turned slightly sideways to the circle and is farthest from its centre. Alice wears a long dress and ballet pumps. Carol looks tired and impatient. Everyone is distressed by the cold.

'Oh, this is silly.' says Tina. 'We should be talking about, you know, the Richard Julia Jonathan thing.'

Good, brave. To the point, timely. Guaranteed to produce chaos and evasion. But a phone call interrupts us. Five inconsequential minutes pass, the drama in suspense.

Some comment surely is wanted from Richard, who has been silent up to now.'I mean, why does he want to come here? I mean, why?' says Richard.

Knowing the answer. Afraid to voice his feelings. And perhaps insulted because, by starting off on money, we were ignoring his feelings. But then again, he'd been ignoring ours, over the past month, showing disdain for our attempts to discuss and plan our future.

'Well, he's interested in what we are doing here,' Julia offers as a direct confrontation with Richard. Their arguments over splitting have been simmering for months. Richard's eyes flash. Julia needs to neutralise her statement by expanding it into a wider, group reference, hence adds: 'And he'll go out to work.'

'Oh, Great,' leers Richard - sarcastic, ponderous, introverted. He pauses.

For a minute or two we all look around at each other. 'He hasn't got anything better to do, has he?' Richard asks - meaning, he's only coming because you're here. There is some nuance to this, sexual perhaps, that only Julia understands. Then he adds, 'Well, there's lots like him, aren't there?' Here we know what he means. We needed people who would add something, initiate projects - those we hadn't got around to yet, or their own. People who would bring something new, not just help share the load.

Meanwhile Paul has given up hope of turning the conversation towards money, and is now seeking to come over as a Nice Person. So he says: 'Well, look, if Julia wants him to come here, he should just come.'

My god the audacity. It ignores Richard's apprehension (besides pretending there is no financial problem at all.)

'Pass,' says the next person.

We have started 'going round the circle.' This way of talking precludes the worst of the two-person exchanges. It includes everyone - how democratic - but then it can pressure people into talking when they don't want to, making them very boring. And when someone interrupts for a moment, someone else is sure to say: 'Well I think now we've started, we should continue going round ...'

A diversion springs up over whether it is OK to 'pass' on such an important matter.

'Well I think, now we've started.' says Paul.

'Well all I was going to say,' blurts Alice, 'was that it's a bit strange how when he first came here he was pretty much against what we're doing, but now he wants to join.' This was pure noise. As though we didn't all experience the same ambivalent feelings towards Laurieston, every day.

Tina says: 'Besides, Julia's lent him some money.' Probably alluding to Julia's inheritance - it had come through and she'd repaid Maureen her £1800 money-in-the-house. But was keeping the balance in a private account of her own. The money thing could take us anywhere. Perhaps Julia's purchase of a new hi-fi, before she arrived. Or Richard's new hi-fi. Or even Carol and Dave's lack of capital, or Stuart's. Or the way Stuart seemed to be drifting out of the Group (he isn't here at this meeting.)

'Yes, what about your living expenses, Julia. You haven't paid for yourself for this year yet. Nor has Richard,' says the Accountant. Referring to the old agreement we had, to provide equal shares of the income. Note the pompous bureaucrat-speak - 'living expenses.' This was nervous, gutless criticism.

Julia would normally have walked out of a meeting like this, pleading exhaustion. But though threatened and probably frightened, this one is too important for her.

'I'll pay the money in, anytime,' she says.

'Jonathan won't be a money-earner, though, will he? I mean, we have plenty of gardeners,' says Patrick. The gardener. He slumped back, looking bored and sleepy, raised his eyes from taking the minutes and says what he then summarises as 'This is a strange conversation. Right up in the money-clouded skies.'

Minute-taker's licence. It also shows however a scornful line with regard to money which those with no money in the house, no particular involvement in money-earning and, usually, no children - i.e. with little to lose - will come to share.

Nicky mutters: 'I hardly know him.'

Another diversion. Most of us don't know Jonathan - we hardly know each other - and so we will have to work on what we do know, or can work out: Julia and Richard's feelings, the money, projects.

Julia is next in the circle. 'So,' says Richard, 'let's hear why you want him to come then.'

'Well I like living with him. He's a nice person to live with.' Understatement, euphemism.

'Yes, but he won't get anything going,' replies Richard.

'There seems to be no reason for him coming except to be with you,

Jools,' says Mike, out of turn. 'So why don't we ask him to pay his way here, like Tony, and see how things go?'

Agreed OK. He pays his way, say the minutes. This means, if he comes at all.

But the meeting isn't over yet. Alice, who has disdained to speak about money, asks Julia, 'Is it going to make you happy, his being here?' (The PO guesses this means, 'Can I carry on fucking Richard without you interfering?)

'Well,' Julia admits. 'I feel more positive. There's been lots wrong with me here. It's true, I find living with so many people difficult. It's destructive, the way I deal with it. I cut myself off.'

She certainly did. Brave of her to say so.

'Yes,' says Dave, in the manner of a TV philosopher, 'we're a very large group. But also we need more people.'

Julia looks horrified.

Richard says: 'He's only coming for love. But that's a good enough reason, isn't it?' Pause. Then, impulsively: 'I can take him personally. I mean, it doesn't freak me out, him and Julia. Interesting, that, isn't it? Julia's going to find it hard, anyway.' And to Julia: 'What if he lets you down? You'd find it hard without him.'

Richard was right to worry. Julia and Jon never really became a couple: they fought for a year or more.

In the Radical Commune, everyone who wants to join will have to do so for love. In this way, we will take over the world. And we'll always party.

Jonathan was a Cambridge graduate. Thoughtful, bespectacled, he should have become a don. Maybe he still will. He'd worked for a year as a road-sweeper in London. Manual labour as the penance of the disillusioned middle-class academic. Then moved to Liverpool where he'd taught Liberal Studies and met Julia and Richard. Lost his way again. Depression caught him. But he'd got it fairly well parcelled up and deposited in the left luggage. Since July, he'd been working in a bakery. He arrived with his wages, which he paid in. And two absurdly white, crisp, and clean boiler suits, with the bakery's logo in red on the breast-pockets.

'Of course, he didn't really bring in any money,' grumbled some, 'he only managed to save his wages by living on what Julia gave him.' Still. That first week, he worked, mostly on out-door jobs, especially the garden, as though we were all watching and assessing. Perhaps we were. Learning about our new communard. He beamed, looked puzzled, pushed his hair back off his face. And worked.

Tim and Bridget, not tempted at all by communal living, moved to Flosh Cottage, on the coast beyond Dumfries, rent-free in return for a couple of days' farm work a week. We kept in touch. When Paul started his new Job, at the Mackintosh, he stayed with friends of theirs in Glasgow - Nigel and Meg. So did Stuart, who, to our general surprise, also landed a teaching job at the Mackintosh, joining Paul in the Architecture Department.

Tina and I - and we didn't do much together - held what Tina called a 'political soirée' in her room. This was an attempt at something different from our ordinary meetings - whose tempo had slowed as if we had a thousand years to get everything sorted out.

We just talked about bits and pieces of our lives. Jonathan about student demos. Patrick about Nepal. Carol described the theatre group she and Dave had met in. Dave spoke about his early life - the time, when he'd misbehaved at home, that his parents had rung the school and asked them to beat him! And his father being a missionary priest who died when he was thirteen. (I was gobsmacked and felt a lot closer to him, after that, though it's quite possible he didn't notice).

Julia talked about her sister, Patsy, and her family.

And Nicky, about how he didn't understand our political stuff. Feminism, Ecology. He'd still, after ten months, little connection with our exotic set of radical notions. (Here was an opportunity explain, but we missed it.)

We were pissed off with him - always off, doing god knows what, on his own, costing us money, bringing none in. In fact, Nicky was the new Stuart.

But it was a good evening. 'We should have done this long ago.'

A small group of us talked about a Kids Project. Tina had always wanted to 'work with children.' And Patrick was keen, too. We didn't know quite what this could, or should, involve. Which children? Those in trouble, in care, on probation? Community groups? School parties? Special Needs? And who would pay? Tina, Alice, Richard and Patrick fixed up to visit Formby Hall, near Liverpool, a full-time centre for children's holidays, to exchange ideas, or pinch them.

Do you remember - just before you left for Formby Hall, I asked you, though maybe I'd no longer a right to: 'Well, do you think you'll?' Sleep with Richard, was what I meant.

And you replied, hastily, making a promise you'd no need to, 'No. Definitely.' I think we both knew there was doubt, there.

When you got back.' I asked, 'Well?' You looked flustered and apprehensive and said, 'No. Well, yes. But not Richard. Patrick. It was the roundabouts...'

I still had my romance with Rose to work out. 'The worst part is over now,' she'd written, 'He's stopped beating me up.' Bloody hell, I thought. But the letters which followed - every couple of days - were chatty and cheerful. It was four weeks before I went to see her. I got one hitch from the end of the drive to Dumfries, then a second to outside her door in Finchley. Fate lending a hand to this ludicrous, stubby knight errant, come to save his lady from the dreadful, violent Catch.

But it turned out, things weren't like that. It was obvious I was just a bit part player in their ongoing, antagonistic scene. I'll spare you the details. I never saw Rose again.

At this low point - this was shopping therapy - I bought a cheap car. A Morris Minor: £100. And we needed a car - Paul was always off in the Ami, the Landy was usually busy, and Nicky's car, which he'd converted to run on propane as well as petrol, was not an option. With the Capital issue still not resolved, I felt OK about spending some of mine. But, true, it was a totally non-communal decision. Dave still goes on about it.

Later you told me what happened. You spent a day at the seaside, at a funfair. Then Richard and Alice were into making love, but you'd all been given one big room to sleep in. So Patrick and you had moved over to the farthest corner to be unobtrusive. And one thing had led to another.

It hurt me to hear it, so it hurt you to tell me. But I wanted to know, in a way I hadn't with Paul, with Nicky.

I had a vague theory, 'Liberated Post-Scarcity Sexuality in The Communal Loving Group' about how whatever you did and enjoyed, would go around, come around. Crudely - the more sex people had, the more there would be to share. Something like that. It wasn't fully-worked-out.

So much for my head.

My heart banged and my stomach recoiled. I would picture imaginary scenes from this weekend. The journey in the Ami. A mealtime. The room where it all happened. The fuck, with orgasms and all. Curiously, this last bit was reassuring. I was thrown by romance, love - but not by the physical, sexual part of it. The genitals bit. Maybe that was because my own fucking around hadn't changed my love for you one iota.

And at first, it all worked. OK, Patrick was a shade aloof from the Group, but I liked him and that helped. Besides, you and I still slept together, made love, most of the time. Patrick was your weekend affair. 'It's been a week,' he'd say to you. And you'd spend a couple of nights with him. You made it look, at first, as though it was just a friendly, casual attachment. It was ages before I figured out this wasn't quite right. Wasn't right at all. He was your main lover - the one you felt jealous about, the one you thought about all the time.

That second Autumn, we noticed the trees below the wood, between us and the Top Field, along the west edge of the lawn, had been carefully selected, more than a hundred years before, to give a breath-taking autumn spectrum running from red (post-office, magenta), through browns and yellows (earth, sand, canary), to gold.

Alternative Technology Week arrived. Stuart spent the Sunday morning showing the twenty or so visitors around. Vague plans were made for what to do with the week. By Monday lunchtime, the visitors were lost, bemused by the notion of 'self-structuring.'

It was supposed to be Stuart's week. Have you seen him, I asked Alice. 'Haven't you heard,' she replied, 'he's gone to work as usual,with Paul.'

'But I thought he was taking this week off.'

'Well, it seems not.' said Alice. She sounded cross, but she was smiling.

And of course, there was no point in being annoyed anymore. We'd given up expecting anything from Stuart. He'd become, since getting his Glasgow job, more like a visitor. When he did something for the Group, like cook, you almost felt like thanking him.

It had always been difficult to see Stuart as one of the collective. It wasn't just that he acted on his own, rarely worked with anyone or discussed his plans (though this didn't help). It was what he did and didn't do.

He'd spent a lot of time away. Sprung visitors on us. Written a sizeable cheque as a loan to Veronica. - and then, when he'd started to earn his Mackintosh salary, opened his own bank account. He'd been consistently unpredictable and erratic. And with his talk of art galleries and marinas and caravan sites - he'd begun to sound like a regular hip-capitalist.

There was one afternoon in early summer when we'd eaten lunch on the lawn and were lolling in the sun. Stuart in smart white Levis and his 'I'm a Leo' T-shirt. I forget what started the conversation off, but I know he stopped me dead with some remark - about the women's movement, possibly. Anyway, something I couldn't take.

'Look.' I said, 'when you joined us, you said you were an anarchist.'

'Oh all right then, I'm not,' he said.

Stuart had been lonely and beset by problems - we knew that. At first, we'd tried - we really had - to understand and to help. But that hadn't worked. Now, we really didn't care anymore.

The money from his flat came through - around £3000. No-one was too surprised when he immediately bought an absurdly expensive hi-fi and kept the rest. He rarely came to meetings. He missed meals, preferring to take bread and cheese, or leftovers, up to his room. He had left the group - we just weren't too good at recognising this.

Alternative Technology week, meanwhile, turned out well, without Stuart. There were more experiments to make methane - Nicky had arranged a load of chicken-shit 'fuel' to be delivered. A group including Peter H. made a home movie, a skittish "methane promotion" picture (but the methane effects - eating beans then farting in the bath - were faked using Calor gas.) There were detailed calculations about hydro-electricity by a group of men - the whole week was predominantly male - excitedly spouting about 'constant head, flow rate, pipe diameter, coefficient of friction, kilowatts'.

All very interesting. But for our lives, the whole business was fraught with dilemmas. Were we really going to cut down our dependence on mains electricity or bottled gas by making a regular contract for chicken manure supplied by a battery farm? An unnecessary, squalid, high tech factory, which disfigured the gentle valley down towards Kirkcudbright? We thought not.

Or buy an expensive, precision-made turbine as the centrepiece of a hydro-generator? We thought not (but later, we did).

Or build solar heaters incorporating considerable lengths of copper tubing mined by exploited workers in Zambia?

Or construct windmills, when it was clear that if only the system would stop its lunacies, e.g. burning up electricity to make yet more cars and office buildings, the national grid plus coal would do for several years yet.

Stuart spent only a couple of days in Glasgow. He returned to take a part in the rest of the AT Week. But shortly after that he bought a flat in Glasgow and moved out. All this without a word. 'So is this you,' I asked him, as he loaded stuff into his hired car, 'are you really leaving?'

'What do you think?', he asked back. I have no idea as to why he was so belligerent. Contemptuous, also. He didn't say goodbye to anyone.

In the Radical Commune, we'll have a wake, when some-one leaves.

It was colder still. Billiard Room kitchen was nearly complete. We sanded the floor and lacquered it with polyurethane - which took a week to dry. Dave had worked out how to run the old central heating system using wood, and short-circuited the system so that only the radiators in the billiard room were linked. But it was still chilly.

The stables east-side roof sagged alarmingly. Up at the house, we just about kept pace with Billiard Room roof leaks, as the wind caused slates to slip. Gales brought down one of the biggest beeches in the drive, snapping the phone line and flattening twenty yards of Farmer Henty's fence. Nicky borrowed a chainsaw and we spent three days clearing up.

This was Nicky's last communal effort. He left quickly, once he'd made up his mind. There was a meeting that he didn't come to - he just slipped a note under the door, saying he had to leave and how much money could he take with him? We couldn't agree. Some felt he'd been quite a drain on us already, financially and emotionally. In the end I gave him £50 out of 'my capital' - enough, with the cash he already had, to give him a start. He went to Edinburgh to do odd-jobbing there. It must have been a bleak winter for him.

Later, in the spring, Nicky asked to rejoin. We said no, we didn't want that. He found a place to live nearby and became a neighbour.

We painted rooms and corridors, sawed wood for the big boiler, kept the Hydresse burning, ferried children to school and playgroup. Repelled door-to-door salesmen with their brushes and detergents. Swept leaves into heaps, for yet more leaf-mould. There was still a flow of visitors and a flood of questions. We were as difficult to interview as someone fighting a fire or giving birth.

In the mornings, cobwebs were frosted.

.

14

And Earning A Living? Not to mention Multiple Relationships?
The Kids Project, after all the planning, hosted its first group. By now we called it, 'Freefall Project.' But to ourselves, because this name never quite flew with the customers. (We were good at sales, but rubbish at marketing.)

Sue C. rang from Penrith. The van bringing her, John H. and the Somerstown kids had broken down, so Jonathan and I took the Ami and the Morris to pick them up. It was 10 p.m. when we got there. We found them telling stories, singing songs. I'd met Sue C. in London, earlier in the year, to fix up this visit. She climbed into the Morris with me and three kids.

We got everyone sorted out and off to bed. It was by now about 2 a.m. I went to find you, but you were asleep with Patrick. So I slept with Sue C. Wow! Romance having developed on the long drive home.

It was a beautiful week. The kids were older than we'd expected - between 14 and 16 - and they fitted as easily as any other visitors into our lives. We took them to Loch Whinyeon. Up the Merrick (leaving behind some girls wearing high heels). Down to the beach, where we gathered up driftwood, made a fire, cooked sausages and made cocoa. Over to the cinema in CD. We couldn't have had a friendlier, more reassuring start to the Kids Project. Everyone enjoyed the week, including those - Julia, Paul - who had been apprehensive and sceptical.

And at the weekend, we were hosts to a 'Potlatch' - a gathering of Peace News readers. We hadn't known how many to expect - by the Saturday night, the house held, someone reckoned, 140 people. The Somerstown kids were lovely, looking after babies, falling in love, being mature and warm. Sunday was a day of tearful farewells.

'I'll come and see you soon as I can,' I said to Sue C.

Then you and Pat went to Greenock and Glasgow to see Social Work departments, Education Departments and community groups including the Milton Community Project, to look for business for the Kids Project. You were gone for about a week.

Later, I'll reproach you (won't I just): 'You went on holiday with Patrick first.' This was only half-true, too; it was a working holiday, perhaps

89

not a holiday at all. But it was two more years before you and I got away together, without the children.

Meanwhile, I began to hitch to and from London, to see Sue C. I was bewitched by Sue. But if you were upset by these carryings on, you didn't say.

There was a PeopleCentre meeting, soon after. For once the terse style of the minutes says it all: "November 24th. Proposed: If everyone wants to do the PeopleCentre and it's going to make a reasonable amount of money, let's do it!"

"All: AGREED!"

"Julia: It isn't that easy."

But it was a decision that's lasted. And this is not just for conferences but for battered wives, groups of 'under-privileged' children, the lot. Hmm, I thought

But so it has turned out. The PeopleCentre project is currently (1977) due to host a Gay Men's Week, and, with AIDS a big deal, I find myself proud of you fuckers, all of a sudden.

And Self-Sufficiency:
No, but Dave erected an electric fence for the goats, round the tennis court bit. Carol fixed up more chicken-roosts in the stables.

And Communal Childcare?
Carol complained loud and long about our lack of communal childcare, by which she meant childcare for Tam and Tiffy. She didn't seem to notice that most of us looked after the other seven children just fine - sharing cooking, clothes-washing, school-taking bed-putting and, for George, Polly and Sophie, playgroup type stuff.

'Besides,' we said to each other, 'Dave does seem to do his share, even if she thinks he doesn't do it right. And we all take one or other of Tam and Tiff on every shopping trip.'

And Do You Ever Have Meetings?
By now, we had a notion of 'People Meetings' - times when we could, we hoped, talk more about our feelings and perhaps leave Business Meetings free to get stuff done - instead of collapsing, as they so often still did, into a trough of confused irritation. In fact, both sorts of meeting will remain meandering and inconclusive. We don't know how to separate 'feelings' from 'decisions.'

Close to Christmas, for example, we sat around the Morning Room fire in separate chairs: Alice, Patrick, Jon, Carol, Dave, Tina, Mike. Distant as electrons. Paul is in Glasgow. Julia hadn't stirred from bed all day, perhaps feeling - as I suddenly did - that everything was pointless. There's an odd lack of flow. Richard's absence is noted.

'He's in a fantasy world,' observes Dave (so it's not just the PA, then)

Mike: 'We are avoiding talking about the important questions.'

Tina: 'I can talk about projects without letting my real feelings come out. Group Therapy might change that.' So, to Tina, credit for the first proposal of group therapy. However we didn't know how to take it up.

Dave: 'Nobody seems to think what they are doing is very important - they don't get up in the mornings.'

Alice: 'It's like the early years of marriage, you stick at it till you find the real common ground.'

Jon: 'Mike, why are you shutting yourself in your room?'

Mike: 'Because life doesn't make sense.'

In fact we have two main responses to our loss of direction - physical idleness coupled with mental turmoil - or, more often, frantic activity, anything to keep busy, plus intellectual sloth.

Mike: 'I'm waiting for the kind of understanding that makes people get on.'

Tina: 'In a commune, or a community?'

Mike: 'Move towards being a loving group of people?'

Dave: 'You talk about wanting a loving group, but you do nothing about it - at least, not to me.'

Jon: 'Some people cannot talk about it, can't bring it out.'

Dave: 'I don't think twelve people can live together without some people not getting on.'

Mike: 'What we have now isn't my dreams.'

Carol: 'Are you aware that other people have dreams?

Pat: 'What?.'

Dave: 'Help with the painting?'

(It maybe made more sense at the time.)

And Women's Meetings?

Sue G. had fled Knockengarroch shortly after Women's Week and moved to Newton Stewart to work in a children's home. The women drove there once a week, meeting as the 'Galloway Women's Liberation Group.' (The Accountant would think 'it's a sixty-mile round trip' - but wouldn't dare say so.)

And Men's Meetings?

No, no men's meetings. Some evenings, after getting the kids off to bed, Patrick and I would talk. But I was becoming irritated with his distant attitude towards the Group; and the way he had, it seemed, developed a way of being counted with those who wanted a lot more discussion and argument about what we were doing, without ever actually initiating any. Another time, Richard and Tony came to my room and we explored stuff about relationships and sexuality. 'We must get together again,' we agreed. But it didn't happen.

The Capital.
We had another go at the capital.

Julia says: 'Well, my capital is pooled.' She had, indeed, finally paid in her remaining cash balance.

'I thought all the capital was pooled,' says Dave. He was always very insistent on this, even though his and Carol's money was still tied up at their former house - and looked like it would be forever. True, they wanted help with a legal framework so they could transfer this interest to Laurieston. But we were too busy and anyway, a bit fed up dealing with Carol-and-Dave problems.

'I still want to spend mine on the Building Project,' says Paul. (We could never shift him from this, even after Richard and Tim had built an entire barn, Dave had done a house conversion and Richard supervised the Mair's house-painting - all without spending any capital - Paul couldn't see that we already had a working project. He talked in thousands for stocks and equipment.

I say: 'The capital isn't pooled. It's sort of loaned. It isn't really clear just whose money the balance of the capital is. Anyway I want to pool mine, if there's something here I want to do.'

Tina turned the discussion round to income, rather than capital. 'Well, we've agreed not to live off capital. So people not earning an income here should go out to work.'

'Richard and Julia haven't provided any income,' says Dave. I agree with Dave on that. And it's curious how, if you're feeling too tired or indifferent to say what you want, someone else will say it for you.) 'And Mike bought the Morris without consulting the group.'

'Well, what about Stuart's hi-fi,' Tina promptly countered. Alice, Jon and later Jay claim that Tina always defends me. I only notice when she doesn't.

And what about Richard's and Julia's hi-fis?,' I offer.

Not really fair, because they'd bought them just before arriving, If Stuart had stayed, we'd have had five new-ish hi-fi systems. Dave and Carol were generous with theirs - it often sat wherever we were mainly living. The others stayed in their 'owners' rooms.

We had talked of pooling huge sums of money, never our possessions.

Some more alternative technology we could have done with: a way of relaying a few channels of music cheaply round the house.

It had taken about three hours to get this far. Julia and Patrick had left. The rest of us were numb, stiff, cold. Shaken with emotional plague and deafened by anomie.

'I think we should fix the little Land Rover,' says Dave.

Why Did You Leave?

No Idea. Meanwhile, I'm putting together Communes Network Spring 1977 edition. I know it's absurd. Communes Network, being edited by a recluse - Tom C. is away and I'm living with J&S in an isolated farmhouse in North Yorkshire. But no-one else at Laurieston offered to take on the job when I left, and I thought it would be a shame to let the mag die.

So I type up jolly and gossipy accounts of life at Wheatstone, Crabapple, Lifespan, People-In-Common, Birchwood and Glaneirw. And muse on the banner - which has mutated from Communes 'Network' via 'Netwrok' to 'Netrock'. Maybe this time it'll be: Communes Don'tWork?

Meanwhile, the PA claims the term 'networking' as his invention.

15

Christmas 1973/New Year 1974

17th December. Billiard Room kitchen being finished, we moved in, with the old central heating boiler going and a big log fire in the giant hearth. We're needing a Business Meeting, but, in celebration, this evening's agenda begins with several bottles of Nukie Brown.

Meeting minutes are still written in the rice-paper accounts book we inherited with the house. They're often illegible and anyway fragile. But they seem to say:

Jonathan and Patrick will *definitely* look at the roof, as soon as it is dry.

Goats: we are looking at £89 to fence them in properly.

Feeding the boiler is a two-person job. Next week, Dave and Julia. Also, Jon needs help wood collecting.

Kids Project: children from Greenock and other groups are coming in the New Year. Now that we have spread through the house, which bedrooms can they have? Can we get a record player? Could Paul's students, coming in February, build an Adventure Playground?

Vehicles: 'Someone,' said Paul - meaning Dave - 'poured cold water into the Land Rover's engine when it was hot and it's cracked the cylinder block and it will have to be towed to Glasgow for repair and it'll cost hundreds.' Bit of a downer, that.

'Christ that's two Land Rovers we've gone through,' says Carol.

'Plenty more where they came from,' says The Accountant, giggling.

Staff nurse: Tony, dispensing Benylin.

Billiard Room wasn't cosy, but it was liveable.

Knock knock, says Tina. Who's there? Luke. Luke who?

Luke Warmth.

Tina off with Patrick. Cold.

Next day it's Carol, Mike, Dave and Jonathan's turn for a Turnip Day.

To feed the goats, Dave has fixed up turnip-picking at Matt McTaggart's farm. A typical morning shift would see four of us, cold and wet, spending three hours or so pitch-forking turnips- 'neeps' - onto a trailer. Then eating 'neeps-wi-mince-n-tatties' - which Mrs. M. serves up for dinner. While, as tradition demands, waiting for her own meal later. (And we clock other differences. Lunch being Dinner. Dinner being Tea.)

We are rewarded with conversation and all the turnips we could carry home in the Morris and trailer, for us and the goats.

19th December. Dave fixes a huge new notice board to the main 1st-floor landing and pins up his 'Money Store For The People' idea. This would be an alternative bank-cum-building society which would favour communal and other politically OK but financially iffy projects (later this thought will help engender the "Maxi-coop" discussions and later still the Ecology Building Society.) I really like this idea.

And I then post proposals for next year's PeopleCentre events - to be called our 'Alternative University' - for Summer 1974. To no great excitement, I note.

Actually all I want for myself is to have a door marked "Department Of Rock N' Roll," behind which I lurk. I never achieve this.

But since the Alt. U. will need a library, I spend another of my nights alone sorting everyone's contributions to the Morning Room library. With the result that we have two or three copies, sometimes four, of the books of Colin Wilson (does anyone even remember him?), The Alexandria Quartet, Donne's poetry, Catch 22, Camus, Sartre, Saul Bellow, John Updike, Doris Lessing, Marge Piercy's Woman On The Edge Of Time, R.D.Laing's 'Knots.'

And so forth. At the time, I remember feeling cross that people had clearly kept their newer, still favourite books to themselves (but now, I think, why-ever not?).

On Christmas Eve morning I was up a step ladder, quite cheerful, finishing off painting Billiard Room, worrying about the usual: daughter, son, chord changes, wife, girlfriend, Christmas presents. I was watching paint dry as a new thought sloped in. Low, slow and black as a cormorant.

"Of course, one day, you're going to be leaving here."

I nearly fell off the ladder.

I'd previously thought, this is it. This is me. Here. Forever.

It was Alice who asked me what was the matter. I mumbled something about having to leave the group sometime. Which left Alice never quite trusting me afterwards (didn't it, Alice?). A seed had been sown: one day, I'd be moving on.

This was an elephant-in-the-room of a realisation. I recall I had to meander on the front lawn for half an hour.

That evening, with all the over-excited kids finally in bed, we were briefly all together.

Billiard Room still reasonably comfortable. And we had a tinselled, glittered, paper-chained, roof-scraping, twenty-foot Xmas tree! Nobody in the world has a tree like us!

Christmas booze came out. It's a great night. Nicky re-appears, unannounced, with his usual malt whisky and serious spliffs. He's OK, no longer suicidal, it seems. But since he has 'left,' we don't quite know how to deal with him.

It was a night which left you, me, Patrick and Sue C. by the fire. Sue C., and her son, Barney, were staying for Christmas and New Year. But this was Christmas Eve. I wanted so much to be with you, make love with you, sleep with you, wake and have Christmas morning with you, with Joel and Sophie crawling over us, opening their stocking pressies. I'd checked with Sue C. that she wouldn't mind that.

But you were hesitant.

Not least because Sue C., sussing out the difficulty, had offered: 'Patrick - will you sleep with me?'

She was being helpful here, not trying to pinch your boyfriend - well, just for a night - and wanting to make space for you and me. But you were jealous of Patrick. He was your man - not allowed to stray - whereas I was just your occasional lover (and not so constrained).

'Come on Patrick, yes or no,' said Sue.

'Well, er, yes,' said Patrick. Until, looking at you, he understood what to say. 'Or, no.'

Creep.

So you chose Patrick. Not that I minded sleeping with Sue C. again. Not at all, at all. But this was the first Christmas Eve you and I hadn't spent together and it seems now that this was the beginning of the end of our marriage. The "Christmas Eve train-wreck", is how I tend to think of it.

Then Christmas Day - our first proper, communal, Christmas-at-home together - was disastrous.

We'd meant to ignore this 'bourgeois consumer-fest', hadn't we, and develop a Winter Solstice ritual. But the kids knew, from school - they'd come home asking about the Baby Jesus - that Christmas was a big deal. And grandparents and their gifts had interfered.

By lunchtime, Billiard Room floor was inches deep with boxes, torn tissue and piles of junk toys. The kids were squalling. Sonya was crowing - 'mine's better than yours.' Joel was in tears.

All the Groans were maudlin and squiffy. Lunch was local turkey or (imported) cashew nut roast, plus all our own veg. I tried to say an atheist grace, wanting to mark this occasion, but it didn't really come out right.

Afterwards, paper hats and silly games. Suddenly we are just like the regular world (where in Belfast, scarcely a hundred miles west, people didn't stop killing one another).

Then Carol & Dave went off to parents. Tina, Patrick, Alice and Julia took ill for a week.

This didn't leave too many to cope with the Hogmanay. The house filled with assorted friends. Everyone capable went down the pub and first-footed in the village, finishing up in Rosie and Neill's wee cottage. This was to try and prevent a repeat of last year.

It didn't work. Party, village and sundry collected in Billiard Room at 2 a.m. Some have received new LPs for Xmas - The Who, David Bowie, 'Derek And The Dominoes.' We boogied, with huge energy, until late. Typical Hogmanay accidents included sprained ankles, cut fingers, drunk bodies in heaps, people sleeping in the wrong beds.

So here we are, gang, it's 1974, toot toot! And it's face-stretching, tit-freezing, mind-blocking, pipe-bursting cold. Julia wrote:

"It snowed Monday and Tuesday and a bit on Wednesday, then froze and every night froze more. The windows had frost fingers all over them every morning and I kept the curtains closed all day. On Saturday and Sunday Billy fell about with cold feet and cried for his Daddy. Then George cried Daddy and he cried Jon. On Friday I went with Sonya, Bill and George onto the ice on the pond. It was very thick and made no sound."

Meanwhile:

Laurieston Hall is a massive country house - pink, yellow, green and other muted jukebox colours - which once shrank to a doll's house and soared away in the direction of Mossdale, glowing orange.

Some nights it's black as the Titanic, steaming westwards, grainy and jerky like an old silent movie, light streaming from the portholes.

Now in the sodden mists of winter it's mainly grey as Ghormenghast.

And the people are:

Alice, who enjoys Circle Dancing. She is also court photographer.

Carol, who makes lampshades by modelling tissue paper on giant balloons. Plays guitar, sings a bit, makes mordantly witty remarks. Might occasionally clean up the stables yard. But this winter, yawns a lot.

Dave, who admits proudly he is 'hard on shoe leather.' He's bought three pairs of shoes so far, while the Accountant has bought none. Heaps his dinner plate, talks while he eats, stays slim. Struts about like a scoutmaster, doesn't he? There's no side to him. Dave actually says things in public like "Not now, Tiffy. Daddy's busy," or "Come along, Tammy,

97

it's lovely muesli," quite without realising how some sophisticates do mock. If it wasn't for the Goats, Dave and the PO would get on well.

Jonathan, who wears a sweater full of darns, one colour for warp, another for weft; who has put trays of seed potatoes to sprout in all the downstairs south-facing windows. Jonathan likes to appear more than a little dopey but is, in fact, not so.

Julia, who knows the names of all the trees and wild flowers but whose ego, via za-zen, is in the going-out-of-business-business. She never runs. Her sweater, like Jon's, is also neatly darned at the elbows. Over that, she has a new, green boilersuit. And on these really cold days, a bright woolly skull-cap and heavy-duty blue quilted coat. She's more feline every day: rubs her cheekbones with the backs of her hands. She's overdue on the cooking rota but refuses to negotiate on this.

Mike: The PO. I play sax and do a lot of brooding. And I am Cottage Bookings person. And when we had some dissatisfied holiday visitors in the cottages, demanding to see the Manager, Carol directed them to me. So that's me then, I'm also the fucking Manager of this clown outfit.

Nicky: but no, Nicky has at last definitely left. In fact, he's moved in with John O., a writer, living up the road at Ullioch cottage.

Patrick, who wrote 'Is This A Book Or Something' for the kids for Christmas, which should become an international bestseller. He is magic at football. Also can whistle tunelessly, a skill your PO cannot master. Bastard!

Paul, of whom Jonathan says, "He treats us like his collective wife." And indeed, sometimes he is "tied up in Glasgow, won't be home till tomorrow." When he's here, he cooks, beautifully, but always what he wants to make. He'll look sideways at a bag of beginning-to-rot parsnips, which need eating. A talented architect, he is only rarely violent.

Richard, who is still thinking about building a proper post box for the front door. And who is all the gether too good-looking. In a hurry he does run, if he has to. But mostly, he glides. He does not appear dopey, but, at this point in time, he is. On the other hand, when a pipe burst in Billiard Room, flooding it, it is Rich who in about thirty seconds, severs the leaking pipe and hammers it flat, closing off the gush, while the rest of us faff about wondering where the supply taps are.

Sue G., back from working in Newton Stewart, who is wanting to join us. She seems solid. I cannot imagine a problem.

Tina, who makes jokes, coughs, and has never been seen to run anywhere at all and spends a lot of time ill in bed. These days she's wearing patched jeans, torn sneakers and a new (jumble) sweater.

Tony, still obsessed with his attempt to build a man-powered-flight machine. He and I have a slender Birmingham (Birbigub) connection so naturally I call him 'Tone-eye' and he calls me 'Moikl'. Officially, Tony is still a "resident visitor;" unofficially he's by now a de facto member. He's also a wee bit asthmatic - we worry that if he builds his machine, he won't have the puff to fly it.

And then we are our Relationships. First up, you, me and Patrick. We seem to be living in a novel themed on Jules Et Jim, with you playing Jeanne Moreau (and looking the part, darling).

You're the hardest to describe. Now 32, you're a mum, first. And you do the Kids Project, which is like being a mega-mother. Sometimes you write - a poem, a short story, even a political piece. But much of you is hidden. At least from me. You would do anything to avoid a serious personal conversation. You deal in ciphers and wave invisible wands. I can't think of anything else that engages or amuses you. I'm your co-parent and we have a daughter who's physically not quite right - but I can never use that, or anything else, to get any closer to you.

And there's Patrick. On whom I have very little take. Originally, he seemed to agree with our communal rhetoric and presumed politics. He does the Kids Project with you and a lot of gardening; but he's never found a voice of his own. He waits and watches.

He's still only 24. Basically, super-teenage. He's tall, dark, handsome, slim. No surprise that you're shagging him, really. Your trophy boyfriend. We would've called him your "toy-boy", but that phrase comes later.

Whereas I am at this point mainly low. For the benefit of future generations, I would recommend not consenting to your wife/ main lover/ mother of your children/ all of those starting, let alone maintaining, a sexual relationship with anyone else, especially not someone who you are going to have to go on living with, in the same house, day after day, even if …

But this is your PO getting angry here. Needing to take a breath.

…even if it does mean you can yourself have other partners and you think this might be a step along the way to a totally free and liberated, ecstatic and harmonious society.

Paul Smoker, of the University Of Lancaster's Peace Programme, will say later that we have achieved an extraordinary situation which elsewhere in society would have led to 'straightforward murder.' (Indeed, I do wonder whether Straightforward Murder wouldn't have been a wonderful simplification.) (And a great name for a band.)

From here on, our triangle was never even remotely comfortable. I had this 3/4 beat going: "*Even* Christmas *Eve*, Even *Christmas* Eve." It was the start of the stomach-kicking, face screwing rift between us. Which, most days, I still feel.

Since then, seems to me all we had were different degrees of comfort-fuck. Not unpleasant: on the contrary. Indeed we still had this quite intense sexual relationship didn't we? Even if we don't talk about our relationship anymore. Which we don't. But I think for you, it was keeping me, your old man and co-parent, sort-of happy. You always had another agenda.

I would have been happy to just be with you. In fact I pressured you on that. 'Why don't we all just leave,' I asked you? 'Be a nuclear family again?' But you were too in-love with Patrick. Utterly besotted. Which I alone was too stupid to see (everyone else knew, but they weren't saying).

And you loved Patrick jealously - you didn't want him sleeping with any other women. Which of course he wanted to, and sometimes did. To your obvious chagrin.

Meanwhile I was still struggling with whether 'love' was a one-on-one thing or something we should all try for universally. My agape had gone ape. I had fallen on my caritas.

January 3rd 1974. Patrick and I were cleaning up the scullery, which had become a dumping ground for jars, bottles, tins, cardboard boxes, chicken food, broken kettles, unmatched wellies and children's cast-offs. It was a job you could never finish. We broke off for a cuppa in the Old Kitchen.

'I suppose we should talk,' I said, 'about … you know …'

So here I am, in this famous triangle thing, trying to negotiate with your lover.

Except it wasn't a triangle, three-sided and strong. Has there ever in fact been such an arrangement? It was more of a see-saw, Patrick and me on the ends and you teetering on the middle.

The basic mechanics never worked, for a kick-off.

Sometimes you would make it plain that you planned to sleep alone, thank you very much. I thought those were the simple nights, until I realised you cheated. I mean, Patrick would knock and you wouldn't turn him away.

Or we tried being 'spontaneous,' which was supposed to feel free and easy and light-hearted, but which actually meant - who, spontaneously, got to you first?

Then we had drifted through a time when the general idea was that our days would determine our nights. So if you and Pat worked together with a Kids group, I would make myself scarce. Or if you and I worked on - but that was the snag, we didn't really work on much together, did we?

Phrases come back, triggering memories like the titles on a jukebox full of sad songs: 'What are you doing tonight?' 'It's been a while.' 'I'm going away tomorrow.' 'It's your first night back.' 'You don't mind, do you?'

'I mean, where do you think we are going?' I asked.

'Don't know, really,' he says. Hard to get a word out of him, this English graduate. We sipped our tea and shivered. We were dancing on glue.

'But anyway,' I said to Patrick. Pause. 'I suppose I feel all our relationships should be equal.'

Now this was hardly likely. You and I had the children and thirteen years' backlog of living and working and a raft of shared assumptions. You and Patrick had arguments, which you spoke of, and sex, which you didn't.

'Yeah,' said Patrick

But these were delicate negotiations, bound to produce embarassing nonsense.

One way in which things were equal: if I came into Billiard Room, you'd jump out of Patrick's clasp, or off his lap. And the same the other way round.

'It's a shame we don't seem to be able to be easy with each other in public,' I offered.

Plus there was me and Sue C. 'Of course, Tina being with Patrick left you free to develop your relationship with Sue C.,' comments the PO. Well, theoretically, yes. But it's hard to be 'long-distance' lovers.

Then, theoretically, there is Alice and Paul. There is by now diddly-squat left of the original Paul-Alice-Mike-Tina axis. Paul and Tina hardly speak. Nor, it turns out much later, do Paul and Alice, because Paul has taken up with Meg in Glasgow. But the rest of us didn't know this.

And Alice: I thought you were happily free-ing up from Paul: I didn't realise just how much you were hurting. I wish you had been better at asking for support. - and that I had been better at empathising. But we didn't have those skills then, did we?

Meanwhile, back in '74, Paul was still breadwinner on high and you, ducks, are seen as powerful. Anon in the diary - not me - has you "scheming and dreaming."

Next, we have Julia and Jonathan. And Richard and Kate B. Who seemed to be telling us that (a) Richard and Julia have split up amicably and (b) Julia and Jonathan are therefore the new couple on the block. All very simple.

In fact, George was crying Daddy because Richard was away such a lot - he'd gone back to work in Liverpool for three months. Of course, we needed the money, but it did seem he just wanted to get away from Julia-with-Jonathan.

Meanwhile it wasn't Julia-with-Jonathan. When Richard went away, Jonathan moved to Tower Room, in the West Wing room, far away from Julia's. As though Richard's presence had been a protection. Suddenly expected to commit himself totally to Julia, he couldn't.

'It never was any good after that,' said Julia later, 'we only had about one fuck a week. Plus, I was still jealous of Dick.'

Not least, we have Carol and Dave. Laurieston's remaining, 'together' couple. What to say? Most of us have your standard protestant work ethic, but Dave, who, like Tina, has a heavy-duty C of E background, has it in depth.

One result is, he's always on the go. He's wonderfully productive.

Snag 1 is, almost everything he does, Paul doesn't like. It's the same old clash of styles - Dave the Bodger vs. Paul the Stickler. The Accountant sides with Dave, liking his wooden bed-bases for the PeopleCentre. And his Mark I sawing horse is indispensable.

Snag 2 is that even when Dave has Tiff and Tam, Carol is always - flawlessly - the struggling single parent. In fact, most of us spend loads of time looking after Tiff and Tam - and fully share looking after the older kids, with zero interest or input from Carol and Dave.

But Carol had decided she couldn't stand the pulls anymore. She wanted her nuclear family back. Just have her own children and Dave to deal with. They'd thought of leaving - but instead, could they move into one of the cottages?

And of course we thought:

'It'll split the Group.'

'Cottage bookings are coming through and we need the money.'

'If you move out, it'll be hard for you to move back in later.'

'It won't solve the problems between you.'

But none of us made any definite objection. And none of the practical problems were insuperable. So they moved to the near cottage.

On January 4th, 1974, we have a 'Meetings Meeting.' Despite sore throats, colds, flu and persistent hangovers we were in a busy, energetic phase again. We made New Year Resolutions:

Business and Project meetings every week.

Keep diaries of how we spent our time (Dave and Mike will analyse).

Co-ordinators for all the Projects. Goats, Dave. Chickens, Carol. Garden, Julia Jon Alice. PeopleCentre, Mike Tina Patrick. Design and Building, Paul and maybe Rich. Grounds, Patrick and Jon. House Maintenance - unfilled vacancy.

And we'd do the 'Big Question' meetings - Money, Aims, People Wanting To Join - urgently.

9th January 1974. More snow. A crisp day. Patrick, up really early, has trodden out a huge 'GOOD MORNING' on the lawn. Jonathan meanwhile feeds the goats, rekindles the boiler, opens up Hydresse. We are scheduled to have a

Morning Meeting. Amazingly, everyone shows. Except that Richard is still away. And Tony and Sue G. are not expected to surface quite yet.

Right. Shall we start?

Jonathan takes the whimsical minutes.

1. Dave suggests we start by consulting the I Ching. Or something else to 'lift us above the mundane.' Unfortunately, he hasn't brought the book.
2. Paul goes off to look for milk of magnesia.
3. PeopleCentre: Dave W. is bringing another group of students from the Jake, in Leeds. The Kids Project is to have girls, for a change, from Greenock. And more kids from Barrowfield. It's all go.
4. We need to make a new compost stack, renew the youth club rota, patch the roof, fix the West Wing drain, demolish the lean-to, repair the chicken houses, make marmalade.
5. Paul is to jet off to Australia. Distant relative. Has arranged six week's leave. Returning via India, to meet up with his friend Mahdu. Jesus, we can't even afford a holiday in this country, say some. His parents are paying, says Mike. This trip was always part of the deal.
6. Mike says cash loss from petty cash is increasing all the time. Then he goes to take a call from Sue C.
7. Julia will be sawing logs later. She has finished her electrically-heated propagation box.
8. Mike has had to deal with authority in the form of the local rat-catcher. Who found no vermin but was duly shocked by our stacked-up junk. More 'filthy hippy' stories will circulate locally and we will have to set them right in the pub.
9. Julia and Paul think Patrick should have hitched from Dumfries, rather than getting Tina to fetch him.
10. Welcome to the meeting Tony P. and Sue G.
11. Dave will collect yet more turnips. He's bought yet another new pair of jeans - but OK, *cheap* jeans.
12. Everybody will cook. Even Julia (I don't think so.)

January 22nd, and we do have a Big Issue, Money Meeting. Richard is still away in Liverpool, Julia is ill in bed, otherwise we're all present. Wow!

So: shall we start?

Cue for a thick gloom to descend. Bodies sag, smokers roll ciggies. Big Question meetings always start like this.

The main problems are that we aren't really earning our living, expenditure exceeds income. We might be "the richest commune in world" - someone's denigratory comment - but actually we were living hand to mouth like Mr Micawber.

"Result, misery," quotes Tina. And we don't want to spend the Capital to live on. The small problem is that the 'kitty loss' - unaccounted for petty cash - is increasing. We opt for the small problem. First topic, then: Personal Allowances.

We have been here before, and know all the arguments. The PO is working on the idea that we pick different roles each time, more as a reflection of how we are getting on with each other than as serious discussion.

'Maybe having a fixed amount of pocket money would limit total spending,' says Alice.

'But people will only go and spend it', Paul responds. [He and Alice are having difficulties].

'I agree with Alice,' says Dave. [He often did, yet this was years before he and Alice got together]. 'Pocket money would stop us feeling guilty every time we spend anything.'

'And we wouldn't have to remember every little item when we write up the cash book,' Alice adds.

'Well I think pocket money would be a retrograde step,' says Carol. [She and Dave were quarrelling a lot. And Alice and Carol never did get on particularly well]. 'I mean, I think we *should* be anxious when we spend money.'

'I agree with that,' says Mike [feeling distant from Dave for several reasons].

'Besides, how do we define what is personal spending?' asks Jonathan.

Aha, the personal spending issue. Any minute now, Paul will mention tobacco and Mike will admit, of course tobacco is indefensible, but Paul's addiction to buying woodworking tools is more expensive. Dave will refer obscurely to Mike's trips to London and Mike will say Dave buys more shoes than the rest of us put together.

But not this time. 'I don't think we should get into making value judgements,' Dave sidesteps.

'What's wrong with value judgements?' Mike wonders aloud. But then, agreeing to change tack, says 'Anyway, we should really be talking about earning enough the money in the first place.'

'Yes,' Tina agrees, 'I can't feel responsible about spending money unless I'm earning it myself.' [An interpretation of this in the light of Tina and Mike's relationship is left as an exercise for the reader].

'That's what I think, too,' says Patrick. [Easy, this one].

Have we had an update on Lothlorien?

Chuck and Jill had inveigled a Corsock farmer, fourteen miles from us into the north-east hills, into selling them 9 acres of land. Then extracted a Planning Department OK for a communal house, for which Paul would be architect. Then they'd vapourised - to Tenerife - presumably profitably. With no hard feelings.

Meanwhile the new owners, the putative Lothlorien Community, who planned a residential situation for looking after people with mental health problems, were even more simpatico. The house Paul designed is beautiful and I expect it will feature in Architectural Design and his retro show.

In March, there was a meeting to talk about whether Sue G. could join us.

Most people didn't have much to say, but were generally in favour.

Mike said he really liked Sue. G and wanted her to join.

Alice revealed that, in the women's group, Sue had said she wanted to get pregnant. And Alice thought that as Laurieston wasn't a good place to have a baby just now, Sue shouldn't join. For her own good. So concerned for others, Alice.

Tony kept quiet. Didn't say that he was a bit worried that, since he and Sue G. had become lovers, she might be joining more to be with him than join the group.

And if Alice was the teeniest bit jealous on account of this, 'cos she and Tony were still lovers, too, she wasn't saying.

Anyway the rule was that we all had to be in favour. Alice wasn't, and wasn't about to change her mind, so that was that.

Sue G. left shortly afterwards.

I felt steamrollered.

Mike worked on the next summer bash - still tentatively titled the 'Alternative University' or Alt U. Dave planned a Spring conference on Legal Frameworks For Collectives.

Tony finished his sleek flying machine and assembled it on the lawn one day for the benefit of all the kids from the Village school. Later, he tried a test-flight at Gloucester Airport. He was towed by a fire engine - but finished ignominiously - literally arse over tit - in front of gloating TV cameras. But he lived with us through the summer of '74 before drifting away. He'll return later, but we didn't know that.

16

And How D'You Get On With The Locals?
Of course, what some people rather hope to hear about is mayhem. Perhaps even Easy Rider type near-lynchings, as if we had moved, long hair and ten years earlier, to the USA's bible belt. These people asking were nearly always city-dwelling academics - who generally do not even know their own neighbours.

'Well look,' we'd say. 'Farmer Gordon gave us a load of manure. His sons come to fill churns with our burn water in a dry spell. Colin the blacksmith gave us some fencing stobs, Tony Garrod mowed the grass and the local Medical Officer of Health gave us a flock of Indian game hens.'

'Right now, Farmer Henty isn't too pleased with us because one of his twins broke an arm falling off our rope swing, and there've been a few days when our goats have got into his fields, but basically things are OK there. One night, two of his farm workers, George Hall and Ian Gilchrist, turned out at 3 a.m., with tractors, when a visitor had mis-directed his hitch, a 20-ton truck, down the Long Drive and got bogged down.'

'And we are regular customers of the vet, who has spayed the cats; fixed goat's sore udders; put down Thurber (Jonathan's old hound-dog, who became irascible in old age); and ditto Lucy (never productive as a milker).'

By now, our enquirer is listening only out of politeness. But we are on a roll.

'Meanwhile, four people have just founded Woodfoot Collective in Lochhill cottage down by Ringford to start a mini-commune. And the new Lothlorien owners are installed in various caravans and huts on their sites, while their house was starting to be built. And Lally who's our yoga teacher, has moved with Jackson, her old man, and her kids to Drumglass cottage. And we just sold a spare gas cooker to our new friend and neighbour, Nessa...'

Momentarily, it felt as though Galloway was becoming an Alternative Development Area.

Of Course, You'll Have Communal Childcare?
Whatever we did, there were usually children right there with you.

We shared the everyday, daytime, optional and generally pleasant times with children. But the inevitable tasks, pleasant or not - attention in the night - were mainly the domain of parents or lovers.

So everyone would cook kids' tea, take them to the beach, fetch them from school, read stories, help them make a play. But parents cleaned their rooms, took them to the doctor and dentist, got them up in the morning, put them to bed. Even then there were overlaps:

'Come on Sonya, bed-time,' calls Alice.

'Oh go away, Patrick's putting me to bed tonight.'

Everyone enjoyed Polly's giggles, mischief and drawings; Sophie's precocious jokes; Joel's cuddles and his up-to-the-minute knowledge of the football league table; Sonya's self-confident moods, and her writing; Billy's smiley charm.

But it was Richard, Julia or Jon who looked after George when he pulled a kitchen bowl onto his head; who consoled Billy for a bruise, a broken toy.

Paul or Alice who applied plasters to Polly's every slight scratch, who calmed Sonya when hysterical.

Tina, me or Patrick who did Sophie's washing or soothed Joel back to sleep after a Doctor Who nightmare.

True, the crèche rota (for Tam, Tiffy and George) stayed erratic. Most of us would happily build a pile of bricks for Tam to knock down; walk with the elfin Tiffy when she was fresh and bright, or crouch down with George to watch an insect. But mainly, Tam and Tiffy were with Dave or Carol - who resented this. Whereas most of the time, George was with Julia or Richard - which was what they wanted.

And still there were differences in all of this between the women and the men.

Not in terms of time, particularly. When Paul was away working, Alice had more of Sonya and Polly. But while at home, he more than made up. Richard and Jonathan spent more time than Julia with George. Dave seemed to do as much if not more than Carol with T&T. I think I put J&S to bed more than you (getting them up depended on who you were sleeping with - if Patrick, I would usually work late and sleep in). Here we have the men, on the whole, frantically over-achieving on the childcare front.

The problem - and it was a problem - was still one of attitudes. Because, for most of the men, childcare was 'time off work.' Whereas, for the women, work (e.g. on the PeopleCentre/ Kids Project/ garden) was time when a nagging nervousness about the kids rarely left them.

The PO, benign, thinks we were children of our time, doing the best we could. (You however reduced the PO to tears last Autumn, shrieking at him in a tirade across the lawn that the men had undermined all the women's efforts to - something - and were a useless bunch of shits. Words to that effect.)

So, another meeting - at first, quite a good one. We talked about each of the children, individually. The ways they were growing to resemble us. How we were like, or unlike, our own parents. How we'd been raised.

We talked about how the children held us together. With children you can't move so easily - was that why we'd been, compared to many other groups, quite stable? And as the links between children and adults other than their parents became stronger, the harder it would become for anyone to leave...

'You know, you want to be careful,' Tina told Patrick, referring to Joel and Sophie, 'you may think it's just for now, but they'll think it's for life.'

We talked about the differences between us in relation to the children. We had made a vague arrangement that we would 'back each other up' in front of the children - and argue the toss later if need be. This was especially to do with telling off other people's children and watching them run for comfort to mum or dad. It didn't really work. We were different.

So, round to childcare. Carol said the Crèche Rota wasn't working. She wanted people to commit more time. One full-time person every day, in fact, for the tinies.

A long shifty wriggling silence.

Paul wasn't about to offer. He was thinking about his three days a week teaching, preparation at home, other design work, his long list of vital maintenance jobs - and his own children. Richard and Julia weren't saying anything. Both like to have George out in the garden with them. Jonathan and Patrick did dutiful spells on the rota - but it was planting time and they didn't want to do any more childcare. Tony was packing up to go back to London. That left Alice, Tina and me.

And none of us were up for what Carol was wanting.

So - Carol will moan on to visitors - 'Laurieston Hall doesn't have communal childcare.'

(We should have established the few slots people were willing to commit to, and had a firm schedule for, say, a couple of hours, two or three mornings a week - and progressed from there.)

And now, in June 1977, I am still hearing that newcomers are saying that "we never really got communal childcare together." They mean, we didn't have a Tam and Tiffy rota.

As if childcare isn't mainly washing, cooking, shopping, cleaning, bathing, story-telling, fetching to and from school - all of which we managed quite well collectively, with very little fuss.

(The Radical Commune will of course have 24/7 *adult* care. I figure if the Groans are OK, the children will thrive. And we will not need 'childcare'.) (Alternatively, childcare time will be so desirable it will need to be rationed out.)

The Capital

8.45 p.m. in Morning Room (always warmer than Billiard Room).

Alice, Carol, Paul and Mike present and correct. Tina puts head round the door, withdraws to make coffee. Enter Patrick, Jonathan, Tony and Sue G. We chat about what we've been doing, why people don't come to meetings on time. Children's bedtimes. What's in the paper.

Millions of elms, dying: Dutch Elm disease. The general election campaign - our local SNP candidate just might, for the first time ever, unseat the Tory. Food prices up 26% in a year, company profits ditto. Nationally, we have the 'three-day week.' In saunters Julia.

Jonathan takes tea and coffee orders. Alice disappears. Tina returns. Alice too, but the phone rings, Alice goes to answer it. Dave arrives. Jonathan returns with drinks. Alice bursts back, gabbles: two visitors want to come for a week, will pay £1.50 a day, can I say OK? We say OK, but waffle on about visitor policies and visitor rates. Dave goes to see if T&T are OK. Jonathan remembers he's forgotten to stoke the Hydresse and rushes to see to it. Everyone drifts back in and eventually, at 9.15, Richard, always the last, joins us.

We are, suddenly, family. And this is family business.

'Right, shall we start?'

But it can't be that simple. Capital, income and work were issues which, for each of us, were tied up with deep questions of personal identity and security. And we lacked a way of talking openly, and collectively, about our deepest personal stuff (we still do). (We mainly do that one-to-one.)

In meetings, our language had begun to reflect this. We were becoming bureaucratic, euphemistic, distanced.

We'd begun to say 'This Place' to mean 'the Group,' or 'the rest of you.'

We'd say, 'I'd support' or 'I'd like to see,' meaning 'but I'm not going to do anything myself.'

Keeping pigs, poultry and goats became the grandiose 'Small-Holding Project.'

Paul sitting at his desk was 'The Building And Design Project,' suggesting a degree of co-operation that just wasn't there.

And rarely was anything communal, 'exciting,' 'exhilarating,' 'delicious,' 'beautiful,' or 'peaceful.' It was, at best, 'really nice.'

Anyway, off we go. Again.

'I think we should discuss present arrangements,' says Paul. He can be so pompous, can Paul.

'I'd like us to agree some criteria for spending the capital,' says Mike - who is still under a cloud for having bought the Morris with no discussion.

'I think we should have wider group awareness of how we earn our money,' says Tina.

'I agree with that.' says Alice.

Two hours pass. And we do, in the end, agree, at least, that The Capital, being all in one bank account, is physically, if not psychologically, pooled (with reservations about bank accounts and the ephemerality of money anyway) and will need a communal decision to spend any of it. Won't it?

Jonathan said, 'Some people talk in thousands but what I want to talk about is economising on bog paper.'

Tina said: 'I want everything to be quite clear.' Yes, dear.

Lastly, Dave announced he and Carol would now be getting £33 a month capital repayment from Bickerton Road. Hurrah hurrah. (But it didn't happen.)

11.30 - shall we leave it for now?

And Self-Sufficient, Are You?

No, but we have sources of plant food. Pig shit, as before. Seaweed harvested from Brighouse Bay (a popular 'gardening' trip, even the Accountant sometimes takes part).

Plus a lorry-load of 'municipal compost', ordered from Dumfries by Julia at £1.55 a ton. It was cheap, but, guess what, poor quality – 'over-processed,' said the gardeners. And it meant villagers didn't buy fresh veg from us for a year – Greta, from the pub, being particularly unwilling to trust 'the produce of human shite.'

No, but we have the chickens.

Carol built more chicken perches and bought in another batch of day-old chicks. And wrote up the PR: "From April to December, we have had 4181 eggs, value £133, less cost of food, £119, profit £14. Plus the stock is now worth £62 more than we paid. Plus the eggs are super-fresh and large size. Plus we have had the Christmas goose and a couple or more birds to eat. So are the chickens right on, or what?"

Well, the Accountant mutters, predictably, to himself: nice work, Carol, but stables gates, perches, time and materials, collecting feed, share of Land Rover costs at ten quid a trip...

Completely failing to spot that (a) while church-mouse poor, we regularly have foods which normally only the very rich can afford and (b) PeopleCentre visitors love the chickens.

And no, but we used to keep goats.

My, did we ever keep goats. Some people say you either hate goats or love them, but the Accountant believes he has a more balanced view: whereas he is sceptical as to the value of the Goats Project, given the initial time and cost of constructing fences, gates, stalls and feeding racks, together with the necessary materials including timber, fixings, fenceposts, wire, and various tools such as wire cutters, tensioning equipment and a stob hammer, and taking into account the cost of purchasing the animals themselves, in one inexplicable case involving a round-trip to Wales to acquire Freddy, a billy goat, and then of ongoing costs such as food concentrate and vets' bills, of substantial further goat-related travel, and given that our particular animals were obstreperous, stupid, perverse and stubborn, getting sick by nibbling ivy and yew, in two cases committing suicide (one by overeating, the other, strangulation by tethering rope) or breaking free, for example to leap the garden wall and demolish a season's crop of cabbages in fifteen minutes flat and requiring two hours a day or more, the Accountant estimated, to look after, specifically to lead them, against their fierce resistance, out to graze (causing even Jonathan, on more than one occasion, to lose his cool, start shouting and lash out with a thin piece of rope) and to then heave them back, feed, milk and clear up after them and the fact that, irrespective of the eventual outcome of the minor dispute between Dave, who would insist on the ubiquity of 'gallon-milker' nanny-goats while the Accountant thought them as rare as unicorns, we achieved what would turn out to be a seriously disappointing average yield of milk which, since it never quite lost its creosote, billy-goat tang, was always refused by our children - he considers the wild goats on the Galloway Hills to be just cute.

Here's a typical Goats Meeting (we have this meeting several times over).
    Mike: 'The goats don't make economic sense.'
    Dave: 'What do you mean?'
    Mike: 'They take up so much time and effort'
    Dave: 'Well, that's because you're so negative and hostile. You make it
        all take twice as long.'
    Subtext 1: If you would just stop criticising me, I would feel better and would get the work done in half the time.
    The PO thinks – that's probably true. There was no pleasing everyone. All of the Projects – pigs, chickens, garden, PeopleCentre, cottage bookings, Freefall and even Paul working away in Glasgow – had quite vocal opposition. We lacked an essential Radical Commune ingredient: communal good vibes.
    Mike: 'And they hardly produce any milk.'
    Dave: 'The milkers know how much they give' - here implying mega-

111

litres - 'and we're only just building up the herd. We'll get a lot more this summer.'

Jon: 'And it doesn't really take so much time.'

Jools: 'And anyway you're just trying to work it out in money terms and it's not like that.'

Subtext 2: Measuring production is part of Capital's value system and we shouldn't do this.

The PO is tired of arguing his case here. Yes, concepts of time, money and efficiency are all warped in the outside world, but we have to make our way.

Tina: 'Keeping goats is nice even if it's not economic.'

Subtext 3: The Kids Project visitors are entranced.

And we're all, even the PO, off into warm-fuzzy land. Goats are part of trying to be self-sufficient, part of living-in-the-country. Milking is a pleasantly calm way to start the day. And visitors generally, not just the Kids Project, love having them around. Freddy, tethered at a safe distance, will obligingly rear up on his hind legs. And keeping Freddy for stud makes a few bob; we get to meet other goat-keepers and you get a whole new insight into the phrase, 'randy as a billy goat.'

Dear Dave,

Now, a long time after the goats are gone, I can still hear you saying 'You spoilt the Goats Project for me.'

And I'm sorry for that. We should have been better at discussing our resentments, the way we worked, how to rotate the jobs we did and share skills.

I'm sorry for all of us and the whole mess.

You might appreciate the irony that here at Dumb Tom's, my daily routine includes looking after and milking Hetty, a placid and delightful goat who nibbles contentedly on roadside grass and gives five pints a day, no problem.

And How Do You Make A Living?

A group of workers and helpers came from Greenock (including Rick H., an ex-Methodist Minister, who confided, cheerfully, 'I'm the only person to be tried for heresy this century.)' They liked us and, over the years, brought a dozen or more groups of kids.

Our first Greenock group was an education for us. The kids will eat none of our food. We have to buy in crisps, white bread and bacon. And apples and bananas, which they will at least class as packaged food.

It's about now we are challenged by certain right-on politicos that the term 'kids' is, in fact - since it refers to young goats - offensive. We should always use the term 'children,' unless 'teenager' is more appropriate. I am proud to say we tell said persons to fuck off.

A week later, we get a crisp, computer printed, council cheque.

We hosted another Greenock group, then Sue C. brought a second group from Somerstown, but this time all boys and much younger. They fought each other, thieved from the village shop and were generally obnoxious and we had to sit up late in a sort of police role. I hardly saw Sue. The only good time was taking a few of them, with Jonathan, to the snow covered top of the Merrick.

On their way home, the more enterprising lads managed to steal guns from the gun shop in CD - and so got intercepted by the police on their way down the M6.

And Of Course, You'll Have Women's Meetings? And Maybe Men's Meetings?

The women's group based in Newton Stewart dissolved but a new one started with the Laurieston women, some women from Kilquhanity, and Betty, a playwright at whose house most meetings were held. Laurieston 'internal' women's meetings continued, too.

Back in 1969, when Tina first started going to a women's group, I remember my reactions of incomprehension, amusement, fright and anger and - only much later - acceptance and enthusiasm.

And I wasn't the only man to have gone through this or some similar set of responses.

And so men's groups had started up; to talk about 'how to support the women's movement' or to 'look at our own sexism.' Or - 'Why don't we stop all this hair-shirt stuff and just have a good time?' Times when we could simply relax with other men in a way that matched the closeness within the women's groups. I went to occasional meetings in London but my old job, then the move, meant that I'd never been in a regular group.

So men's meetings were something I wanted very much at Laurieston. When the men started complaining about the women's meetings - that they took up a lot of time, cost money, and were secretive - the Accountant defended the women.

'They're one of the most important aspects of Laurieston,' he said. And he suggested men's meetings. Mike the anti-sexist, feminist, radical man.

And bullshitter. I also thought that the women met too often - taking up time we needed for group meetings. And were too secretive. Dammit, the meetings were partly about us men - we needed some feedback. And the women were becoming a clique. They covered things which should have been everybody's to discuss, just because they happened to be together.)

The PA had called one or two men's meetings. But they hadn't taken off. The PA felt it was someone else's turn to have a go. Dave started an irritating habit - calling for men's meetings in the full group, but never arranging one.

17
Spring 1974

This Spring was suddenly boom-time for the Kids Project.

Leeds Free School came to stay, self-catering in the Old Kitchen. They had brought all their own food and bedding and were paying us just 30p a day each for electricity and hot water. So - no Kids Project wages in it for us. I volunteered to be link-person - and so got luxury breakfasts - bacon, eggs and real coffee!

Your PO took them, singing, to the seaside and joined in their games. And up the Back Track, in the J4 - this being a van which Dave had bought for £25 - to scavenge wood.

And he had a short-lived romance with Bridget R., tra la. Tina was cool: Patrick was furious. (The Reader will by now familiar with this situation.)

Otherwise, we tried to integrate the visitors into our own lives, in Billiard Room. First, we had Richard's brother, a teacher, who brought kids from his school in Portsmouth.

And teenagers from Milton - their gang name was 'The Milton Tongs' - began to come regularly.

Through one Tony Hoskyns, a colleague of Sue C's., we received an entire backline of amps, mikes, speakers and drum-kit, which is to be ours to look after. It was installed in the top of the tower - the deal being we will host embryonic rock ('Hoskyns') groups from Somerstown and elsewhere. (Which we did. None have become rich enough to keep us in our old age.)

We thought about setting up Freefall as a charity - and about a 'Freefall living group,' which didn't happen either.

And we had teenagers from Dumfries for a weekend - we were trying to give Freefall a local focus, but it didn't really work out. They or their youth workers didnae like us, y'ken.

And Leeds Free returned again, but without Bridget R. The Accountant sighed.

We were basically still pretending these kids could live in with us: share our work and play. Billiard Room was a constant huge mess. Julia more or less stopped eating with us. Others kept firmly out of the way. The kids' music and style dominated. Nights with Milton meant putting drunk teenagers to bed.

Nights with Somerstown, who also came again about now, were worse. They formed factions, victimised individual kids, set fire to a mattress, ran riot round the house, broke things (often deliberately) and ripped off anything they thought they could sell.

We knew we had to re-think the Freefall Project.

I think this came down to, simply vetoing further groups from Somerstown, and Dumfries. Surprisingly, we elected to keep on with the Milton Tongs, who, on their home territory, were the most terrifying street gang of all.

Sue C. and I burned up watts and money on the phone and I was always first in the queue for the postman. We swapped flying visits. Twice, Sue scrambled north. Three or four times, I gravitated south (once, in fact, along with Tina and Patrick, and we talked with assorted groups of people about starting new communes - something like that - but actually I felt disloyal all along to my real co-communards.)

The last day of my last trip, we sipped Cinzano and lamented the fact that Laurieston is not only hundreds of miles away but is also - since Sue C. is a film-maker - devoid of film studios, contacts, PR people, and funders.

Meanwhile, London is short on wild moorland which - I am amazed to realise - I do now like to be close to. While still liking the bustle of London for a few days, Galloway has become my home.

John H. comes round for my farewell. Tells the story of his American, situationist lover who just shat publicly on Marx's grave, just around the corner in Highgate Cemetery. The three of us fell giggling into bed.

We're all still friends.

Hitching back, I called you from CD. But you couldn't pick me up because you were tripping. Alice came instead: I dozed as she negotiated the bends and the Laurieston bumps. I was so pleased to see her and of course wanted to sleep with her - but she was otherwise engaged. The Mike-Alice thing was now definitely over.

Next day I was so angry with you, wife.

I thought, if you were going to take acid - so rare at Laurieston - I wanted that to be with me.

Also I wanted to tell you how sad I was feeling about saying goodbye to Sue C. But you were 'feeling fragile.' So I had to look after you instead.

I'll re-frame that. I am looking after you - tea and empathy - while your fucking lover has deserted you and you are totally unfuckingsympathetic to and unfuckinginterested in me. Right, at least that's clear.

On Good Friday, the new goats kidded. Local friends called. We carried food, small children and goat kids in a procession, across the back field and down to the ford, like a nomad tribe gathering for a feast day. Richard had made all the children fishing rods, with lines, weights and stuff (most didn't really try, but George became ace at catching trout). Pulsing, white blossom radiated from the blackthorns. Partridges spiralled by. Snipe looped the loop in mirror-image pairs.

And on Easter Saturday, we hosted the regular Saturday afternoon kickabout. The village vs. the residents at football. Richard would glide, side-together, side together, twice as fast as he seemed. Neill, a skills dazzler, played for our side. He'd pass to the PA - who, lacking both skill and experience - would panic until he could get the ball to Patrick. Then Patrick - who could have been a contender - would slalom his way up the field and score. We always won.

Richard and Kate B. were together and happy. Kate B. didn't live here, just was here all the time, NQA. Like we'd adopted a daughter. She looked after children, cooked and worked with us. We of course teased Richard about cradle-snatching: he didn't care.

Richard and Julia were still very tense with each other. 'But Dick,' Julia admits, 'does make a lovely seed-bed,'.

Julia and Jonathan, however, were hopeless. They'd work a long, hard shift together, planting seedlings, potting herbs to sell, then reward themselves with planting marigolds round the central herb-circle.

Then Jonathan would disappear. The next day, he'd be slogging grimly at heavy digging while Julia lay rigid, in bed all day, curtains closed. I'd take her tea and ask: 'So shall I kick your bum out of bed, then.' Some days she'd laugh and say OK. Other days, she wouldn't acknowledge me at all.

Richard and Jonathan seemed friendly with each other. Patrick and me, too. The four of us went to a national Men's conference in Leeds. I remember a magical meal, above an Indian restaurant - in their upstairs store-room, the restaurant below being fully booked. - sitting on sacks of rice, with some beer and Thai grass. Leeds United beating Derby City 2-0 helped the mood. I wondered why everyone there came from Laurieston, Lifespan, Leeds, Liverpool, Lancaster or London. ('What the L,' said Pat.)

You seemed in good spirits. Your existential depression of last year had passed; you were busy with the Kids Project. True, you me and Patrick bounced off each other like spinning tops - that wasn't getting any easier.

Paul went willingly enough off to Glasgow. I think by now we do all know he has a relationship there with Meg.

As for Dave and Carol, the move to the cottage had relieved Carol of one set of problems and substituted another. From the outside it looked like a typical nuclear family battle. But things couldn't be laid at the communal door anymore. Arguing over who's looking after T&T. 'Standards' with regard to nappy washing. Carol went on to anyone who would listen. We were fed up of her moaning on.

And suddenly, Dave's Legal Frameworks conference is upon us.

A visitor wrote: "Mind-blowing stuff. There were 25 of us visitors from co-ops and communes, struggling with this Legal stuff - Housing co-op rules, trusts, partnerships, charity law and so on - but taking time out to play games, hold women's/ men's meetings, give / receive massages, find out about Laurieston.

"Resident Dave was great, focusing, fixing, time-tabling, nagging us to do chores, keeping the momentum rolling. Fantastic."

But it didn't help when Carol, refusing all offers from the rest of us, burst into a group meeting to dump Tam and Tiffany, crying, onto Dave's lap. Yeah, yeah, point taken, Carol.

Afterwards, we became legal 'experts.' Dave will spend months drafting all the material into a handbook.

And the big questions - do we want to be a commune, or a community? Should we expand to say 50 adults? Which legal framework would really suit us? - were shelved. Meanwhile, Laurieston Hall was still owned simply by Alice, Tina, Carol and Maureen.

The Legal Frameworks conference and the Freefall Groups left us with an after-the-party feeling of needing to get on with our own lives. On the whole, we avoided visitors.

But there were exceptions. The Living Theatre (London) people returned, to rehearse a play to take to the streets of Belfast. They stayed for a few months. They taught us their way of massage and led sound and movement workshops. They were lovely, but quite mad.

And Julian G. parked his beautiful old caravan, which, it was said, had once belonged to Coco The Clown, down by the stables while he served an apprenticeship at an agricultural engineering firm in CD. He helped with the bees.

We planted the garden, fenced the tennis court field, serviced the Ami and the J4 van, did more Freefall letter-writing. Mike began finalising the programme for the 'Alt U.'

We'd decided on the schedule for the Summer Weeks. Somehow, the uniting phrase, 'Alt. U.' didn't stick. It became a series of themed weeks. For the 'simultaneous but separate Women's Liberation/ Men Against Sexism week', Alice and I were sharing the work. Paul was co-ordinating activities for Glasgow week and Towns/ Community/ Environment week. I was also doing Social/ Political and Science/ Technology Weeks. The bookings rolled in.

Mainly, via Richard's rather beautiful, red post-box. To the right-hand side of the front double-doors. (Previous minutes had said: "27 February - Richard offered to build a post-box." "27 March, post-box still to do." "13 April, Richard has nearly finished post-box." "29 May, Richard reminded about post-box." Obviously, Rich had been waiting for the perfect moment.)

Dave and Carol went on holiday to London, leaving Jonathan, who moved into their cottage for the week, to look after Tiffy and Tam. Richard went away with Alice and you, me and Pat looked after Sonya and Polly. ('When are you and I ever going to get a holiday together?' I asked you.)

We took Sophie to the Royal Infirmary in Dumfries. Turns out she has problems we won't go into - but at least her problem is physical, not psychological. Which is sort of a comfort.

The Lochhill people asked to borrow the Versatiller and the gardeners hummed and hawed until Dave dashed off a furious note: "We must support other communes - we're the richest commune in the world." Now, Dave, that is arguable. Even so, off went the Versatiller. It was ages before we got it back.

We bought a tiny pig, the runt of a litter, for £5, from Ed (ignoring Paul's vegetarian protest that he didn't want us to keep pigs).

And the Lothlorien people bought two goats from us: Buttercup and Daisy (their pedigree, Irish Gaelic, names, meant something like 'Liberty' and 'Revolution'). (I should really like goats, the anarchists of the animal world.)

In the garden, there was carrot-thinning, potato-earthing-up. Et cetera. The PO does not pretend to know what goes on in the garden. But he went sea fishing with the Ed, who was a member of the Kirkcudbright Sea Fishing Club and came home, delighted, with three four-pound cod. Later, Richard took over the business, bringing back cod, tope, sea bass, mackerel - and, from the lochs, trout and pike.

We lunched on the lawn and had picnics by the sea. We shopped at auctions for old armchairs and more mattresses. We collected cheeses off the bus in CD, sent from the Stranraer Creamery (I ask you, who else manages that?).

We had a last-minute re-review of the name of the proposed summer events. If not "Alt U," then how about Summer Workshops? Counter Courses? Red Brick? The Politics of Everything Conferences?

Why not call it 'Brian'? says Sophie.

So we made an office, called 'Brian's Office' (obviously), where we duplicated newsletters, confirmed bookings, and nagged Alice and Paul to schedule their weeks properly.

In the last week of school Sonya had been given 'the belt'. She'd run around the village in a fury, seeking any adult willing to beat up Mrs. Laing, the headmistress. Good for Sonya. We went mob-handed to the school, said - 'we can't have this' - and explained our objection to the use of punishment, physical or otherwise. 'It's illegal in England,' we said (wrongly, at the time), 'and we don't see it can do anything but harm.' Mrs. Laing didn't look convinced - but never did it again to any of our kids.

The Accountant kept busy, paying the bills, watching the numbers. Had evenings alone, writing letters to old friends, or playing mournful solos on his tenor sax, down by the pond.

Or spent time down the Laurie. On a moonlit night, the walk out, over Retreat Farm, the spinney of beeches would be stately, grey and green. At closing time - ten-o-clock - would I ever get used to that? - it was black on black, and threatening.

I slept alone a lot. Hooray again for wanking.

18

And do you have, er?

I might say: 'Sweetheart?'

'Mm?'

'I would like to sleep with you sometime…'

'I didn't sleep with Patrick last night, you know.'

'Oh.'

'I was really tired. I fell asleep by myself.'

'Oh, I thought Patrick…'

'Well he came in and woke me up, but I told him I was tired.'

'Oh. Well. Anyway. And tonight?'

'Well…'

'So it's Patrick again, then?'

'Well I've said I would.' You give me a squeeze. 'You don't mind, do you?'

'Um.'

'You offer: Hello'

'Um.'

'What are you doing?'

Waiting for you to call. 'Nothing much.'

You put an arm around my shoulder but I shake it off. I am furious you haven't come to find me sooner. Can't just accept you, now you have.

'Oh well, if you're going to be like that.'

And you leave, and I get into bed and pull the covers over my head in the case the house falls down.

The triangle went all shapes: acute, isosceles, equilateral, obtuse. Mostly, obtuse. Some nights it grew late, while we went through the misery of being 'spontaneous.'

'I'm pretty fed up with wandering around looking for lights under doors,' said Patrick.

'I really should try to be more … to be clear about what I want,' Tina repeats herself.

'Maybe we should, er, *arrange*…' I offered.

I rehearse suspicion, ignorance, approaches, withdrawals, sulkiness, optimism, friendliness, coldness, desperation, distance, depression, and loneliness.

You learned pressure, feeling pulled in two, not having enough time on your own, yet feeling powerful, being 'in charge ' - but still, you said, 'feeling invisible and powerless' - I never understood that.

When you're with me, I sometimes think you really want to be with Patrick - that you're just doing some strange marital 'duty.'

But you will say, I rejected you.

'Hello,' you say, coming to say goodnight before going off to Patrick, as has been arranged.

'Grnhh.'

'What are you doing?'

'Go away.'

'Are you.?'

'Please just go.'

'What about tonight?,' I'd ask of a morning.

And you'd say, 'OK.' Or 'Well.' Meaning I should have asked you the day before.

Or you'd get in first: 'I'm sleeping with Pat tonight. You don't mind, do you?'

In the local dialect, 'to mind' means to know of, remember, be aware of (not - be upset about).

'No,' I'd lie. *But, ken, I dae mind.*

We knew we had to sort something out. We talked in twos. Why don't you stay with Patrick a few days and then spend some time with me after that? Perhaps we could all sleep alone for a while? (It was you who didn't want that.) Perhaps we could all sleep together? (Nobody keen on that.)

In clumsy, highly-quantised steps, we came up with The Arrangement. It still makes me shiver to think of it. You would spend a week with Pat, or by yourself. Then a week with me, similarly.

It didn't work.

The week with you would be a sweet and sour reunion, a glum mid-week, a last-night-before-we-part mixture of careless, depersonalised effervescence or desperate, angry loving.

The week without you, loss at first. Non-committal, alienated hugs in the middle, exaggerated friendliness at the end.

Patrick and I at least shared a similar situation; it made our matey alliance a little easier. We continued to work together - I recall making a compost heap cover using the corrugated iron off the laundry's lean-to.

It was harder for you - your 'free time' element never materialised. And you had no-one to share problems with - the other women, certainly, being pre-occupied. It would never have lasted long. And it didn't have to, because the rush of Summer was about to hit us.

(In all of this, I never realised that what I was supposed to do was scream, shout and - you said later - hit you.)

We had a meeting about relationships. To talk about our feelings; about being upset, depressed, jealous, uncertain - or, elated, even.

About our infancy and childhoods; our parents. Being brought up as girl or boy.

Our feelings about monogamy, nuclear families, possessiveness. How we'd all read Laing and Cooper, Freud and Reich, Firestone, Figes, Greer and others - and their impact on us.

And the nitty-gritty middle ground. Living in a group where some relationships were so bad - that we divided off into emotionally-based sub-sets.

How outside lovers affected the group. How it makes you feel guilty if you're close to someone outside the group. How the vibes in the amorphous, external 'movement' over-spilled to us and vice versa. How it feels to sit down to every meal with your lover's lover. And how close couples fit in.

Fleshing out the desiccated, delicate, bird-skull pictures of our relationships with the tissue and the juices.

Sexuality. Sensuality. The differences between women and men, straight and gay.

Stereotypes. Attractiveness. Style. How it was becoming difficult for a man to tell someone - especially a woman - that they're beautiful.

And exhaustion, boredom, VD, contraception (coils, heavy periods, floods of chemical greases, side-effective pills, condoms).

The elusiveness of, not just coming, but notionally earth-shaking orgasms.

No. Right on the button, Dear Reader. We avoided all this. Gave up after half an hour of mumbling, chilly and speechless. The muscle, fat and bone of this 'relationship' creature remained a mystery.

Nights you spent with Patrick were still horrid for me. But on one of them, I worked right through, then left the house shortly before dawn. Walked north, along the west bank of Woodhall loch, the rising sun filtering gently through the canopy of tall, mature larches. Struggled north-westerly across the moors to Loch Skerrow. Contemplated birds. Turning south, I climbed the hills on the far side of the stream known as Grobdale Lane - used by smugglers 200 years before, while hounded by the Excise-men (to whom, rhymester R. Burns belonged). I descended to the Gatehouse Road, hitched to Gatehouse, then back the long way round, via Ringford, talking enthusiastically to the driver about communal living.

Cuckolded? Try long-distance walking!

And Do You Have A Legal Framework?
June 1977 - Dear Alice and Dave, I gather you are having a go at 'The Constitution' again. Brilliant. I suggest (I know, I know, what's it got to do with me?) you should start off with a 'Preamble.' This would be the heart and soul of the matter. It would say - for us, mainly, but for visitors, friends and possible new members too - just why we are living at Laurieston.

At last, The Aims!

It would just take those old, one-line headings we always had, on living together, feminism, socialism, anarchism, personal growth, communal development, ruralism, adult/childcare etc. - and flesh them out with our experience over the last five years,

This would be the part of the 'Constitution' most frequently discussed, and liable to change. The point is to know what we are doing - not to create the Communal Ten Commandments. To promote and make room for discussion.

Without this preamble, the way would be open to interpret 'the rules' any old way - and our whole history says this would be timidly, conservatively, with the minimum of public discussion and the maximum of private agony. Without it, a housing association or whatever could drift towards becoming your typical, bourgeois, nuclear-family, co-ownership community, without discussion. Do we really want to ratify the positions of Rosie/Neill and Bridget/Tim down in the cottages?

Second. You will need to work out critical agreements. The more interesting, practical extensions of the main preamble. The real rules. For example. Do new people joining have to bring in some money, as Patrick and Catriona did, or what? And what about people's capital - it does get up my nose that mine is tied up in LH while Nigel, Meg, Tim & Bridget have kept theirs separate. When do children become full members? What happens when people leave? Who does the breakfast dishes? Surely if we are ready to agree anything, we could make some decisions here.

And only third, the small-print, People-In-Common type, detailed housing association rules. Membership, governance, quorums and so forth.

19
Summer 1974

'We're in the alternative hotel business,' Jonathan sniffs, 'The Revolutionary as Landlord.'

'No, we're the People's Republic of Scotland, Galloway Autonomous Region PeopleCentre, not £3 a day, not £2, just £1 a day per adult, half for kids, more if you can afford it, can't say fairer than that, my son,' says the Accountant.

It was a terrible, crazy, lovely, mad summer, which ended up in a panic and disaster and in which I was up and down like a bat in the dusk and which I began with a weep, just over the burn where the cleared scrub tends exponentially into a small cliff. I ran up, clutched onto a little silver birch, consulted a blue flower the size of a baby's fingernail and sobbed vertically for a few minutes. I can't remember what I was crying about. Something academic about if only we had ten times the land and a tenth of the house we'd be a different economic fish all the gether and swim against the whole of Galloway. But in this house? I came back over the beech mound and the damn thing was still there. Full of people, was the only way it could ever work. Fifty more members - or else, endless streams of visitors.

I walked back into the house and it was Women's/ Men's week.

In retrospect this was a daft idea - we should just have had separate weeks.

The women had the Old Kitchen, the front rooms and the lawn. The men were kept firmly out of sight in Billiard room, and looked after all 28 children.

Even so, some of the Lesbian Separatists said - well, shrieked - that we shouldn't be around at all. Why come to a combined week, then, we wondered? And some of the gay men complicated matters by claiming - loudly - that 'politically, we're women.' Chaos.

But then again, there were trust games - leaping off an eight-foot pile of tables to be caught by eight men. A convoy to Carrick beach (seven men, seventeen children). Yoga. Friendly meetings, even if we didn't push back the frontiers of sexism. Play-lets, bonfires in the evenings. Nudges and winks in the Laurie, references to the lawn-full of nude women.

Tina and Alice had a much harder time, trying to reconcile all the overlapping and exhausting arguments amongst the women. Straight versus lesbian. Child-haters vs. mothers (a.k.a. "breeders.")

We had a week's rest. Some of the group went away, the rest cleared up. Some graffiti remained:

'Tao is the source of ten thousand things.'

'Yes and most of them are lying around in the Hall.'

Next up was Glasgow Week. 'Glasgow week was rather small and where the bloody hell was Paul?' We had problems, problems. The man who was shocked by the buckets Jonathan has put in all the loos, to collect piss for the compost heaps. The folk terrified by lack of meat in the diet. Integrating a group of 'battered women', also from Glasgow, who were supposed to be camping, self-contained, in the grounds but who got rained out and asked to 'camp in the house.' Still, things worked out. Party night, Friday. Saturday morning, farewells and football.

Stupidly, the Kids Project team - Mike, Tina, Pat and Jon - thought this would be a good moment to start fostering kids in care. In Morning Room, thoroughly hoovered and wiped, and wearing our original, now rather fading, 'smart' clothes, we gave the local Children's Panel our performance as nice, normal, concerned middle-class folk.

Immediately, we were asked by Social Workers to take on a sixteen-year-old lad, Laurence, 'for a couple of weeks.' He stayed two months, nicked from us and visitors, terrorised the children, once really hurting Joel, wet his bed, lied pathologically and was altogether a sad case. 'Your Laurence,' said one visitor, 'locked our Gordon in the top of the tower, and him with a weak heart.' 'He's not ours,' we said. Tina kept an eye out for him more than Patrick. Never again, she said afterwards. Not for ten times the money.

The third Summer week was 'Social/ Political' week. We had academics, professionals, assembly-line workers from Ford at Halewood and from Chrysler - Big Flame people. Hippies working in movement bookshops, cafés or on little magazines. Some old friends. People who say they are 'just his girlfriend' or they 'just want to walk in the hills.' And some of our parents mixed in with all of this, too. Culture shock all round. Even a bewildered couple who'd booked the near cottage months before - and couldn't stay there because Carol and Dave were in it, so had accepted a room in the house instead. A recent, jokey phrase from cheap coffee bars applied to us: "You don't have to be mad to work here, but it helps."

'I came here to talk politics.'

'Right, but I'd just like to hang around with people, a few at a time, and get to know them first.'

The splits in Soc/ Pol week began at the first meeting.

We had, on my left: academics, Marxists and those who worked on 'revolutionary socialist' journals and papers - all determined to align themselves with the car workers and be legitimate, serious revolutionaries. Mostly men, of course. With their agendas and chairpersons, they wanted to discuss - in fact they thought we should *all* discuss - shop floor politics, union tactics, pay and conditions, attacks on the working class's standard of living, the forces of repression, Worker's Control. I seem to remember the academics offering to take on extra childcare so 'the workers' could catch up on Marxist theory (quite a 'lifestyle' move, for them). One of their lead questions was: "Where is the class struggle?"

This lot were also upset about the lack of meat and the piss buckets.

And then we had, on my left: situationists, libertarians, students, anarchists, community project workers, far-out academics, writers, loonies and freaks. Who wanted to set up ongoing small groups to talk about ecology, the environment, utopian dreams, revolutionary culture, what happened to the 60's, the power of symbols, the politics of food, Zen, mysticism, sexuality and such. And to do all this 'while sitting comfortably.' Typical lead question: "Who's your favourite poet?"

The straight left versus the alternative. The party and the movement. Rough caricatures these, and it wasn't such a simple division, because women and men, adults and children, 'born-into' class differences and suchlike cut into everything. So we had a network of camps and alliances.

There could have been a coming-together; or a useful debate. Either way, a step towards understanding, perhaps a more harmonious co-existence. But the two broad groups kept a polite distance, almost as though there were, as in women's/men's week, two 'simultaneous but separate' conferences.

The sun shone - that helped. There were the usual summer things - swimming, playing, visits to the pub. But between the groups, most communication was by graffiti:

'The ecology movement is middle class and apolitical.'

'The unions are macho, bureaucratic and hierarchical.'

'We have got to struggle for the right to work.'

'What about the right not to work?'

'No revolution without a broad-based, working-class movement.'

'No revolution without Women's Liberation.'

'Fight the attack on our living standards.'

'What about the Third World - compared to them, we're all rich.'

'That's a middle-class wank.'

'Well, you should know.'

'And you're ignoring history.'

'Be cruel with your past and those who would keep you there.'

I was in the middle of the week, as co-ordinator. Considering the differences amongst this bunch, it was going OK.

Except I'd thought we'd have a few Laurieston contributions on the bill. Because our pre-summer rhetoric (well, OK, *my* pre-summer rhetoric) had expected us to be giving to and learning from the Alt. U.

Perhaps not 'Towards Loving/ Living Groups.' Nor 'Putting Women's Liberation into practice' - we'd be a bit shaky on that.

But maybe 'Primitive Communism' - after all, we'd made income sharing work.

Or 'Yes, we have no, ring-leader' - about voluntary co-operation and consensus decision-making. I thought that would connect over to workers' control. Or maybe even 'Voluntary Poverty,' though this would have romanticised a necessity.

But I was a little short on confidence.

Besides, the straights had dismissed us and the softs knew most of it already.

Meanwhile, I rehearsed my spiel, for when I was going to be asked something like: 'You don't seriously think you can be political out here, do you? Capital must be fought at the Point Of Production. All the real problems are in the cities.'

'Ah,' I'd reply, 'but don't you see, there isn't any countryside anymore. It's all one vast, squalid factory. In fact, the oldest and biggest there is. Capital has its first roots in agriculture.'

Then I'd take off on The grain production belts. Mutton assembly shops. Deathly quiet wood-pulp incubation units, dumped anyhow on the landscape.

Great green garages for the meat and milk machines, each one individually numbered through this new ear-stapling technique. Wrecked, broken, and anyway inexplicable machinery on every farm; sometimes screened with a little tasteful woodland and blue-bells in season.

In this factory, *comrades*, (I might introduce an ironical tinge, there) the people are scattered and divided. Closed shops and negotiating rights are meaningless. Unions are scarcely visible. Unemployment is massive. Pay is low. In fact, just about the lowest. Hours, long. Conditions, poor. Accident rates at work, high.'

Here, citizens, public transport is minimal, shop prices are higher than in the city, public amenities few. Schools are still catching up with the 60's. Housing is scarce and this worsens every year as rich townies buy up

128

cottages for their second homes. People still live without mains electricity, gas, water (charming for a short break, not so funny in summer when the well dries up or in the cold and wet of winter). Whole families live in small caravans. The chooksters of Argyllshire, in corrugated iron and polythene shacks. Many in cottages are tied to jobs, to particular landowners. The situation is still feudal.

And there's no anonymity. Everyone knows your business. You're more vulnerable to intrusions here.

And you say, 'Well at least there's no pollution.'

You must be joking. Here is the guts of eco-disaster. No, not traffic and fumes. But here is where they put the tank-testing grounds, nuclear power stations, motorways, pipe-lines; here where they won't clutter up your leafy suburbs. Here is where the land is mined and quarried like there's no tomorrow. Here is where land is set to pasture for beef, where it could be fifty times more protein-efficient, growing grains and pulses. Here is where chickens are caged, for life, in batteries. Here is where hedges and walls are razed. Whole species falter while businessmen pay £500 a week to shoot already-tame game.

Oh it's beautiful, Galloway.

Incidentally, *brothers*. You have new cars. We have an old J4. You earn about twelve times what we do…

'But you're privileged. Not everyone can live like this.'

Too right. But we have room for more people. We are screaming for members - even half-arsed union shits such as you (no, we don't say this out loud). The problem is with you - I notice you're not asking to come and live here. You won't leave your town, with its comfortable pubs, clubs, discos, community bookshop, law centre, whatever. And the latest films and late-night, Mediterranean restaurants.

Well, you're escapist.

Look shitface - I become increasingly aggressive in these paranoid imaginings -as the silence went on - you sit there in you brick wigwam with your colour TV and central heating. And you call us escapist. How dare you.

Or sometimes, I just think: 'Of course we're trying to escape. Aren't you?'

Sadly, no-one really challenges me on these issues.

Friday Night, Party Night.

And on a typical Saturday morning, SS Laurieston, docked in the small hours by a skeleton crew, sees the passengers disembarking. On the quayside, fond farewells all round.

All morning the Hall will have reverberated with the kids' shouts, adults calling people into cars, mop buckets clanking, hoovering, the duplicator in Morning Room cranking out address lists, trolley-loads of breakfast dishes creaking through to the Old Kitchen. And mounds of cases, rucksacks and sleeping bags being dumped and picked up. People shuffling around, drinking last-cups-of-coffee. The stuck-record rhythm of Bye! Bye! Someone - maybe even Julia - taking money for our bunches of dried flowers. People fixing last-minute lifts, promising to write, keep in touch, see you soon, meet next year. Last kisses of holiday romances - with each other, sometimes with the crew - and off they go down the drive.

As they do so, the local guys arrive to play football. Your car workers are impressed. Plainly we middle class wankers in fact relate to local, working class persons. We have a few hours, just about coping, to replenish supplies, clean up the bedrooms, before we welcomed the next week's punters (aka fellow revolutionaries).

Personal/ Political week nearly sank in a storm on the first night. Some Primal Therapy visitors demanded - while others were still arriving - that they were only interested in doing encounter work - and why not start immediately. It was too soon, and everyone was tired - but the business of planning the week was rushed through, skimped, and twenty or more of us went up to Warm Room for what was, for most of us, a first experience.

One of the therapists, Jenny J., was definitely in charge.

There were too many people. They should have known that, if they're so expert, I thought later.

We exchanged names, each person in turn round the circle repeating the list and adding their own - we'd all done that before. Then breathing and loosening-up exercises - ditto. Then we split into pairs and had to look into each other's eyes and find out, not using words, who most needed to be looked after and who would do the looking. I got Kate B. I thought: all the time I've known Kate and this is the first time I've ever really contacted her. I felt sheepish about that; it got in the way.

But then a woman started crying and quickly the pairs broke up and attention focussed on her. Pretty soon, she left the room. Next, another of the therapist team went into the business of talking about bits of his past. He started crying, banging a pillow, yelling...

It appeared real and immediate, yet in a curious way it looked phoney, or rehearsed. As though we were being shown what to do when it was our turn. Except it never could have been everybody's turn, there were so many of us. I left. And more and more people kept leaving.

The Therapists left the same night. They thought we were, and I quote, "dead, dishonest and more hung-up than a bunch of policemen."

Yep, Jenny, that's me to a T.

The rest of the week was fabulous: one of the best of this or any summer.

Self-organising worked. The timetable of workshops stayed full. There was more discussion of the issues of Sexual Politics than there had been in Women's / Men's week (and much more than in our own, home-based attempt.) Certainly we were less inhibited talking about sexuality and relationships - about attraction and jealousy, orgasms, desires, fantasies and the peculiarities of our bodies, making love.

A radical psych's group - various 'radical professionals' - some psychologists, teachers, lecturers, a doctor, a journalist, social workers - debated the merits of 'fighting the system from within' with their dropped-out counterparts.

There was an evening when we talked about our spiritual natures and needs, our various religious upbringings, living and dying, our responses to and need for rituals. But we faltered here, unable to develop a 'ritual' that would suit us all.

And we created a 'non-violent action group' which began as a circle in the sunshine and finished late into the night.

Throughout, there were games and dancing. Swims in the loch, walks, visits to the seaside. A rhythm of activity and rest. People 'falling in love.' All familiar by now but still pleasing. The children complemented this week, putting on plays and puppet shows, running wild, their bodies painted (a new idea at the time), all round the lawns.

At the same time, in Billiard room, Freefall hosted another Greenock Group. Most evenings, everyone came together in a curious, cheerful mixture. Party night, Friday

It's August, by now. Days were hot or wet. The season's new rabbits, bigger now, sprang down slopes, across skylines - and under your wheels. Nights began to draw in; cold and clear, or overcast with smoky cloud. Soon there would be shameless autumnal moons. Owls.

I changed my name to Sam. The difference between Mike and Sam was that Sam didn't smoke tobacco. It was a game, like spending a day or two in silence, communicating, if mime didn't work, by scribbled notes. Like abstaining from tea and coffee. Or dressing up. I'd started it suddenly, spur of the moment.

'Mike,' Richard called, 'have you seen the pig bucket?'

'My name's Sam.'

'Sorry, Sam. Have you seen the pig bucket?'

Richard never queried it and never missed, during the month or so I kept it up. Just did it. Others needed the explanation. And it felt strange at first. I liked the alertness which came from waiting for, and avoiding, the deep habitual response to 'Mike.'

Paul couldn't get the hang of it. Alice did a thorough, deliberate, learning job. Tina managed it easily as far as the bedroom door; where I became Michael again (and thank god for a ciggy). Carol played the game conspiratorially (I quite liked that). Dave jocularly, Julia with curiosity, Jonathan with permanent disbelief, Patrick with irritation.

'Well, Sam, what's the matter with you?'

'Too many things.'

'Like what?'

'I'm lonely, I suppose. Ridiculous, isn't it, all these people here, the house more like I've always hoped it would be, the benefits of living in the country but with lots of company, yet I still feel lonely. I go around at night, you know, switching off lights, putting out cats. And in the mornings, in the noisy breakfast scene, I don't know who to go and sit with. Don't want to get into heavy conversations so early in the day.'

But what about all these women you've been sleeping with? You seem to be having a second teenage.'

'Never had a first one, you know that. Nothing really until I met Tina at college.'

'How are you getting on with Tina, anyway?'

'Sometimes, OK.'

'You don't sound very sure.'

'Well. It feels like I hardly ever see her. We get on, but don't sleep together much. I mean, we don't make love much. It's always so late, we're both so tired. And she sees Patrick more than me. And now the Arrangement's finished, it's back to random nights. And that's how it happens - these other women. I often seem to find myself hanging about with the crowd, dancing, boozing, talking. And what with one thing and another.'

'Sounds like you're just taking advantage.'

Oh balls. It's more the other way round. I'm sort of their holiday fantasy - their Greek Waiter.'

'So you don't enjoy it?'

'Well, it's mainly rubbish, sexually. And, if you must know, one-night stands are quite hard to relax into and enjoy. Too much other stuff going on. I mean, it takes a bit of practice to - oh, never mind. Then sometimes there's mornings, when you're not sure who you've just woken up next to. Not good, that.'

'And?'

'Well, I don't want another long-distance relationship. I want my friends and lovers here. Sometimes I feel I'm being unfaithful to the group, like Julia used to say. So that's another reason for drawing back.

'Tell you what, Michael.'

'What's that, Sam?'

'Well, Michael. We'll go round the twist talking to ourselves like this. Let's both go down the boozer.'

Education Week's programme was the familiar, over-ambitious list of topics: The State System vs. Free Schooling, Sexism in education, The Mystification Of Knowledge, 'Theorising As Life And Play.' And though the week was dominated by the presence of a gang of Manchester Free School children, there was the usual pattern of games, meetings. But by now I was keeping out of the way. The Alt U had become a chore, almost.

'How's it going,' I asked Patrick, who was co-ordinating the week. We were in Brian's Office. 'Well there's one lot criticising us for even thinking of taking our own kids out of school - you know, how will the system ever change if all its critics leave and do their own thing - and another lot who are shocked we haven't done it already - how could we have turned the kids over to the state for so long. Et cetera.'

Then came 'Octopus,' the group which had been the year before. A holiday group - not part of the Alt U. The residents grumbled about 'just catering' for this group. 'But that's all most people have done all summer,' I said to Patrick. Or was it Tina. 'I suppose what it really is, people are fed up with so many visitors.'

By the end of August, The group had, again, disintegrated. We'd talked about the Alt U weeks as 'an extension of the commune' - with all jobs shared, so that we could all spend time in the talking, the 'learning' and 'teaching'. So that the Alt U would inform and change our lives. It hadn't worked.

Confronted with blank lists for cooking, clearing up and vegetable-picking, the visitors dutifully signed up. But there were a hundred other jobs which would take longer to explain than to do. We kept running, rarely meeting each other, looking after the garden, the goats, Freefall, our own children. Paul used his holidays from work in Glasgow with a flurry of trips to local builder's merchants, planning offices and potential design clients.

Spending time with the conference people fell largely to Alice and me. Alice had the harder time of it, looking after the more demanding visitors.

The visitors had swamped us. Asking searching, intelligent, un-answerable, routine or just plain damn-fool questions, trying to find the 'real Laurieston.' But that, if it existed, had gone to earth.

Most visitors were, fortunately, physically well. A few would bring us a cold or something similar. A few would come down with our version, as Alternative Scotland's Costa Del Sol, of the runs.

But one woman, Gill C., collapsed with something which puzzled the local GP for a crucial week. Then tests came through. It was Hepatitis A (no, we'd have to explain, endlessly, it's the one you catch by touch, like, through food. Not Hepatitis B, the one which druggies get from sharing needles).

Oh dear. We despatched Gill C. off to hospital and wrote letters warning people of the risk of infection. Guiltily we got rid of the piss buckets - though there was no indication they did anything worse than niff a bit on a hot day. We became extra-careful in the kitchen. Used floods of sterilising fluid. Every sink, hand basin, bog, bucket and even the washing machine reeked of chlorine. All hands were scrubbed red.

Some visitors cancelled, but there were still around twenty visitors to the final Alt U Leftovers week, which was supposed to discuss vast topics (Science, Technology, Arts, Media) but during which we mainly felt panic.

We had a week of grace. Then Edinburgh's Theatre Workshop came for a holiday and taught us the basics of tumbling and juggling - those of us who weren't too dazed and exhausted. And Glasgow International Socialists (or IS, which later mutated into the SWP) came for a week.

The children went back at school - Billy, Sonya and Joel now joined by Sophie and Polly.

Alice and Dave hitched off to the Comtek (Alternative Technology) festival in Bath and I set off to work, with John H., on the parallel Bath Arts Workshop community festival. It wouldn't leave many people to help with the group of Freefall kids from Newcastle who were due to arrive – these would be our last visitors for four months. We turned away a Greenock Group we'd forgotten to forewarn.

Tina looked anxious and dejected as I left.

'Cheer up,' I said, 'things could be worse'.

And sure enough, things were worse.

We weren't about to have just a Laurieston Crisis Week. It was going to be a Crisis Autumn and Winter.

20

And Do You…?

In Women's/ Men's Week, the Arrangement decreed, you'd be with Patrick. I saw you only fleetingly, putting the kids to bed. I felt horrible about this, and sought you out late one night by sending word into the Old Kitchen. You seemed surprised that I needed to see you.

There was nothing to keep our relationship going. I liked your notion, that relationships are normally made up of daily acts for each other - cooking, shopping, fetching cups of tea to an ill partner. We had none of that. No daily bread, you might say. And we didn't go out together, hardly at all. Anyway you didn't like the Laurie and there was nowhere else to go.

It was then that it really sank in how low I came on your list of priorities. In some order the children, your mother, the Group, the Women of the Group, the Kids Project and Patrick all came first.

And I'm only realising now that, while you had Patrick crashing into your life, demanding your time, competing with me, the Group, the Projects for your attention, creating the reality he wanted by sheer determination - you had me pathetically sulking, telling you, in effect: 'If you cared for me, you'd come to find me.' I can see now why you'd take the easy route. Feel guilty, but choose to be obsessed with Patrick.

(Here at Dumb Toms, three years later, substitute Jay for Patrick and I still feel the same. Yet even now, you still sometimes say, that you love me. And that you'll visit. I'm wondering why that is.)

And are you self, er..?

No, but we make our own honey.

The bees swarmed. We banged pots and pans, sprayed the garden hose and hurled grit. This, I explain to the assembled, astonished visitors, is to make the bees think there's a thunderstorm, so they'll settle quickly (I had just learned this from Patrick and Julian G).

Using the big ladder, I climbed up the tree and sawed off the branch where the swarm had settled. Amazingly, magically, it re-settled on a pole near the hives which Patrick, in his white boilersuit, hat and veil, had just set up. Then they obligingly crawl up a blanket and into an empty hive he's prepared. Clever, that. Nobody was stung. 'Swarming bees are happy bees.'

No, but we keep pigs.

We hadn't agreed it, but Richard bought two breeding sows. 'Paul won't like it,' says the Accountant. 'But, he's not here, is he?' said Richard. Not unreasonably, but I doubt that Richard is ever quite going to fully get the hang of communal decision-making.

He and Kate B. build huts for them. And name them: they are Brigitte and Bardot, apparently.

No, but we have goats' milk. I went out with Jonathan, collecting hay from the roadside in Ed's trailer. I still thought keeping goats was daft, but it was pleasant work. I wondered why the council mowed the verges - were they keeping the countryside neat, like a municipal park? Jonathan patiently explains it's to prevent weeds spreading to the fields, the drains from choking and trees and shrubs from establishing themselves and growing out over the road. All quite simple. How come I can't work out things like that, after two years' country living?

No, but we have potatoes to live on.

Three varieties of potato, in fact, plus seventeen different kinds of green vegetable, six of legumes, six of pulses and twenty-seven herb and blossom teas, not counting the blended mixes.

Richard's fresh-caught fish. Smoked salmon and mussels. Eggs. Hare, rabbit, woodpigeon, pheasant, chicken. Rosehips, rowanberries, hazelnuts, crabapples. Home-made jams, preserves, pickles, chutneys. Home-made bread, always.

Blewits, chanterelles, puffballs, boletus, parasol and horse mushrooms. Elderflower, parsnip, nettle, and banana wine (the bananas came cheap, over-ripe, from the wholesaler in Dumfries). Friends shared their bottles of Malt whisky and herbal products from Thailand, Nepal, Tibet, Lebanon, Zaire and Devon. Amanita muscaria and psilocybe semilanceata were also available.

We were the New Poor, it says in the Sunday Supps. We dined, in fact, like the rich rarely do.

And would you say you have been, on the whole, healthy?
'To become and stay healthy' - would have been another of The Aims.

Mainly because it feels better, of course, but also because how can a garden, a Kids Project, a commune or a revolution be made by sick and tired bodies?

Good Health, we had thought, would be part of the package deal, following on from hard work, the out-door life, a wholefood diet. We wouldn't need the NHS, in the end. We'd learn first aid and midwifery and perhaps naturopathy, herbalism, acupuncture...

'Western Allopathic Medicine,' insisted various friends, and their pamphlets, 'with its emphasis on antibiotics and other so-called wonder drugs, and on surgical intervention, and in its ignorance of what constitutes positive health, causes more illness than it cures.'

What a fatuous overstatement. But the basic theory seemed unshakeable: better to live right, eat properly and avoid getting ill in the first place. Except it didn't work out.

Several of us had prolonged and enervating bouts of colds and flu every winter.

We had stomach upsets, scabies and impetigo.

The children passed around German measles, chickenpox, mumps, the general run.

Adults had headaches and migraines, unspecified fevers and infections. The women, thrush and cystitis. We had the pill, the coil, the cap, the condom - but even so, a couple of unwanted pregnancies and hence abortions. Not to mention gonorrhoea and NSU.

And we remained addicted, to differing degrees, to tobacco and the hauf and hauf (a Scottish psychedelic). And Mars bars.

'We're healthier than we would have been,' some argued.

Or: 'We're not as bad as the average visitor.'

Or: 'Living communally, and with all the visitors, puts us at greater risk.'

Either way, we stayed regular customers at the Health Centre in CD. And are just about to make serious demands on the NHS.

The Radical Commune would do well to adhere scrupulously to Health & Safety guidelines on kitchen hygiene.

And How Do You Make Your Living?

Well, actually, from you, Dear Visitor. Surely you must realise that?

Over the summer, counting Freefall, we had upwards of 300 visitors. Over the years, we've hosted many thousands. Counting up, visitors have perhaps spent more people-days here than we, the Rezzies, have.

We've had visitors who fitted in beautifully, as though they were already Family, who played with our children, made things, fixed things, slaved in the garden. And who offered criticism and suggestions in a supportive spirit (start free school, manufacture something, link up with other communes, start a federation, all sleep together, call up such and such a therapist or teacher, get away more, stop going away so much.) All things we'd talked about but didn't know how to do - or that we couldn't get started, because we were so dispersed.

Some who embarrassed us with praise -'It's really amazing, what you're doing here.' (Well thanks but actually it's not as smooth as it looks.)

137

These were the ones we were pleased to see coming back (you know who you are).

Then there were those who sat on their arses for a week, who dumped tea leaves in the pig food and pig food in the compost (I mean, how hard can this system be to understand?). Others who had grown old fast and become decidedly bourgeois. Even some who took one look and set off for the nearest proper hotel.

And several who picked up on one or other of our several failings and nagged on about it most unhelpfully. But surprisingly few whom we didn't want back, thank you. (They probably don't realise.)

And we had in-betweens. But, good or bad, we had visitors who kept, and those who broke, all three rules (which were still: No unguarded fires. Watch out for your children. No illegal drugs.)

Almost all of you, dear Visitors, were compelled, it seemed, to tell us either why you wouldn't want to join us: or why you would, but you couldn't.

Those of you who could never think of living with us would say you were 'too individual,' 'too introverted,' or 'too fond of my creature comforts.'

Implying, presumably, we were a bizarre troupe of hair-shirted, extrovert clones.

21
Autumn 1974

It was the smoked salmon, we realised.

We used to get bins of filleted bones from a factory, Newton Stewart way, which made 'Scottish Smoked Salmon' (different of course from Smoked Scottish Salmon). We steamed these, salvaging pounds of salmon pâté. Yummy stuff, hard to keep your fingers out of a bowl of it lying on the kitchen table. Someone later remembered seeing Gill C. working with Patrick in the kitchen, a day or two before she took to her bed.

Hepatitis A has an achingly long, six-week incubation period. And in that crucial sixth week - it must be one of Sod's laws - Patrick and Polly collapsed. Just as a Newcastle Freefall week was ending.

On a Grandparents trip with Joel and Sophie, Tina and I extended our trip to London, visited our former GP - the famous Dr. Hindley of Highgate, who had delivered Sophie - and were promptly given gamma globulin shots. Back in Laurieston, the Medical Officer of Health prevaricated. Supplies would have to be fetched from Glasgow. And, says he, medical opinion is divided; some say it has no benefit.

We kept the children home from school. Quarantined ourselves. And waited. As if we didn't have trouble enough.

By the middle of October, Paul, Meg (who had been planning only a short, first visit), Dave and Richard were all seriously ill with the hep. Alice too, but she was away at her parents' house for the worst part.

And our GP, Dr. Kerr, finally came up with gamma globulin shots for everyone else (meanwhile making plain his distaste for treating Paul and Meg, an unmarried couple, sleeping in the same bed).

The shots worked. At least, no-one else came down sick.

Let's hear it for Western Allopathic Medicine.

We had two blank, grey months. Days when the sun, if it peeped through the early morning clouds at all, would retire again, obviously distressed by the state of us.

The Well - those with the strength left to murmur 'actually I don't feel too good, myself' - nursed The Sick. Several times, I shouldered Paul from his bed to the loo and back. And he is one big, heavy guy.

And we coped with the children home all day - because of course we'd to keep them off school. We did the chores, fed the animals, chopped wood. Which left little time or energy for much else.

We had no work, no visitors, no income. Not even garden sales. Only Paul's sick pay. We talked about claiming the Social and what the village would think (because they'd certainly find out.) But we lacked the energy to get to the SS office in Dumfries. We lived on the summer income, but it was running out fast.

There was nothing to be done except keep going, day to day. Physically and financially we were near to collapse.

When the MOH said it was safe, the children went back to school. But this, it turned out, was too soon. First one village child caught the hep, then, three weeks later, so did Ken and Greta's kids at the pub. They were petrified; obviously if they caught it, they'd have to close down. We explained again, it wasn't our fault. And no, it wasn't Hepatitis B.

This threat passed. Even so, newcomers to the village will sometimes get the impression we live in squalor.

By the end of October, The Sick were over the worst, physical phase of the illness. But their troubles continued. They entered a period of convalescence, lasting through the winter, in which they were weak, easily tired and 'jaundiced' - a combination of being irritable, depressed, hysterical, flustered and unable to think straight. Like a four-month hangover.

We lived with no purpose except survival. The disputes of the spring and a catalogue of issues and incidents from the long summer waited impatiently to devour any emerging vitality.

An external adversity might have given us some strength, some unity. This invisible, treacherous, internal sickness left us wrecked and divided.
There was rarely more than half the group at a meeting - having half-hearted discussions. Not least, because 'we can't decide anything with so many missing.'

We might begin with the children. They're not happy, are they? Perhaps make them a proper playroom? In Tony's old room, maybe? Or a communal bedroom?

And there we are, talking instead about rooms and spaces. Living space first of all for new people, if we indeed going to have new people, which most of us think will be all right, if it is limited to a few at a time, a process described as 'organic' growth; anything organic is good at this point.

We remind ourselves that the stables – it's roof still needing attention – will eventually be made to provide more living and/ or work space and there we are, adding existing and hypothetical work projects into the discussion.

First, space is needed specifically for the PeopleCentre, Freefall and the occasional Youth Club disco, although the latter is not pressing, as during our isolation, Neill has been running the weekly club back at the school. And we remind ourselves that some folk do not want to share their living space with Freefall and the Youth Club, so these must be elsewhere.

But before anything else – and here we slip softly into fantasies - we need a plan of how we're going to use the whole property. And allow for Paul's building project. And make space for a furniture-making workshop, which could become a Co-op, employ local people whose kids could join ours, in our Free School, when it's up and running. And we should really start an Alternative local newspaper, because we need wider contacts.

'We're not getting very far with talking about the children.'

It takes two hours to meander through this and similar territory. We don't explore detail, just deal ghosts of ideas from the communal pack. Trumping, finessing and back-stabbing as we go.

And of course we cannot decide anything, because there are too many missing.

Except that, another evening, in Billiard Room, again discussing Freefall, someone proposes:

'Well, they'll have to be based somewhere else, like the Front Living Room.'

'But it's so cold in there.'

'Well it's cold in here.'

'Ah,' Dave steps in, 'I'm in agreement with Paul on this. I think we should buy a Jotul.' (This being a Norwegian-designed, quality woodstove.) (Paul wasn't present.)

Everyone agrees, apart from the PO, who objects: 'I thought we couldn't decide anything'?

'S'alright,' says Dave, 'I'll check it out with everyone who's not here.'

Leaving the PO speechless.

November mornings, the sky would be light pink, patterned with rainclouds and geese. It wasn't all that cold. Wet, though. A deer or two visited from the hills.

We picked up the pieces.

Richard worked with Tim (still based at Flosh), building a barn for rich, eccentric Henry, whose farm was at Dunscore, over by Dumfries. The barn was to be a garage for Henry's huge steam lorry, which, meanwhile, was currently located down at the stables, being repaired and renovated by Julian G.

Do pay attention at the back.

Patrick and Tina fixed Freefall groups for the new year. Dave wrote a draft Legal Frameworks booklet - the material coming from Dave himself, People-In-Common in Burnley and Radtech in Sheffield. Tina and I struggled to edit it into something readable.

Jonathan and Patrick did the goats and the garden: I helped Jonathan plant some fruit saplings (ruined a year later by Freddy in ten minutes of billy-goat vandalism). Paul resumed his weekly commuting to and from Glasgow.

The women spent time (really, a lot of time, thought the Accountant) - creating the first issue of their, new, feminist, rurally-based little mag: 'Country Women.' Tina wrote a bleak but funny story, "Putting Down Roots;" Carol a piece on keeping chickens; Alice one on moving to the country and Julia about being raised in it as a farmer's daughter. The PA typed up and duplicated the whole thing.

Carol's flocks of poultry multiplied. Even the ducks were laying well. And Carol had developed a new skill: making slip-on leather clogs.

And this was when, at Tom C.'s suggestion, the PA became the PO and wrote the 'research proposal' for the P&CRP, saying: "We have no guiding principle, ideology, activity, or guru. We are committed to living sustainably in a rural environment - beyond this we have a complex, overlapping set of aims and intentions which vary for each member of the group."

Some people staying temporarily near Stranraer asked to come and stay for six months, to continue practising being a commune. This chimed with an idea some of us had championed - using the house as a base for other groups to get started. 'Because surely we wouldn't want them to jump into it like we did?' But we couldn't decide. Pretty soon they divided and scattered - some of them, later, setting up Wheatstone commune near Shrewsbury.

While we, more than ever, needed new members.

Catriona came to stay, as a possible joiner. She'd done a post-grad course in Town Planning then worked for two years in London, joining a women's group but otherwise growing to hate the city. She'd called to see a friend at B.R.A.D., a short-lived alternative technology commune in Wales, and visited other groups. She was living semi-collectively - points for that.

We were just right for her, she thought. The women's group, sharing work between the women and the men, pooling income. Careful, we said, things aren't all they seem, we're in a terrible state. This led to a strange meeting where we pointed out all our defects and Catriona told us we weren't that bad.

And we liked her. At least, many of us positively did and nobody positively didn't, which is as good as it gets. She was independent, feminist, committed to communal living. And I remember her smile, half-hidden behind her glasses and long dark hair. And the first time I heard her singing, with such a clear, folksinger's voice - I thought it was the radio.

We told her to come back in the New Year.

Tim, Bridget, and Angus called back, too. They'd been working hard on their smallholding, but were finding it difficult financially. Lonely, too.

We'd known and liked them for two years. The snag was, they didn't want to live communally. They wanted their own nuclear space and saw their relationship to the rest of us as mainly an economic one. They wanted to share our projects, but were hesitant to share our lives.

Paul was very keen they should join, for reasons which will become clear.

'Well we can't seem to decide anything at the moment,' we said, 'come back again after Christmas.'

(The snag was, I thought, bitterly, eighteen months later, they wanted company for Angus and to rip us off.)

And, confusingly, Neill and Rosie had asked to join. Straightaway, some thought it wouldn't work - they spend too much down the pub.

But Neill earns enough to cover it, I said. Feeling touchy - OK, guilty - about my own spending on tobacco and alcohol.

'But will they really go along with income sharing?' Patrick wonders.

Again, we said we couldn't decide until we could all get together.

However, they couldn't wait - they set up home with their children, Ben and Emma, and Norah (Rosie's sister), her partner Davey and their two kids, in Bellymack, a house they rented from Farmer Henty, standing just out of Laurieston on the CD road. Thereby neatly avoiding a serious discussion of how we might have resolved our English middle-class/ Scottish working-class differences.

November 18th, 1974 was our first meeting, all together, for four months. Writing now, it seems such a shame that we didn't have even the simplest of rituals - like, holding hands in a circle - to mark this event. Billiard Room was still chilly.

Paul announces he's ordered some coal - this will be to boost the heat we get from the Billiard room boiler, while we await the fabled Jotul. You should've asked a meeting first, says Jonathan. And we all leap in. We should: think about the miners, not use coal, stop burning green wood, share heated rooms more, replace the wood we burn.

Under attack, Paul is serious. And when he's serious, he's dead handsome, with his long hair tied back in a pony-tail. When he's happy, he looks more goofy.

Richard challenges, 'Come on, what's this meeting about?' How Richard has changed. The debonair film star has gone shaggy and stubbly. He's not stoned, but may not be fully with us.

'Why are we here?' offers Dave, ironically. He's mop haired, wearing another multi-colour dressing gown, newly-made by Carol. Fresh from a bath (funny how that glowing cleanliness puts me off people). Also, the PO notes, there's always hot water down at the cottage. The rest of us depend on the Hydresse - which is unreliable.

What are we here for? Shrugs. Tight little smiles.

'I think it's announcements first,' says Jonathan, who has prepared an agenda. He's dressed entirely out of communal clothes. Baggy pants, thick woollen vest, white linen jacket, died pinkish. Like Julia, he is skinny as a whippet.

'There's a Hoskyns group wanting to come straight after Christmas to use the equipment,' says Tina. Who has craters under her eyes. We are all tired.

'But there aren't any leads left for the amplifiers and I thought, Rich, you were supposed to be...' Mike interrupts. Mike the long-curly-haired bundle of tension and intolerance.

'I'm making some,' Richard replies.

'Also does everybody know there's another band, they're only young, went to school at Killy, who want to come for a month. Is that OK?' wonders Tina.

We suppose so. 'It'll be good to have a few people staying again,' Julia surprises us. Wearing overalls and a padded jacket, and with her hair cropped really short, Julia was anticipating by a couple of years the current feminist fashion statement.

'We should talk about income again,' begins Paul.

Dave says, 'The women spent a lot of time on Country Women and now you're writing this piece for Spare Rib.'

'Well,' says Tina, 'we're going to be paid £50 for that.'

'I'll believe it when I see it,' thinks the Accountant (he never does, because Spare Rib didn't pay up.)

'Anyway we're thinking of starting a Women's Painting and Decorating Collective,' Alice throws in.'

Alice is mainly looking beautiful but sad, these days. With her small eyes and such long hair - maybe waist-length by now - she's apparently puzzled with everything. Unless she laughs.

'Well I'm thinking about finding out whether there's any jobs with the Forestry,' says Jonathan.

'Thinking about finding out' is usually as far as it gets, with Jonathan. And Alice.

And someone asks Carol, 'What's this work you're going to do with Davey? Carol pouts her lips and lifts her nostrils. Kissing air, she's very good-looking. 'Davey has advertised as an odd-job man, I'm going to help.'

Patrick - lean, tall, masses of hair and beard, horrible good looks but still the same tiny eyes – announces: 'I'll sweep the chimneys this week if I feel OK.' And departs to boil the kettle.

'Actually the whole house is really filthy,' says Alice. Mike, Tina and Julia agree to help her clean it.

'The West Wing roof is leaking,' Rich changes tack.

'So's my room,' says Julia.

'And the stables roof is nearly gone,' Jonathan adds.

'And I'm worried about this (Billiard) room's roof, too,' says Paul, 'and the gutter downfall pipe in the goat yard. Richard, I thought you…'

'Yes, I'm going to do it,' Richard says.

'And the far greenhouse is getting worse,' says Jonathan. 'So it is,' says Julia, enigmatically.

'So it's three coffees, six teas?' Patrick calls from the kitchen. 'No I'll have tea,' says Alice. 'Why don't you make your mind up,' snaps Patrick.

'I don't want to live here when people can't even make cups of tea for each other,' Alice cries, her face puffy.

We say: calm down, Alice, he didn't mean it. It's just the hepatitis. 'I'm sorry,' says Patrick, passing teas and coffees across the serving counter. We mill about: Alice cheers up, settles down.

'A thing I'd like us to agree on,' she says, 'is building another kitchen, in the west wing. Maybe in Green Cupboards or Nurses Dining Room.'

'Well, at least they face south,' says Mike.

Nobody else comments. Nobody raises the time and effort that will be needed, the cost, the eventual location and how it might affect other projects. The how, the why, the when. The Group, the PO now realises, was giving its tacit assent to splitting into two. Have two kitchens. Hence two Living Groups – this phrase enters the lexicon immediately. It's a momentous decision. Yet we were all smiles.

The meeting is over, everyone moves to go. Paul sneaks in: 'The Ami needs servicing, but I haven't really got the time to do it.' Tina steps forward. My wife, the car mechanic.

Still, for the moment, united, we set off towards Christmas with some colour back in our collective cheeks.

22

And you get on with the Locals?

We have a new couple, Liz and Arthur, both actually Scots, living in the far cottage, empty since the last summer let. Liz works alongside Neill, so we now are friends with two Art teachers at CD High. Arthur is quiet to the point of being unintelligible, but works for the Gas Board. Or similar.

Julia has started work at Lybro's in Dalbeattie as a trainee machinist, making jeans. It means getting up at 6, walking into the village to get the works bus with other local women and not getting home until 6 p.m. And bringing home £15 on a Friday.

Julia, Carol, Mike and sometimes Julian G., are going to Lally's new Yoga Class in CD. (It's officially "Yoga for Women", a counterpart to Car Maintenance for Men.) Even Neill and Davey sometimes go too.

The Woodfoot lot are surviving OK. Andy the Potter is wanting a goat from us.

And How Do You Make Decisions?

'If we're going to talk about Projects,' I said, 'couldn't we refer to my notes?'

'Oh, they're just your picture.'

'But they're not, I've tried to include what everyone has said.'

'But they're so long.'

'Yes but it's all in Sections.'

'Anyway, how can we talk about things if you've already written everything down?'

'Well the idea was that we don't talk very well about things anyway and there's so much to remember.'

'Well what I feel is that if we refer to your notes, that sort of makes you The Leader.'

'Oh, piss off.'

'The Radical Commune' - I addressed the middle distance, the Cairn on Ullioch Hill - 'needs a leader, anyway. Someone brave, strong, clear-headed and funny. Someone to call people together, suggest what to do. She or he'd make us laugh, help us cry, guide, inspire, push, cajole. Tease and teach us, bully and love us. Make decisions when consensus fails. And, of course, pass the job on to the next person after a couple of weeks. If we can have a cook-of-the-day, do boiler duty for a week, why not be leader for a fortnight?'

Patrick did however read my notes, in the end. Him and Tina and Julia. What a waste of time they were. but then he only read them as a duty, because of me and Tina and the triangle. And he's so petulant and huffy and you can't tell him off about it because it's still the hep, his liver, talking.

And Do You, Er.
With both Jonathan and Tina away, Julia came to my room one evening and we talked about yoga, meditation and her planned visit to Throssel Hole (newly re-formed as a Buddhist retreat). And why her thing with Jonathan had 'never worked here.' Then I found I could say it - come to bed. And I thought, maybe our little romance will blossom.

It had been eighteen months in abeyance, I thought in the morning. Felt across the bed and of course she was gone. Off to Lybro's.

She was gone for three days; working, never lingering after supper, retiring without a word to her room where, presumably, she wanted to be left alone. 'Hey, Jools, what's happening,' I asked, following her down the corridor on the third day. She came to bed again. Then never again. Whatever was happening between Julia and Jonathan, it was a full-time pre-occupation. Later Jonathan explained that whenever Julia got interested in somebody else, he'd be attracted to her again. So I'd just been a little warmth on a lonely night. I felt cross and a bit cheated.

And Do You Have Meetings?
We tried a new style of meeting. Dave had got the idea from a book about Oneida, an American community founded over a century ago. The idea was to focus on one person at a time, while the rest of the group would criticise - we added comment on and compliment - the one in the hot seat. First Julia, then Tina volunteered.

It didn't really work. People told Julia she shouldn't spend so much time in bed - she pointed out she'd been going out to work for a month. They told Tina it was hard to get to know the person behind the mask - but there were no great revelations about the triangle or its interaction with the group. We kept to surface emotions. Said we'd try it again sometime, not meaning it.

Dave especially wanted another try - but wanted the rest of us to show willing - for somebody else to call the meeting. The same as me with men's meetings. the real problem here was while say cooking and cleaning were recognised as communal tasks, organising, initiating, calling meetings, answering the phone, replying to letters, being 'front' to official callers, planning, budgeting - weren't. they were left to those who began willingly enough but carried on, as these jobs were left to them, in a spirit of martyrdom.

And Do You?
One night, late, I took a phone message for Carol and strolled, deliberately rather slowly, down to the cottage to deliver it. Dave being away at a Land Trust meeting in London. You were with Pat.

Message delivered, I kissed Carol goodnight and turned to leave. And she asks: 'Is that all?'

'Well,' I said. And spent the night with Carol.

'Pleasure and confusion' - it ought to be one of the I Ching answers. The pleasure of a new lover; confusion, because Tina wouldn't like it, because she didn't get on too well with Carol. And because I didn't, with Dave. And because I was still a bit cross with Carol for not being the perfect communard.

Dave returned the next day, and that was that for a while.

23
Winter 1974/75

Little pig had become known, ominously for him, as 'Christmas.'
Back in the Spring, Richard had fenced off a wee patch for him, built a sty, and fed him scraps and fattening meal. He'd survived and grown, rooting out everything except nettles. By the first week in December he was big enough.

I dreamt that Richard and I had agreed how to do the deed.

Richard would say, 'It might as well be now.' And he'd go to sharpen the knife. I would tie a piece of soft cloth over the flat, circular head of the stob hammer.

Tempting Christmas with a bucket of scraps, I'd lead him - following enthusiastically - from his sty to a stall in Goat Yard (I'm still looking for the human equivalent of that bucket of scraps).

We'd feel solemn, wouldn't we.

I'd spill out a few scraps and, as pig put its snout down, one of us would swing the muffled hammer, catching him exactly right, smack on the long forehead - pig would slam flat. The other would slide the knife quick and deep into the neck. Blood would be everywhere. The beast would squeal once - a sound audible in the bones - quiver a few seconds, then be still.

Richard would twirl round silently, his eyes closed. Then we'd string up the carcass by its hind legs and leave it to bleed into a pail. Outside, in the yard, we'd hug each other.

What a dream. In the real world, this would have been mildly illegal. I do not advise you, Dear Reader, to try this for yourselves.

Had we had a slaughtered pig, we'd have done the whole trip. We'd have weighed him in at 84 lbs. of pig chauvinist male. We'd scrape off the bristles with the help of boiling water, gut him, saving the liver and kidneys. Marvel at such fine, deep colours - bright red lungs, silver gristle, soft pastels of intestines. Saw down the backbone and cut away chops, to eat the next day. Deep freeze the larger joints. Cure the belly for bacon with a good-smelling mixture of salt and molasses. With meat from a hare, I'd make pâté de campagne; Dave, brawn from the brains.

Of course, in reality we will have always taken all animals for despatch to the slaughterhouse.

Including a billy kid which I never did slam so hard - I would have been

149

terrified of failing - that it hit the opposite wall, dead instanter.

These days when vegetarians insist: 'If you eat meat, you ought to be prepared to kill it yourself,' I just say, 'You think so?'

Paul and Dave installed the Jotul in the Billiard Room week before Christmas. But it was still cold. Most evenings, we huddled around it, our minds frozen and brittle. Continuing my hopeless campaign, I wrote in the Diary:

Biggest, Coldest Room Research shows:

	°F
Outside temperature	42
Billiard Room, unheated	45
Billiard Room, Jotul burning	55
Big Front Living Room, unheated	54
Sunny Room, unheated	55
Sunny Room with paraffin heater	69

I was still trying to persuade people to move, collectively, to a south-facing room: Big Front, or Sunny Room, for favourite. Both of which, with the help of an occasional sunny day, got comfortably warm by themselves. It was a lost cause - I felt friendless in this attempt, and kept up a flow of negative backchat. I was stubborn and a bore. No change there, then.

In the run-up to Christmas, Bridget, Tim and Angus came to stay again (Bridget would have made ham and egg pies, had we had the ham).

All of a sudden it was Christmas Eve. You and I spent it together - perhaps to make up for last year - frantically wrapping up presents. And fell exhausted into bed.

Christmas Day began with the children tearing open their presents. Still in the shadow of hepatitis, we had been too tired and uneasy with each other to get together and make sure each child got a fair share of presents. We'd just said – let's keep the whole thing to a minimum.

We'd learned nothing from last year. Again, grandparents' parcels were handed over to grandchildren, unopened. Again, Sonya lost no time in bragging. Her Lego kit was 'twice as big as Joel's.' And she'd been given a fishing rod, something Joel would've loved. Again, Joel and others were in tears. Again, welcome to Christmas, the season of full-scale tragedy for kids, anguish for us Groans. All as bad as last year.

But we brighten up. Before lunch, the adults exchanged presents. Julia had made candles, Jonathan, huge collages of pictures, Tina, hand-painted stones. I'd made cards. Patrick settled the children and gave them his first Madame Ethelred hand-written storybook. Dave gave the group a machine involving a weighted pendulum and a biro, which drew swirling patterns on large sheets of paper. Richard handed out envelopes of his herbal produce.

Apart from (again) a cashewnut roast for the veggies, Christmas lunch - roast pork and all - was entirely our own produce. Before we ate, I had (again) wanted to say a grace. But (again) the gathering was too large and embarrassed by this suggestion.

The season of good intentions, possibly. Goodwill is too strong. That evening, Pink Floyd, extending from Thoreau, sang despondently about Quiet Desperation.

Then it was off to parents/ grandparents and back in time for our quietest New Year so far. People chatting in Old Kitchen, listening to Bob Marley. But Carol and I sloped off to share an amorous spliff. Some ash fell into her eye and I ran to fetch the Optrex. Before I got back, Carol had, sensibly, left to sluice her eye with tap water, as the strokes chimed 12. We are in Whitehall farce territory here. It was not the most romantic occasion.

Dave, the Diary, January 15th 1975:

"Alice is digging a drain for the new West Wing kitchen and it's a major excavation. She is keen to plan the conversion without feeling dominated by Paul or me.

"Killy have sold us their old Aga at scrap value, so it seems this will be called: 'Aga Kitchen.'

"But who will live in it is still unclear. Not me, in the foreseeable future.

"True to form, Mike is calling it: the "*Smallest*, Coldest, Darkest Room in the house." He is right in a way, but he's too aggressive with it.

"Last night we planned a few events around Easter on the assumption that this new kitchen will be complete by the end of March. I got stamped on for saying it was impossible.

"I started writing this with the idea of expressing what was on people's minds at the moment as seen from where I sit.

"Paul and I did a survey for leaks and repairs in the cottages, stables and house. Paul has done an illustrated list - at least a year's work. He always seems to think we could find more time to do more as if we were not already working pretty hard.

"I will probably patch the cottages and the stables when it stops raining. It has rained every day for 55 days.

"Paul is still thinking about giving up work at the Mackintosh and starting the building and design project."

"Last night Carol Tina Pat and me talked about the Capital, steadily decaying with inflation. Mike was not there and usually has a lot to say on that subject.

"Tina is busy editing the *Children In Communes* article with Alice, Julia and Carol. As usual I don't know what else is on her mind. In fact I find the hardest minds to read are Tina, Mike and Patrick, though it's getting better.

"Catriona arrived back last night.

"Mike is finalising the *Legal Frameworks Handbook*. We are all pissed off with it one way or another. I want to get it out and finished to clear the decks.

"Mike is concerned we spent a third of a year's income in 10 weeks - we are all supposed to be economising after the hepatitis slump. God knows what caused the spending spree. I want to see the accounts as it bothers me too.

"Julia is back at Lybro's, sewing zips onto elastic material, which is skilled machining. She has nearly rebuilt the hot frame in the greenhouse with help from Jon. I have hardly seen her for weeks.

"Jon is Jon - guru, stoned, wood, food, cycles, growth, feelings, frustrations...

"Pat has done most of the work on the nanny goats we are boarding with help from Jon and Tina. I've done damn all for some reason deep in my head.

"Pat has also been getting the place and his head ready for the groups of kids in the next few weeks. Painted a big Guinness bottle on the wall of Tony's Old Room, which is now the Freefall Playroom. He is calmer now it seems. Plays with Tiff and Tam, helps out all over the place.

"Richard is designing a pig house for when the piglets are born. He's still working on Henry's Barn, over at Dunscore, with Tim Pat Carol and Mike. (*Why doesn't this count as Building and Design, Paul?* - someone scribbled on Dave's Record.)

"Carol is getting into people in the house in a far-reaching way." (Slept once with Mike and a few times with Patrick - typ.) (Tina is of course furious with Patrick - PO.) "All very close to home for me. I know it's a good thing, but I find it hard to adjust to it. I find it exciting tho' it makes me lethargic. I need peace and quiet to sort it out. Things are much better at the cottage - Carol seems less critical, partly because she is more secure, partly 'cos she knows it winds me up and hence the whole atmosphere here.

"Most of what is on my mind can be read from what I've written. It takes a great deal of self-control to stop my mind buzzing especially at times of tension. It buzzes with everything around and with the Land Trust movement.

"I wish others could share this Land Trust thing with me more. It is growing conformist, reformist, establishment and bigger as the months go by, but without my influence it would only do so faster. I wish everyone here was excited by the debate and wanted to talk about it and work on it. I need to work with others - I'm a lousy loner."

Dear Dave, Well, I was excited by the Land Trust possibilities too. The big landowners were scared half to death by the prospect of a Capital Transfer Tax, a Wealth Tax, or both, right? They didn't want their estates broken up and sold off. We hoped they'd prefer to hand them over to a trust. They'd try and keep control, of course, and would have to be fought on that; but we thought the way would be open for huge numbers of new farming collectives. Were we out of our minds?

The meetings you went to must have been fascinating for their make-up. Union leaders and left-wing Labour MPs versus the Gentry, with assorted Land-For-The-People hopefuls and eco-buffs angling for the balance of power.

And I shared your interest in finding out who owns all the land, in working towards a federation of Communes, a Communes Building Society, connections with urban collectives and so on. I looked forward to the time when Laurieston would get off its collective arse, stop navel-gazing and Do Something Out There.

But I did think you were spending too much time and money on this. I didn't realise you were making contacts that would lead to two good and full conferences.

Well. We get on better now, nicht? Though I was close - probably the closest - to you on your wider political stuff, I felt far away on almost everything else. But the point, I think, was that I felt comfortable with this distance.

Catriona had indeed arrived back with us, and stayed on in some undefined status, bewildered, and, though not ignored, left very much to find her own way. It was well into February before we got around to having what we called her 'Joining Meeting' - during which she has to wait outside. At least it only took two minutes.

Julia proposes, straightaway, that Catriona 'should join and be like everybody else.' We all immediately say yes.

So: welcome, Catriona. Or, 'Kate (S)'. (She is dithering between these options and needs to be different from Kate B.) There was no special do. Catriona just dropped easily into living in Billiard Room and pitched in with Freefall and the Garden.

(And paid in at least a year's money. The Accountant approved!)

(The Radical Commune will always party when someone joins.)

Meanwhile, we'd had Jay, Lesley and Molly to visit.

Jay had known Jonathan at college, before he'd dropped-out (from his architecture course! Why is this Movement crawling with architects?)

He'd lived communally with friends in London; met Lesley when she moved in toward the end of that group. They'd gone to Devon together, where Jay had worked as a farmhand and Lesley bore Molly. He was tallish, with long black curly hair and a fluent line of chat about the politics of agri-business, ecology, the alternative and nuclear families. I remember him saying: 'We're not a very tight couple.' (Lesley had just had an affair with someone else – typ.) And he was a skilled gardener and builder. Just the man we need, I thought.

And Molly was a delightful, self-possessed, almost two-year-old, with a gorgeous smile. I really wanted Molly to join.

Lesley was quiet. I didn't really meet her, but built an idealised mental picture. She'd worked in a factory. Working class, I interpreted. Wrong. Was in a women's group. Strong feminist, I thought. Wrong.

She'd a soft, moony face; long straight hair; voluptuous figure. Attractive or what.

'You mustn't let that count,' said the Feminist Policeperson in my head (the FP), 'that would be so totally sexist.' And I didn't. I liked Jay and Molly - Lesley was OK by association.

They returned home but wrote immediately, asking to join us. Paul was hesitant. He asked what Projects they'd be into. Jay replied: "your Building Project." Top marks! Lesley - who said she felt "very young in comparison with everyone else" - said "the Dairy Project" (maybe meant the goats?) We made, for us, a quick decision. Jay, Lesley and sorted out their affairs and they and Molly joined us before February was out.

(Dear Lesley, are you ever going to come and see me here at Dumb Toms?)

But we were accelerating towards the spring - and had a run of bright, clear, spirit-lifting days. Billiard Room felt busy. You cheered up and offered: 'Maybe it isn't all struggle?'.

We had, if not a meeting, at least a get-together. Dave and Carol had been baking bread and what with that, the Jotul's full-blast pine-wood aromas, joss sticks and a woodfire in the huge, old, Baronial fireplace place itself - Billiard Room smelt and felt almost comfortable.

Richard wrote beautiful, rounded, green-ink, slightly oblique, entirely lower case, unpunctuated notes:

"march 2nd 1975

by the way this is me as I am in case you're interested

oh I know you're not

but what's all this screaming for coffee tea etc.
what I'd like is something else"

We were chatty, never quite serious. Swapped light-hearted exchanges - jokes, even. Initially, the only argument was over which record to play as background (ELP, or Crosby Stills Nash and Young?) Julia and Jonathan were knitting; Tina, sewing.

Alice cartwheels in, triumphant from having retrieved a whole cheese from Ullioch Cottage, which the people there had nicked from us. We had thought them friends, but they were just more people who thought we were rich: to be stolen from. Alice had sorted them out on that. Such bravery! What a star! I wouldn't have dared do what Alice did. Incroyable. What's more, she's brought along the last of her Christmas envelope from Richard.

Carol smiled, Dave positively beamed. Pat was pretty vacant. Paul looked cheerful, considering he needed to talk urgently about the drainpipe in goat yard, the leak in Patrick's old room roof, the stables roof, the Morris gearbox, the van's clutch, and more.

Richard continues:
"lot of chat going on
peoplecentre - we are all thinking about –
loads of visitors over easter –
dave's conference - living in the country - we are short of tables
tineke and ben from last summer want to visit again we all say good"

You went off to bed with Patrick, but I could hardly mind. Carol had sought me out and we made love for the second time and I felt happy and wanted her to stay and talk - but she had to sneak back to the Cottage.

Two weeks later, different story. Julia wrote:
"I resent the jolly tone of this diary as I am in bed with flu and it is sunny outside of Jon's window where I am lying. So here is gloom, gloom for a change.

"I will write a totally biased record of a People Meeting that happened on Tuesday, 15/3/75, after yoga, in Passion Room. Present were Richard, Micheal," - she always got it wrong - "Patrick, Carol, Tina, Alice, Dave, me and the New People - Catriona, Jay and Lesley. Paul was in Glasgow; he came back last night and was told about the meeting. Jon is in St. Lucia with his mum and dad and transparent lizards and tree frogs on the ceiling, big as George's hand.

"The meeting was about the move to the west wing. Mike yattered about loving groups as an ideal, and how this split is not along these lines. In the

155

middle it was decided that we would each say what we see as the reason for having the move.

"Dave started - said he felt isolated, living down at the cottage and alienated from the whole thing, and more...

"Lesley said she didn't think we should split as it seems to be making us unhappy, and more...

"I said I found it horrible to look around and judge personalities and say, 'I want to live with you and you but not with you.' In fact it is easier to be negative - I am moving because it's ludicrous to live with the people in the Kids Project - bad for me and bad for George. We both need a structured life.

"I was terrified when the idea of expansion came up - I hate change. Then, after a bit, it seemed a lovely idea. We need more people to expand our lives here, make life more joyful - stop all our energies being sapped in maintenance - let us feel our work brings in income, feels good, smells good. With more people coming it seems sensible to live in smaller groups which might make some bits of life simpler and there will be lots of people around, like a village. But now the crunch has come and we are actually creating the (to begin with) two groups - I realise I don't want to split up. (All this is not what I said, it's what I'm saying now.)

"Then I talked about my fears for the precarious Billy, George, Richard and Julia set-up. I have a lurking suspicion I am just a monster ego.

"Alice said she had wanted to get right away, after the hepatitis. But as her depression lifted, she found herself wanting a living group in the stables. Which switched to building a kitchen in the West Wing and accepting who comes along - except that she wants Tim and Bridget to come and wants it quiet and she has said before that she would not be happy if Carol, Dave, Tam and Tiff went into the West Wing with the move. Alice is in trouble for saying that, which is unfair. I also don't want T & T.

"Catriona thought the move was a simple thing - she has not been here long.

"I am not conveying it very well but by now the whole feeling of the meeting was very grey and negative. It was as if each one of us resented being shoved into the move by the others.

"Dick said he felt we were being organised for the Kids Project and not for living a good life together

"Tina said she was sick that the move was being put at the feet of the Kids Project, which she said could be stopped after June. She said she had tried to be close and loving with people over the last year (not with me, you haven't).

"I didn't say that, as a matter of fact," Tina scribbled in later.

"Carol was hurt and tearful. She had wanted to move down the West

Wing but felt unwanted so will just wait and see. I felt a right bastard that me and Dick do not positively want George to go down the cottage a lot and neither of us has any urge to look after Tam and Tiffany. We like George being with us when we work. Jesus must I write all this in the Diary. Mike says I must.

"Who's next. Jay. Can't remember what he said. Something sensible. Oh yes - we should do things together. So we did.

"On Wednesday morning we all collected wood up the Back Track and got lots. Very nice bit of old oak. At about twelve I was fixing to die and went to bed and Alice felt sick and went to bed. So I do not know if it brought us together or not.

"Then afterwards, in the kitchen, Patrick put his arms around me, that was lovely. He said something like - if reality is sad, have happy games. I had wanted to hug people all evening…"

I was preoccupied with the notion of becoming a student again. I'd sent in my research proposal and was keen to go and see the P&CRP people. Mainly because a student grant would let me obsess about LH - which I would be doing anyway. Jonathan, Tina and sometimes Patrick seemed keen, too. I thought we could share out the time, pay ourselves 'wages' out of the grant.

But also, the possibility of leaving Laurieston hadn't left me and I thought the academic caper might be a handy bridge back to the outside world.

But what to say? I hadn't a clue what Peace and Conflict research was. I imagined it to be about the arms race, international relations. How did the 'alternative' fit in? Tom C. assured me that others in the Programme were interested in the whole self-sufficiency/ alternative technology trip - but then, we weren't, especially. Would they accept that in trying to live the way we did, the problems were not the technicalities of solar power and pumps, but of relationships and people?

'Our main windmills and waterfalls are ourselves, gyrating and sploshing in emotional squalls' - no Michael, that won't do.

'For example,' I rehearsed, 'we are trying to work out at a practical level the differences between us as women and men. Different conditioning, blah, working on men not oppressing women, blah, surely implications for a peaceful society?'

The bloody women can't even get their so-called 'Decorating Collective' together, is what I really thought.

All this time and petrol (and money) spent on outside meetings. The women's group had grown so large it had to split - the 'original' women in one group, Lesley, Catriona and 'outside' recruits making up the other. They were planning a joint trip to the Manchester National Conference. But there were no 'internal' women's meetings, hardly. What's happened to the idea politics begins at home, I wanted to ask. And when are the women ever going to talk about Alice's quarrel with Julia and her antipathy to having Carol and Dave back in the house. And aren't Lesley and Catriona being left out in the cold?

None of your business, snaps the FP. Looks like you're still waiting for the women to give a lead, instead of getting together with the men and sorting things out for yourselves. Mmm, I thought, and felt resentful, confused and guilty. I didn't dare make any open comment.

(Much later, in another context, I did venture a question about what the women were doing and Alice promptly wrote that I was "stomping all over women's feelings, defining what qualifies as being a liberated woman." Yes, Alice, sure you're right. Love that 'stomping.' Have you ever tried stomping on a feeling?)

This confusion was on my mind as I hitched down to Dumb Tom's, the night before going to see the P&CRP. For the – er – interview? I arrived late, and tired. A women's group from Lancaster, visiting for the day, was deciding who was going to clear up. 'Why doesn't he do it?,' demanded one of them, before I'd even said hello. Bloody women.

24

Laurieston Hall is twelve acres and stables and two cottages and a pond with herons and ducks and bees and mortuary and laundry and woods and rhododendrons and a big cold house adrift at dead of night on the Solway Firth. And Coco The Clown's old caravan and surrounding knockouts. (Jonathan, The Diary.)

And Presumably You Have Communal Childcare?
Is this a commune, Sophie had asked. Yes. What's a commune? Well, a lot of people living together. Oh you mean, like flats?
Mmm. The children.

Sophie wanted to be an 'acrobat-mummy - its father can look after it while I'm at the circus.'

'Is it true fathers mostly drive and mothers mostly cook?', Joel wants to know.

Sonya wrote minutes: "Kids meating (sic) at 4 o'clock on Wednesday. School - Billy off on Monday, Sonya off on Wednesday, Joel off on Friday. If I get my sums right tomorro I will be good. If mummy sleeps with Richard I will put something on the door."

Well past Christmas, Billy was still missing his two front teeth. His face framed by dashing long hair. George had gorgeous platinum curls. Polly wriggled and giggled. Tam was 'easy going and resilient.' Tiffany, 'highly strung and clinging, but enchanting.'

Tina had finished putting together the *Children In Communes* piece for *Spare Rib*. It had, plainly, been hard with the children at first. "We came together as a living group and communal childminding was immediately talked about, experimented with and despaired over," said Alice.

Carol remembered the early months with Tiffany and later with Tam as "fraught with tension, anxiety and guilt." And Tina summed up: "It's hard to nurse a new baby and a new collective: maybe it's daft to attempt both at the same time."

And she didn't underplay the present, writing: "It's a daily, often painful collision between theory and practice. Every day throws up murky situations where ideals are jockeying for priority and expedience threatens to beat them all. Nothing stops while we work out the ideology. We make it hard for ourselves, living like this - and we don't even know if it's worth it yet."

Well, maybe there's been a spacetime warp. Maybe in some other, unimaginable universe, there's a Laurieston that follows on from the concluding optimism.

Tina: "More and more the initial roles and situations get reversed. Now, daily, people, other than parents, comfort children. Play with them, arbitrate, wash, bed-put, of course cook for. Take them to school, football matches, the dentist, whatever."

Where, according to Alice, "Effectively communal childcare may be operating for days at a time, but mostly it is not organised and visitors who can't see a rota can't see there is communal awareness of the children. But we question and criticise within the group, observe and are sensitive to the children's ways. How we organise childcare reflects these complexities in a way a rota would not."

Where Carol, who had "Longed simply to get into the mum bit, for a cosy, rural nuclear place" still lives down the cottage "Where Dave and I can make a place that's easy to care for babies in, still work communally and be with other adults and children."

Where Tina's relationship to Sophie and Joel "Is still comparatively effortless. Before, it was built up of one-way acts of service - cooking, cleaning, transporting, amusing. In return, I couldn't help expecting something - gratitude? - at least that they be content. It was a system of obligations. Now the relationship is built of talking, playing, messing about together. It's a voluntary, spontaneous system. Though they're older, too, it has everything to do with living communally. We're not thrown together, we come together. It feels lovely."

And where Julia, speaking of Bill and George, can say: "There's a lot more messing at the edges. Bill and George are friends with the other people in the house. They honestly seem very happy and busy most of the time. They can get angry and miserable, but don't often seem bored or irritable."

Meanwhile, in this neck of the universe - Terra, June 1977 - the children sleep:

Molly in Lesley's room. George and Billy in Julia and Arthur's caravan up at Lothlorien. Tam and Tiffy in Carol and Roger L.'s cottage, Syllodioch, over by Gatehouse. Polly and Sonya in the converted Goat Yard with Alice. Robbie in Meg's room - Teapot - with her and Paul. Angus in the cottage with Mr and Mrs. D. (oh all right, Bridget and Tim).

Joel and Sophie, at Dumb Tom's next door to your PO, who would like to nip out to the Brown Cow in Bentham but who doesn't have a baby-sitter.

160

And Do You All?

The back of that Winter, I kept desperately, compulsively, obsessively busy. It was work as therapy. Gales fetched down two more beeches in the drive and with them - again - the phone line. Jonathan and I spent three days working in cold swirling rain, sawing up the sappy wood. Simple, not unpleasant days. Anything to block out the Tina-Patrick equation was OK.

I was depressed-ish. Ish here means down, listless, anguished: but seeking neither pills nor psychiatric help just yet, thank you. Able still to get out of bed.

(In "Home Comfort - Life On Total Loss Farm" - an American communes book - it isn't until p.130 that anyone is less than ecstatically happy. Dishonesty, or from another universe, I wonder?)

And therefore, you, too, were more-than-ish-depressed.

I never figured out how it worked. But if I felt depressed, you'd loop the loop and come out even more down than me. At which times, we were no help to each other. It had always been like that.

I'd try, but I couldn't help you. And, natch, feeling worse, you couldn't help me.

So actually, our Tina, I don't recall feeling looked after by you, hardly for a moment, at this stage.

Or any other I can remember.

So How Do New People Join?

Tim Bridget and Angus kept calling too. The problem remained the same - they wanted to work, but not live with us. Tim was openly sceptical about the point of living communally.

Tina wrote a long, powerful, and personal justification of our need to change ourselves and social/ political structures concurrently.

"Culture, consciousness, whatever you like to call it, is as crucial to the quality of change as the mode and relations of production are integral to bringing it about."

She described the domestic issues within the living/ working collective as "The most potent catalysts of self-examination and I hope, immediate channels for change. While the daily jolts to your awareness inform and colour whatever, if any, macro-theories you're working on."

"And what chance when the millennium dawns of accepting and co-operating however remotely with persons of a different skin, culture, just class even, if we can't accept positive conflict with others, much closer to us in culture and taste, over the washing up? No chance. The latter is easier and incredibly difficult. We're learning it."

This was magic stuff, at the time.

It wasn't new to us, but it was a long time since anyone had tried to re-state what living together was about. It was sustained, intelligent and well put. The tone of the ending was almost euphoric:

"OK, it was very hard at first. Even after a year it felt like pushing water uphill. And I thought what is the point of trying to live with people you seem to have very little in common with. But to me it now feels good to accept, have faith in, feel secure with, and that probably means love, a number of people whose ways and tastes are not mine - that wouldn't have happened if I'd waited to fall in love with them first. I've found it personally enriching. I've often been depressed, often irritated beyond endurance, sometimes really happy - but never bored."

People went around smiling for a few days after this.

"*At least it's never boring*" – Tina here creating the definition, the much-quoted raison d'être of Collective Living.

Not me, though. It seemed to me that your theory - that living together generated strength and solidarity - was a pile of dead bones. We were still in a communal waste land. About to split in two. (And, now, of course, you say I "led you" into this?)

How About Really Complicated Stuff, Like Resource Planning?
Hoping for the mythical space masterplan, I'd meticulously copied Paul's plans of the house, showing all the rooms, and made cardboard tickets in various colours for all the activities we needed space for. I thought this kit would help us play around with different possibilities - whatever happened in 'The Split.'

Patrick wrecked this game. Knocked it over and immediately, sweeping up, junked most of the pieces. Sorry, bit of an accident, says Patrick. My co-communards thought, charitably: bless, not his fault, accident, could've been anyone.

I knew in my heart: it was deliberate. The cunt!

How can this fucking so-called triangle ever possibly work?

Sorry, what was the question again?

So How Do New People Join?
Bridget and Tim didn't reply - by the time Tina's letter was sent, we'd decided they could join. They were such hard workers: busy, energetic and strong people. And they would try living collectively for six months. They could keep their £3000 or so capital separate to start with. After that - well, it was a typical Laurieston hazy deal.

(As Tim struggled to define the limits of their involvement, the PA remembers telling him how communal living might work. For example, if he and Bridget had another child, that would seriously affect our

162

economy; so the very brand of contraception they used would, theoretically, be a communal matter. I meant to shock, and think I succeeded. Wish I hadn't been so heavy, just now.)

And How Do You Make Decisions?
When we'd been a couple, we'd had resources to get us through hard times. In the triangle, I got resentful. I imagined that Patrick got all the easy and pleasant times, while I was just someone to lean on.

To put that another way: if there were ever easy and pleasant times, Patrick got them. Because we had none. Just hard times. I became less tolerant, of course I did, of your continual illnesses. You'd come for help, and I'd snap that you should take more care of yourself, not knock yourself out being the commune's Cheerful Stalwart.

I blamed you instead of supporting you (but actually this was also part of the triangle dynamic.)

And you couldn't help me, because - well, you couldn't.

And How Do You Make Decisions?
Fuck knows. Apparently, the location of the West Wing kitchen has indeed moved to the coldest, darkest room and has become known as the Aga Kitchen as we have bought the said Aga. And it seems it's an open chequebook for anything the new kitchen people might want. Even though we do not officially know who is going to live there.

The Accountant begins to doubt the centre can hold.

And How About Multiple Er?
Tina, much later, wrote:

"The day before Patrick got Mary, Michael said Patrick is after Mary.

"And when Michael wanted to talk to Carol because they had slept together he complained that there was never a natural opportunity though he was on the look-out for it because Patrick was always there, it was uncanny."

Well, prescience or no, this was such a bad time. And I couldn't fathom what was going on. We had hardly made love for six months. You said it was the same with him - I didn't believe you. Suddenly I was jealous. Spent days robotically getting the children out of bed, keeping them amused, then back to bed. Washing clothes, tidying, doodling. Lying still in bed, shoulders hunched. Or hitting the pillow.

I suppose I put all the blame on you. You-and-Patrick. It's been eighteen months now. Him always pressuring you to be a couple, to cut me out.

I put all the blame on you because I was sorry for myself because I was depressed because our relationship was in a mess because for example I put all the blame on you. Shame, eh?

163

And Presumably You Have Communal Childcare?

Suddenly, Paul and Alice went to a conference together! In Newcastle! About 'Children at Conferences!' Heavens Above. I think now, Paul perhaps had some romantic interest but.

And how do you make decisions? Well, in this case, it's clearly Paul and Alice just leaping in and spending the cash.

They brought back the papers. These, and the women's article, sparked off renewed discussion about the children. What had happened to the idea that, living communally and rurally, the children would have the chance, even at a very young age, to be useful, a chance denied them everywhere else?

We resolved to encourage them to feed the chickens and the pigs.

And weren't they developing boy/ girl sex-roles? And instead of being 'polymorphously perverse' - exploring and playing sexually - they were becoming almost prudish. 'They've started saying such and such is "rude".' The disturbing thought occurred that they might be growing up exactly like us adults.

It's the other kids at school, we said. We really will have to start own school.

And are we 'adultist.' We control, direct, constrain the children's lives. Theirs was the power to amuse, delight and surprise - or exasperate, annoy, frighten. It still felt more natural to speak of x adults and y children, rather than x+y people. The way the adults behaved set patterns for the children. No wonder they didn't want a communal bedroom, when the adults all had their own rooms. No wonder they call things mine, when we still had our favourite possessions shut away.

Should we have more meetings with the children? In the long run, when they're teenage, will they want their own teenage space, like in the Kibbutzim, or Twin Oaks? There were no answers.

The children continued to be a huge part of life at Laurieston. Demanding, preoccupying, permeating - days, nights, rooms, structures, the consciousness of the Groans. One day they'll have their own story. At this point we adults, having racked and filtered our ideas, laid them down again, to mature for another year or so.

And. Er.

You took off on a wee holiday at Rose Castle in the Lakes, with Tom. C., Jonathan and assorted friends. You then went on to London because you 'couldn't cope.' (I could, obviously).

I brooded. Jonathan told me that at Rose Castle, you'd revealed you'd have to choose between Patrick and me. This was one of those supersonic needles of outrageous data, passing straight through the skull, leaving only echoes that don't cohere for hours or weeks. Unthinkable information you can't believe. Which gelled while you were away.

Oh god. Could you really think of choosing him? The complete El Bastardo? You ring up, ask for me, he doesn't even fucking tell me?

The PA was, as we now know to say: 'In denial.' Whereas now, with a bit of distance, he thinks: Well, that could be quite sensible of you. We all get to choose some options.

And so he did, about now, start wondering if whether he could. If he could maybe. Find a lover. A happy, uncomplicated relationship. Are they still making them? A steady lover, anyway. Someone to sleep with more than one night running.

Because it's been so long.

And How Self-Sufficient Are You?

In the Garden, Julia, who had by now left Lybro's, began a meticulous recording of the year.

In the heated boxes we apparently have: Onion A1, Broad Beans Aquadulce, Cauli A.Y.R., Lettuce Premier, Leek Musselborough and Tomato Ailsa Craig. And chamomile, basil, balm, caraway, parsley, winter savory, chives and fennel.

Juggling between the paraffin-heated tent and the electric bit is apparently a constant worry. Onions, cauli and lettuce had been getting "a bit drawn" in the electric, so were moved to the tent.

Gosh it's all such drama down there.

Outside we have: Pea Feltham, more Broad Bean Aquadulce, and tree seedlings - Sweet Chestnut, Box, Walnut and Holm Oak.

Pig shit, fine, but Rock Phosphate, iffy, have been spread everywhere back in January. Whispers in corridors go: 'Rock Phosphate. Can we still say we're Organic?

We are strong on whispers in corridors.

But basically you're a Kids Holiday Project, Right?

Well no, but.

We were sticking with the Old Kitchen for cooking, and making the former Dining Room - Tony's Old Room - into Freefall/ PeopleCentre Room (featuring table tennis and hanging out). Patrick was very firm we should be offering a home from home.

(Dear Patrick, I believed it at the time, too, it had such an emotive pull to it. Of course we shouldn't be a dreary youth hostel! Though I did think you came across school-master-ish at times. It was much later I realised that being a 'home' was impossible and not what the kids wanted, either. They wanted a sort of residential discotheque, a live-in youth club and chip-shop. We could have built a complete fantasy room.

I'm not saying we shouldn't have tried to show the kids our lifestyle (brown bread, women out working, men cooking and minding small children). But they'd notice all that, anyway; and our main propaganda (if we had the confidence) should have been aimed at the adult helpers, I think.)

We had the first groups since last summer. First up, the Milton Tongs, who gave us the 'Four Crowns, The Wine For Men!' mural. We hosted Leeds Free School, Manchester ditto, some more Dumfries kids. Then Somerstown again, but no Sue C.

The Somerstown girls wrote afterwards how they hadn't stopped crying yet, they were missing us so, wanted to come back. We must be doing something right. And it had been coats-on-in-the-kitchen weather, too.

Plus, for a few months, we had Howard, Fergy, Frank and Neil - 'The Band' - four ex-Kilquhanity lads, somehow self-catering in Warm Room, to use the Hoskyns equipment up the tower. Intending to become rich, famous. But.

Then there was Dave W. with another group of Jacob Kramer students, who painted more murals including 'Guinness Is Good For You.' They were fantastic.

Less so, another group of Paul's Mackintosh students - middle-class kids who paid peanuts, but expected a hotel lifestyle. Officially they were to work on the Galloway Mill Trust project which Nicky, back in the area, had nagged various local worthies into setting up.

And The Locals?
I would sometimes type up Nicky's letters and minutes, from his dyslexic notes; as would Alice, here observed by Richard:

Poem for the princess and the princess disappeared

> Tonight i saw the princess
> lonely in her kitchen
> and felt her so far away
> person from another planet
> and last night
> with the incredible Nicky
> and his shadow dog Leaf
> her gentle fingers resting
> on letters, floating
> and flying across them so surely
> her long hair so darkly
> and her eyes scanning quickly

the back to front message
and it all comes out
carefully so surely so quickly
with me standing there quietly
rough beard so murky
her asking direction
to make it lie neatly
across the white paper
destined for millers
concerning machinery
that museum curators
have stored in their basements.
It all passes briefly
so briefly, so briefly
me leaving early
these two who are working
the princess, the artisan
and the shadow dog lurking

(Richard - 'The Caretaker' in the Diary, 31/1/75)

So How Do You Make Decisions?
More specifically, from friends aware of the plan: "How are you deciding who will be in what group?"

We of course attempt a meeting. False memory is a frequent first tactic, as in, 'I thought all this was agreed ages ago.' (Because meeting minutes are meaningless. Anyway we never refer back to them.)

But not so, say some of us. Because although two Living Groups are shaping up, Julia, Tina, Patrick and Mike want more people to join before we split up, otherwise the separate groups would be too small and deciding which way to split, too acrimonious. And what if, having divided, we get into problems like one living group being keen on a new person and the other one not?

Alice and Paul wanted to split straight away but Mike said we had to solve our problems first, otherwise it'd be unfair to newcomers, what would they be joining?' This threatened to become another Alice vs. Mike thing, but Julia said it wasn't and told Alice that anyway, she wouldn't escape it by living in a different group.

Temporary conclusion: we have to get on with the Split because we can't agree on how and when. What nonsense we went through.

How do we decide? Another answer we might as well offer is: 'By magic.'

Because for March 24-26, we were 'closed for alterations.' It was musical rooms time again, the house looking like a hippy furniture warehouse. All this without, as far as the PO was aware, much further discussion at all. Someone had put up a 'which animal does everyone remind you of?' questionnaire – that was about it. After the static had calmed, and we cleaned up, we found ourselves - with everyone, if not wildly enthusiastic, at least accepting of the situation - in the following new layout of the Zoo:

First, in the new, 'Aga Kitchen' in the West Wing, were:

Alice (kangaroo, cat, giraffe). Well, of course, having argued for and driven the Split, Alice would be moving to the Aga Kitchen. It was her idea! Alice is getting what she wants, as usual! – is what, uncharitably, I would have thought initially. But realise now that I had no idea – I would say none of us really knew - what it was Alice wanted. Perhaps to get away from the Kids Project, or from some other Project, or Person? Or away from us all? Alice had once suggested that she and Paul should remove their 'collective nuisance' from the group, and Julia had reproved her: 'don't say we don't want you, when it's you who don't want us.'

We know neither what Alice really wants, nor what she does, other than look after Polly. It certainly wasn't just the Accountant who asked. To which she replied: 'I could give a reasonable account of how I spend my time. But I don't want this way of talking. I find it oppressive. Because I'm a woman.' The PO, with the FP looking over his shoulder, makes no comment.

I'm sad how far apart we've become. We used to be the two who held it together. Things like calling meetings, she doesn't do anymore. She must be miserable. God knows how she's getting on with Paul these days. Suppose I could ask. Does she see the split as a way to get back together with Paul? Got to say, that doesn't look like it's - but I can never say what I think anymore. I'm a male heavy, making 'snide remarks.'

Paul (penguin, hen, griffin, neurotic rhinoceros). I was not going to miss living with Paul. Paul with his blathering, convoluted speech: 'I would like some predetermination of living structures.' He wants his happy little home, Alice, his daughters, Meg as well soon and of course to get back to Glasgow and his work - he's only here 'cos he's still ill.

It is true, I run people down. Miserable sod, that I am. Always moaning and criticising (but not always wrong). Fuck it though, I run myself down, too. And besides, says the Accountant, don't forget Paul still earns half our income, singlehanded. And you'll miss his omelettes.

Julia (eel, ostrich, salmon, lemming, scorpion). I wouldn't mind living with Jools, but she's the one who really can't stand the mess of the Freefall Project, needs the calm, hence she's really into yoga (I must stop saying

168

'really into'). Julia still came to lean on my shoulder and blether about Jonathan. Sometimes, not often, I ran across her, commuting between the garden and her room. She was strong and busy again: I fancied her, but what was the point.

Richard, (king-fisher, circus elephant, polar bear, duck-billed platypus). I did like his style uniqueness authenticity clothes writings and so forth and he coped much better than I did with being on his own. But he was just too, what's the word, exasperating? to live with. Unless he changed or I did, I didn't really want to try it anymore. I'd enjoy having Rich as a near neighbour and hoped we could go fishing again sometime.

(As the PO, I wrote notes – Rich and Jul to live in same Living Group - wonder how they get on? - star split-up couple - 'Yes folks, in communal living there's no need for lawyers, court rulings, custody arrangements. Couples can split up and still be co-communards.') (Possibly a delusion. But no lawyers so far.)

Catriona (anteater, lark, swan, turkey). Whom I hardly knew, but she seemed nice. It must have been awkward for her, choosing where to live.

Bridget (carthorse, racehorse) and Tim (heron, goat, penguin, Donald Duck), expected in Aga Kitchen but for the moment still in Flosh Cottage, packing.

Meg (sheepdog, brown bear, kangaroo), still in Glasgow, would, we imagine, soon follow as might *Nigel* (bat, koala bear, chimp, skylark).

Meanwhile remaining in Billiard Room were:

Mike (rhino, centaur, goat, baboon) and *Tina* (porpoise, swallow, zebra, chameleon). Again we disagreed. You were against the Split all the gether, insisting it would all come out right in the end and knocking yourself out, being the jolly, sympathetic, 'let's keep it together' communard - and again ill and tired. It never crossed my mind we wouldn't always live together. Easy mistake to make.

Jonathan (brown bear, mole, mule, St. Bernard). I was OK with Jonathan. He talked sense, was on the same frequency, politically, was wise and witty, sometimes both at the same time. He intended, re the shop-in-CD proposal, to 'talk about the ideology': to write something for 'Alternative Scotland': to call a Men's meeting. Did none of these things but. Yet still he blethers on my shoulder about Julia. Also told me, en passant, 'I think I'm in love with your wife' – we'll let that go. Join the club.

Patrick (gibbon, giraffe, parrot, crow, busy bee). I'm not the only one to think: world of his own, cut off from the real problems, pretends they don't exist. Doesn't call a Men's meeting. Well, none of them do. Jonathan finds him unreal, too, so it's not just me. Alice says she can't stand the way we are with each other and Patrick says he thinks we're all fine. Touch of weirdness, there.

Still, Patrick does agree about getting more people: is very strong on the Kids Project: is really good with Joel and Sophie. Were I to wish Pat that would simply vapourise in the night, that might be understood. In fact, though I wanted his R. with T. to finish, it didn't occur to me that we might not share the same Living Group.

Lesley (moth, guinea pig, lizard ("for its retarded grace"), otter, puma) and *Jay* (salmon, squirrel, bullfinch, beaver, border collie) were, like Catriona, still unknown quantities. Good vibes from Jay so far, however.

While down at Near cottage were:

Carol (tortoise, albatross, mouse, terrier, angel fish) and *Dave* (beaver, sparrow, Mr. Toad, dachshund, duck). The Accountant, miserable sod, never quite managed to forget the loss of cottage rent this arrangement entailed. But it seemed to be working. Chickens, goats, Tam and Tiffy were looked after.

Carol taught me to crochet. I still fancied her. Purely superficial, said the FP. Beat yourself up. But what's the chances, said the PA. On the work front, Carol was thinking of becoming a Yoga teacher.

And Dave, too, was OK. Although the Accountant still bristles about Dave's actually paying for a train from Bath to London to 'save time', instead of hitching. And the way he kept going on about two living groups when of course there were now three, with him and Carol still down the cottage. Workwise, Dave has a big conference coming up.

Finally, distributed nuclear family fashion amongst these three Living Groups were:

Angus Billy George Joel Sophie Molly Polly Sonya Tam and Tiffany (no zoo info). Will they commute? It would be a shame not to continue to see them all.

And a shame not to celebrate. I bought a bottle of wine, never going to go very far between us but the first time anyone had ever done so, thinks the Accountant. Jay thought it excessive. It was a month before we drank it.

25
Spring 1975

'But I heard you'd split into two groups?'
'We have, it's just that it's easier for us all to be in with you lot while the conference is on.'

The big move had taken all of a Thursday and Friday, but before we could enjoy, if that's the word, the shock and surprise that we'd made it - visitors started arriving for Dave's 'Living In The Country' week.

Which was busy and optimistic. We channelled our re-discovered, but still limited, post-hep energy into it.

Most of the forty or so visitors were hoping to Move Out Of The City - some formed the instant 'Commune of March 29.' It boosted us to think we might be catalysing new groups (but again, this one was short-lived).

Almost round the clock, everywhere you turned, there was something going on. Days were tightly organised, with loads of Meetings - some with outside speakers, like the man from the Rural Industries Commission. The talk was of how to earn a living - through crafts, rural minibuses, building and decorating, electronics, computer programming, smallholding, gardening, you-name-it.

And visitors helped round the house, worked in the garden, fed the animals, sneaked tasteful murals into the hall - in particular, a pastoral scene, all sun and rainbows, peace n' love sixties - which painted over the previous graffiti: "Milton Tongs Kill."

Later, visitors played guitars, recorders, flutes into the night - folky stuff, half-remembered pops, Beatles, Gerry C.'s impromptu 'Decomposing Brain Blues.' We had visitors drumming, dancing around bonfires and breaking house rule three.

We were collectively inventing what will become an institution - Laurieston Music Week.
It felt wonderful to have the house full again, for the first time since last summer. By the end, I was wishing everyone would just stick around in Galloway. And make their way.

Someone did demand, as a parting note: 'There isn't really anyone here who does actually make their living in the country, is there?'

'Course not,' we replied, 'anyone who does is too busy, this time of year, planting and sowing.'

Next, we had a premature Silly Season.

For a start, Helicopter Man landed on the lawn. He'd heard we might be a place to stay for a few nights. He was ex-navy and currently into yoga and Divine Light - the sect with the Mahara Ji as its guru. His job was to spray the forests with fertiliser.

We said, OK (thinking, what's another couple of contradictions?)

On his last day he gave us all helicopter rides - a dozen or so rapid take-offs and landings.

From the village it must have looked like Vietnam. Half the village drove down to watch. To close the show, he took Rich and Kate B. on a longer tour, circling out along the coast and back over the hills, arriving back just as the Viscount John Arbuthnot, no less, arrived in his Daimler to talk with Dave about the Land Trust thing. They used the Morning Room as the DMZ.

Then 'Crystal Group' arrived. So we had another full house (they self-catered in Big Kitchen while the Aga kitchen lot settled into their new home and in Billiard room, we had a Freefall group from Bordon in Hampshire.)

We knew nothing about the Crystal Group except that they were Buddhists. We had cleaned up first, in our usual, last-minute rush. They put us to shame by re-doing the job thoroughly, then spreading colourful blankets over our tatty jumble-sale armchairs.

They picked hundreds of daffodils. Their beaming guru, Namgyal Rinpoche, arrived and chided them gently: 'It'll be a long time before you see me pick so many.'

He'd jetted in from Canada, and was staying in a local hotel, chauffeured over each day. The first day all he did - it seemed - was stand around while admirers took snaps. Nice business, thought the Accountant. You must be clearing over a Grand. Perhaps he could see what I was thinking: I do believe he winked.

And the punters were seriously happy. Blissed out. Even in the evenings, when the man had gone and when they got into primal screaming - they came out smiling.

It was an infectiously good atmosphere. So much so, Paul and Meg went with the whole gang on a 150-mile round trip out somewhere past Stranraer. Of course, I challenged him on money, petrol and The Ecology.

'But there are so few chances to be with someone like the Rinpoche,' Paul simpered. Paul is obviously on a higher plane and thus floating loftily above this mere Accountant reptile (who wondered again about financially separate living groups…)

The bliss of The Crystals caught our neighbour, Lally, so much so that (the PO believes) she followed the Rinpoche to Greece, his next location, and subsequently back to Canada, thus splitting up with Jackson.

On the Crystals' last day, the guru blessed some oranges and handed them out in pieces. I ate mine, sceptically. But was duly tripped out - happily - indeed, ecstatically - the rest of the day. How does that work?

The following week, Richard's brother, a teacher, was visiting with various friends and kids, under the Freefall umbrella. On their last night Richard baked little cakes, handing them out - I failed to spot - selectively, so I ate mine, went to bed.

Failed to sleep, went back downstairs at 2 a.m., feeling odd, to find a dozen others, all, like me, out of their skulls. Richard had spiked his cakes with acid, hadn't he? Presumably, from his bro?

True, we boogied and played charades until after dawn, then slept for 24 hours but then said: look, Richard, don't you ever fucking do that again.

This had been a Freefall Week in Billiard Room, but with all the Aga people - except Paul, away in Glasgow - eating lunch with us. Catriona and Rich were working with Freefall, but Alice and Jools came, we presumed, just for the company - they brought lunch to share. Maybe we could have continued like that, the PO thinks now.

As it was, Billiard Room Living Group took the hump.

'Look,' we said, 'we have all the Kids Groups, field all the phone calls, deal with all the callers at the door, host all the casual visitors, and this isn't fair....'

So the split was made more real - we agreed we'd eat together just on Sundays. And at last the Billiard Room group had its first evening meal - just the six of us, plus Joel, Soph and Molly.

I fetched out that bottle of wine, bought two months earlier.

'Bit extravagant,' muttered Jay. Fuck me, I thought, one bottle of wine, between us. But then, he and I weren't exactly getting on.

Jay and Jonathan talked gardening. Molly fussed and Lesley snapped at Jay. Tina muttered quietly to Patrick. Jonathan was depressed. Some celebration.

These were, suddenly, stranger-than-usual times.

For a start, we'd agreed to 'try to be more open about our relationships.' By writing in the Diary.

Tina weighed in straightaway with a theory-piece:

"Living collectively screws up notions of what parent, lover, friend, mean. Leaving you not knowing who you are.

"In a nuclear household, commitment is enacted several times a day, It doesn't need to be said, contingency forces it. Love and trust come from repeated acts for each other.

"But share the fabric of a relationship (doing the kids, the cooking, the earning, the shelter) with 13 other people - then what is your relationship with one special person? Everything thing you do is usually for lots of people.

"So if our social structure is aimed at producing positive communal relationships - then they are also loaded against building good, positive, couple relationships. Aren't they?"

The PO, although not currently getting on with Tina, suspects this might be the single most insightful statement it is possible to make about Laurieston Hall at this time.

Alice wrote: "Relationships? I positively don't want to write about them. I spoke once to Mike and he betrayed my confidence. If I spent so many words explaining and didn't get it across, I don't stand an earthly, writing in the Diary."

Whereas, Dear Alice, I have no idea what you are talking about. Unless you mean those five words - 'I do quite fancy Patrick' - which of course I passed on - indirectly - because I thought this was a message you wanted to send. Not a confidence which I could 'betray.'

Richard wrote that he and Alice had recently, as he put it, "done our bit for the revolution." Quite crude, that lad, sometimes.

Then Tina, again, after a trip away with Patrick, staying in a holiday caravan, wrote:

"Mm. Ooh-er. Well, hum.

"Patrick and I had never been on holiday before."

(Nor you and I, dear heart, since before Joel was born.)

"Embarrassed, we escaped outdoors, struggled up a hill to the cloud line, Patrick telling me about the weather, then striggle-straggled home again. Oh wow, leisure. We read our separate books on our separate bunks and fell into separate dozes. Then Patrick made supper, while I read on. Then supper and some wine. Then we made love and thunk, went to sleep before ten o'clock."

No wonder both Jay and Lesley assumed our relationship was over.

And of course - 'made love and thunk' - to me you always made it sound like that.

If there was ever passion, ecstasy, laughter, tenderness, joy, longing between you and Pat - you weren't saying. As though going on holiday with Patrick, fucking with him wasn't 'unfaithful' - but enjoying it and saying so would have been.

(As would be writing a poem, read later on BBC Scotland.)

I pressed you about this. 'Well of course, I've had some lovely fucks with Patrick,' you admitted, and changed the subject.

I didn't put in the diary that Lesley - getting on badly with Jay - had looked lost and sad in the Billiard Room kitchen, so I'd given her a hug. Nor that a few days later, she had come to my room and we had kissed. And the day after that, we had become lovers. (Which, later, Tina welcomed and Patrick hated - another reader exercise, I think).

Nor did I say that I had lent Jay's car - when he wasn't around to ask - to one of the Crystal people. And although I'd warned the guy to keep the radiator topped up, as it leaked - he forgot. No doubt hurrying back to hear a talk on 'every minute zen' or 'right action,' the idiot just forgot. So: water drained away, cylinder block cracked, old car died.

I've felt leery ever since of people who spend their lives seeking 'enlightenment.' Or: wholeness, balance, healing, attunement, focusing, connecting (but OK, I do still meditate and do Tai Chi).

Jay and I towed the wreck to a dump. As we stripped out the useful bits, I could see Jay thinking: no car, no job.

I felt awful. I'd really liked Jay those first few weeks and hadn't wanted to spoil things between us. I apologised for the tenth time.

But then I admitted: 'There's something else I ought to tell you.'

'Oh?'

'Yes.'

'Well?'

'Well you probably know already?'

'No?'

I suddenly realised just how far apart he and Lesley were, but had to go on:

'Well, I've been sleeping with Lesley.'

'Yea well, thanks for telling me.' He spun away into the garden.

We have not talked much since, one to one. And hardly at all since you took up with him.

(November 1977, London. 'It's such a bundle of fun,' I tell my men's group, 'knowing that Tina's now shagging Jay. Down the Mile End Road.)

What I didn't learn until much later was that Jay and Lesley had agreed - as they arrived at Laurieston - that they would not sleep with anyone else for a couple of months.

Jay had been coming home knackered from a hard-working day. Lesley, with Molly no longer a baby, had been off see her women's group, other friends - and another bloke.

So for all his off-handedness, Jay had been hoping that the move to LH would reunite them. But Lesley had broken the agreement after just four weeks. I asked her about that and she said that the four weeks had felt like six months anyway.

This did not, in retrospect, bode well for our, er, relationship.

Before the end of April, we had two Freefall groups from Milton, two from Craigmillar in Edinburgh, keeping the Billiard Room crew at full stretch. Catriona started to turn the former Freefall room - Tony's Old Room - into Craft Room. Paul and Jay did some survey work together. Richard fed the pigs - sometimes, at midnight. Jonathan, Julia, Patrick and Jay gardened. Mike too, on occasion - when not preoccupied sending out invitations to Connections. Tina and Alice planned a Women's Week, also for the summer.

Everyone was busy. I was happy!

Lesley could have been happy. She seemed to like working on the Freefall Project. The sun shone a lot. Laurieston magic springtime. Plus this remarkable, gap-toothed, frying-pan-bellied fellow was in love with her.

But Jay was down, so she was down. Or Jay was mad and she felt guilty. Or Jay sabotaged her attempts to be herself. 'You say that's what you want, but of course, you've got off with Mike.'

(1977: for Lesley read Tina, for Jay read Mike, for Mike, Jay. Heigh ho.)

For the PA, it was so nice to have someone to love. To giggle with, listen to music with, exchange glances with at meals, cuddle with, 'fuck with' - the FP insists you don't just 'fuck' anymore. Except that the fucking wasn't quite right.

With Catriona, Lesley, Jay and Molly already arrived and Bridget Tim and Angus due, we would soon be 15 adults and 11 children. For some of us, still not enough, for others, too many.

These two loose groupings emerged in a meeting. The Ayes, in favour of lots more people, and soon: and the Noes.

Aye: We need more people to share the workload.

Noe: But we can't support any more people. And we don't live as though we're in desperate need of money.

Aye: If we economise, we can support more people.

Noe: If we economise, there'll be no need to support more people.

At the end of Round One, the points are even. Pause to make tea and build up the fire.

Aye: Well I'd like more people, because I feel lonely here. I need more stimulation, more variety. The communal village, like we talked about early on. And the community of communes idea.

Noe-1: I feel lonely here too, but I think we should try to get to know each other better first.

Noe-2: I haven't got to know the new people yet.

Noe-3: I just couldn't cope with any more people (playing ye olde "emotional blackmail" card.)

Aye: But having more people around would take the pressure off. It would be easier to feel closer to more people.

So after Round Two, the Ayes are clearly ahead on moral grounds.

Stalemated on feelings, we return to the practical

Noe: There's no space for New People. We need what we have for the PeopleCentre.

Aye: Like you fucking care about the PeopleCentre - Aye doesn't say that. Instead, we get: We don't have to keep on having groups to stay, if that's what's stopping us getting bigger.

Aye: (Richard) We could easily have a dozen in the stables, if we did it up.'

Noe: (Paul, obviously): But Meg would like to come this summer and perhaps ask to stay on. Then maybe Nigel, too.

No surprise there, then.

Aye: (Patrick): But adding just a few extra will make things worse. We need like 30 or more to make a big difference, and quick.

Paul: If we have separate living group finances, each group could decide'

The Accountant: 'Surely not. We're all here on the same basis. Not chosen by a sub-group.'

Aye: (I imagine Jay): But we don't want any more couples.

Noe: (Probably Paul) 'I certainly think we shouldn't consider more people until after the summer, because the summer is so confusing and new people won't see us as we really are.' Killer argument - the "do nothing now" strategy.

Aye: 'Well, OK, but surely we could ask some people, if they're interested, to come and visit?'

We finish by talking about the sort of people we need. The ideal applicant would be a black, scots, working-class, 20-something, lesbian doctor....

And the meeting is over, apart from the subject of cars. So many meetings end with cars.

There were three more groups of children from Craigmillar. Then a group from Weavers' Field School in London, brought by Pete M., who'd visited the summer before. He said he'd like to join us in a year's time - we said OK, talk to us later.

These were happy visits. The Craigmillars were mainly young children, having their first holiday for a long time - or even their first holiday ever.

The Weavers' Fields, supposedly hard to get on with - 'ESN', they were called - were no problem at all.

The Milton teenagers, friends by now, came back again. Freefall looked more and more solid as a project; once again we talked of setting up a charitable trust, so we could ask for donations. Taking kids to the seaside, the day warm, flowers and meadows shining, I thought: wow, and we're actually getting paid to do this!

Tim Bridget and Angus moved in, joining the Aga kitchen group. But very shortly, Tim began to build a kitchen in one of their three West Wing rooms - the PO does not recall this being agreed, or even discussed.

Meg visited a lot. Alice looked pale and bleak. Still, the two of them organised a self-cater Gingerbread group from Newcastle in the Old Kitchen.

'You realise this lot are actually costing us money,' the Accountant asked Alice.

'Yes, well the better off groups are supposed to subsidise people on SS, said Alice, demurely. (There was never any such agreement.)

'Maybe, but we haven't had a 'better off' group for ages,' said the Accountant.

It was haymaking time again. Dave bought a flat-bed trailer for a few pence at a farm auction and built sides for it with (free) pine slabs. More contradictions - This cheap and elegant hay wain, towed by the big Landy which had cost £250 to fix.

Keith C. visited again and he and Paul stopped the leaks in the Billiard Room roof and put a sky light over its kitchen. When the children's groups were out on a day trip, it felt peaceful and home-like. Evenings saw us sitting around. Tina, Patrick and Jonathan looking very pensive these days. Lesley and I cuddled.

In fact I was away a lot, too, visiting my Dad, who was in hospital, in Birmingham, with leukaemia. Or playing gigs with a Dumfries-based rock-band - Ryder - all over southern Scotland and northern England.

Monday April 21st 1975.

Rain, rain, rain. Solid heavy drizzle. More rain.

A red canoe drifted on the pond. Kids rode bikes into the sagging inflatable on the lawn.

But people fizzed and bubbled. Doing up their new rooms. Planting, milking, going off on trips.

Dave and I went to a gathering of Communes Movement people in Birmingham. We agreed the 'Communes Movement' was barely alive and its constitution was too limiting. Instead, we collectively formed a new, loose organisation. I proposed 'Communes Network' and the name stuck.

26

So How Many Are There Of You?
So in Spring, 1975, there were 15 adults: Alice Bridget Carol Catriona Julia Lesley and Tina. Dave Jay Jon Mike Patrick Paul Rich and Tim.

I rarely spent time with *Alice*, but dimly knew she wasn't happy. She was on her own a lot and had no steady lover. It only became apparent, in dribbled leaks, that she was in fact distraught - for years - over Paul's relationship with Meg.

So now, I cannot imagine why she did everything she could to help Tim and Bridget to join (thus supporting Meg's arrival). She even went to Flosh Cottage to help Bridget pack up while Tim was briefly in hospital.

But then, Alice moves in mysterious ways.

As did Bridget and Tim.

A.k.a "Mr. and Mrs. D., in their Laurieston flat" - they kept themselves to themselves. I remember finding Tim, a year after they'd joined us, wandering lost on the main top floor, looking for Jay's Room. It was the first time he'd been anywhere near. How weird is that?

And they weren't in my living group. I only saw them at work, or in meetings. It feels like I never lived with them, as full and proper members of the LH Group.

But I could give you the background. Blonde giants, they were. Bridget, a daughter of the ruling classes, had been a PA, a super-efficient secretary. With a cut-glass accent. She was always cooking, baking, cleaning, working on the chickens and goats. I found her hard to get to know.

Tim, with some kind of biological science degree behind him, had been a member of the Socialist Labour League or some similar heavy-duty, far left group. But he could take the piss - told a story of being ordered to board a day-trip coach and sell the paper to the faithful: "One person already had a copy. So his minder says, 'Look, there's 55 people on this bus, you've only sold 54 copies, what are you, some kind of fucking liberal?'"

But humour didn't stop him coming on heavy in meetings. He was loud, dogmatic and epitomised the male politico - the stereotype which Alice tried to lay on me (surely you could see a difference, Alice?).

180

He and Bridget were committed to smallholding, outside work, the economics of rural community living. But as Jonathan put it: "The important, personal-is-political, stuff doesn't seem to touch them."

At this point I'd lost touch with *Carol*. Clearly unhappy and frequently rowing with Dave, she fled for a few days to local friends, leaving Dave morosely coping with T&T.

Catriona wasn't unhappy - but lonely, obviously. No lover. And living in the Aga Kitchen group, which met for meals, but for very little else.

With Freefall now back in Billiard Room, Catriona worked in her 'Craft Room.' You could find her in there making 'seed pictures' for sale. There was a loom, with half-finished weavings, and a silk-screen press - both gifted to us, apparently. It was beautiful - so it couldn't last.

Once, I chivvied Catriona to bring her guitar and sing on a mike at a band rehearsal, thinking she might like to play along with/ maybe even join the band. This didn't work.

Julia while not exactly happy, was calm and collected. She had her yoga; meditation; the garden; her smaller, quieter kitchen; candle-making. She took many unannounced trips away, to her mother's and Throssel Hole. The Accountant muttered about her 'stuff the group' attitude - but, out of touch with Julia, he didn't realise it was her survival strategy, mental-health-wise.

(And in any case, when others did ask the group for something, it was often overlaid with such heavy emotional vibes that we were effectively coerced into saying yes. At least Julia's approach spared us that.)

Lesley was realising her new boyfriend could be a bore. All this history - he should just forget it!.

And *Tina*. You were thoughtful and busy with Freefall. I hardly saw you.

Dave, who has bought all the goats, finds them suddenly booming.
He frequently suggests that we should have a Men's Meeting. I agree. But he doesn't call such a meeting. Neither do I.

Like Paul, Dave occasionally puts up 'to do' lists, referring to desperately -needed house maintenance. His lists do seem more achievable and he's often done half of the tasks himself.

Jay was melancholy. I encouraged Lesley to see him and sleep with him - I was, after all, still also lovers with Tina. I didn't understand that Lesley had definitely ended her relationship with Jay. As she explained: 'We just had some things which happened to us.' (These 'things' included Molly. Quite chilling, if you think about it.)

Jay often escaped to London, to work and earn and spend time drinking wine, he said, with his lover, Roma. Whom we never meet. When he wasn't away, Jay laboured in the garden.

181

'It's not you as you, I mind about,' Jay told me, 'it could have been anybody.' I didn't realise his meaning at the time. He was implying Lesley had been frantic to find somebody - anybody - to emphasize her leaving of him. He was right there - I was 'anybody'.

Jonathan returned from a (parents' holiday) trip to St. Lucia, bearing coral and sea-shells. Then went to Belfast, to see his granny. Back home, he wrote in the Diary: "Dream of a bloody hare and Pearl's shit-caked foot in the milking pail, birds and animals fossilised into the road by car wheels - the only dream i remembered for months - i was shaken by it and woke up crying.

"The way i live is bad - not just the smoking but overeating and not enough sleep and constant tension, frustration, fears for me and for everyone around me, my head struck off from my body.

"I'd be shit scared if i saw death up ahead because how can you leave the world when you're struggling with it?

We read this as an oblique comment on Jon's remoteness from Jools. Or hers from him.

Generally, we now regard Jon as Court Philosopher (CP) at this point.

Mike - I probably hardly dared breathe.

Patrick should have been happy, with the garden and the Freefall Project in full swing, his holiday with Tina, his 'happy games,' his made-up world. But he looked sad, perhaps because he'd had letters from Mary L., cooling off their wee romance (and because Tina was still pissed off with him about that).

Paul - I don't know if he was happy. He was off, working in Glasgow, spending time with Meg, presumably driving Nigel as demented as Patrick drove me. Earning money, spending money.

It's so sad we never had a men's meeting. I don't remember Paul ever mentioning them. Or any small meeting, where we might have discussed this. As the Accountant - or as the Politico - I couldn't help assembling the evidence regarding Paul.

His 'leisure' trips in the Ami. Never hitching, when the rest of us always did, except on trips with kids. Hiring a van to bring some shopping home from Glasgow. Spending £250 to get the Big Land Rover back on the road, welcome though that is - but with no discussion - and I compare the J4 van. And buying new crockery, glasses, pots and pans for the PeopleCentre, which he didn't even work on - my idea was to ask every visitor to bring a cup and a plate to leave behind.

It made me furious. And doubly so when, as soon as someone criticised Paul for all this - and it wasn't just me - he'd conveniently get the hep. hangover again and stay out of the way until his next trip away. This was the key thing. Not what he did, but the fact that we could never discuss it.

I was obsessed with living on next to nothing, spending as little cash in the system as possible. The PO would have pointed out we already did - the accounts always showed we lived well below DHSS benefit levels - but in a paid-for house, of course. I was proud of that.

For me, this was this biggest reason for the split: Paul's refusal to talk about money. But also, about identity, about Paul the Architect and Builder, when the rest of us had become primarily communards, and were now only distantly engineer, copywriter, secretary, systems analyst, etc. Sure, Paul earned almost all the outside cash. *But he needed to. We could have managed.*

Richard, who, with Tim, had finished Henry's barn. There'd been the glorious day when, with all the prefabricated supports built, a gang of us had erected the whole shell of the building in a few hardworking hours. The person volunteering to scamper and crawl, foolishly unroped, up to the first apex, with the first bolt, was - The Accountant.

But Richard wasn't happy. Kate B. was in London.

Tim turns out to be a professional gambler. He explains he has a system. He consistently wins, on average. But the amount of time it takes! He'd do as well being a shop assistant.

And Are You Self-sufficient?

Julia wrote, in the Garden Book: "Maxi kidded - a billy. Then Pearl - 2 billies, 1 nanny. We put the billies down, 2 in a bucket, 1 with a knock on the head. Ugh.

"Then Jill - a nanny - she licked it clean - 20 minutes later another, also strong. Afterbirth came a couple of hours later and she ate it all. Finally Heidi kidded, while Lesley and Sonya watched. A billy then a nanny. Mike wants to rear the billy for meat."

The goats at last gave plenty of milk. Yeugh, said our children.

Jools did a new 'Plan Of The Garden,' detailing the exact locations of: Perpetual Spinach, Webbs Wonderful Lettuce, Scarlet Globe Radish, Chives, Chinese Cabbage, Parsley, Lambs Lettuce, Scarlet Emperor Runner Bean. Then she lists 12 types of spud. And four types of fruit bush. And so on, for seven pages. I wish my life was that simple. She continues:

"5/3/75 Sunshine, bright, Patrick's shirt is off while he is puttying and priming the outside of the greenhouse.

"17/3/75 Mary L. forked a strip and moved 8 barrows of compost. Jon's tobacco is not looking very happy. Patrick planted 3 rows of early Scarlet Horn carrot w. help of Leeds F.S.

"21/3/75 everyone worked in the garden yesterday in blazing sunshine. Jay planted two rows of Suttons onion sets. Lesley started weeding round herb garden."

And Are You Self-sufficient?
One way to look at it is that everyone who lives in the city is 100%
dependent on the system. We're slightly less so.

We have so many visitors, it confuses everything. If there were just the
people that live here, we'd be self-sufficient in fresh veg, eggs, meat, maybe
milk and butter if we get a cow. So we'd be a little less than 100%
dependent, food-wise. And anyway, we need the visitors.

And no, we don't produce any tea coffee rice oranges oils sugar whisky
petrol gas tobacco (though Jon is trying) pens paper pencils phones
electricity (but Richard has a plan), hi-fis, garden tools, cars. And we love
the NHS.

We're not trying to be self-sufficient, you see, just trying to make sure
our side of the bargain is a bit less exploitive and harmful.

And do you have meetings?
Oh my.

We have tried 9 a.m. meetings (but some would argue they'd rather get
into their working day, others that they couldn't finish with kids' breakfasts
so early). Coffee time meetings, but these break the rhythm of the day.
Lunchtime meetings, but some people prefer to laze around or retire to their
rooms.

And while we disagreed over organisation, childcare, earning money,
how to use our resources of time and space, new projects, new people - a
typical meeting will just about manage to arrange a cleaning rota for a
conference group, schedule car trips a few days ahead, draw up a tomato-
watering-plan, say yes to a potential visitor, or agree a shopping list (marge
and butter; hard *and* soft loo paper).

Things which needn't come to a meeting at all if we had a few simple
systems. But all systems seem to fail - subverted by forgetfulness, crisis or
sheer cussedness (and the unspoken stuff about 'organisation' being part of
the great, capitalist, anti-life plot, etc.)

So How Do You Make Decisions?
We didn't vote in meetings, of course. Voting would mean 'the majority
could bludgeon the minority.' Voting would have been - part of the
hierarchical, patriarchal set-up.

'Couldn't we sometimes just take a show of hands,' I asked, 'not to make
a final decision but just to see where we're at, it would save an awful lot of
rambling.'

No, we couldn't.

The myth of 'consensus' prevails.

Take the time Paul wanted a new engine for the Ami. Jay thought we should just have one less car. I thought we could buy a whole working vehicle for less than the £250 the Ami engine would cost. Ten people 'passed.' Paul went ahead.

Consensus? The PO doesn't think so.

So Tell Me, How Do You Make Decisions?
Mostly, by omission. Inertia ruled. We never did register as a school, set up a furniture factory, create a charity to run Freefall...

Or *individually*. The smallest personal choices amplified all day, every day, combined to determine how we felt, what we spent, what we achieved - and what we didn't - far more than all our meeting 'decisions' put together.

We could choose to walk 40 yards through a drizzle to shit in the garden loo for compost - or stay in the warm, use an inside loo.

Answer the telephone or let it ring.

Take the children with on a shopping trip or leave them behind.

Cook instant food (eggs, rice, spaghetti) or set to work and clean and scrub a mound of mouldy spuds and onions.

Roll another cigarette, or not. Go down the pub, pick up the gossip, or stay home. Go and offer comfort to someone who's upset. Start a new love affair. Get pregnant...

Choices like these made the fabric of everyday life at Laurieston Hall.

And So How Do You Make Decisions?
Well, in Group Meetings. But there are other ways:

Going round and seeing everyone. Bridget did this when she wanted to put a sign at the end of the drive to advertise her pottery. In a Group Meeting, we might have talked about matters of principle (given that the pottery was Bridget's thing, not at all a collective project, in this case.) It's so much harder to say no, one-to-one. A clever ploy, this one.

Pinning up your piece of paper. The group was so keen to avoid having a 'leader', it was as though any idea that could be clearly identified with just one person wouldn't happen. But write it up, let some time go by and there was a chance the idea would seep subliminally through to the rest of the group. Examples include Alice's original plan for a small, west-wing living group; Tina's proposal for Group Therapy. Buying a cow. Mike's 'living on the first-floor front' - witness platform room and Mix Café.

Calling a small group. Paul called a 'Cars Group' meeting when the price of the new Ami engine leapt up to £400 between ordering and fitting it. Jesus, thought the Accountant. Also, 'what Cars Group?'

'But I called a meeting about it,' said Paul, innocently.

Doing it anyway. Assuming you could do it yourself. Because meetings were so pressured, there was effectively no way you'd get criticised.

Except via gossip.

'Have you heard, Paul's taken the Ami to...'

'Richard didn't put Bill and George to bed last night at all, just left them.'

'Dave's bought *another* new...

'Julia's maybe going to leave.'

For a time, there was even a rule against gossip.

Paul even came to me once and asked if I had any 'grievances'. As though this experiment in living together was some kind of Industrial Tribunal.

'So, How Do You Make Decisions?'

'Well,' I sometimes say, 'I'm the Leader, you see, so I make all the main decisions.' I know, it's pathetic, but as the enquiring faces cloud with suspicion, I do get a laugh to myself out of this.

27

Summer 1975

*Laurieston Hall is a grotesque Edwardian monstrosity, too big for
the ground it squats on. It's the communal home of 15 adult
members, 9 children, assorted long-stay friends and visitors.*

There was a late June, summer, Monday morning.

Imagine it's eight-twenty-five, "British Capitalist Summer Time" - Jay
calls it. The morning sun is insistent.

'You getting up?' mumbles Lesley. Molly, in her second sleep, is on
Lesley's far side. Why's it never Jay, I wonder, to have Molly in the night?

'Wanna see Joel and Sophie off,' I explain. I sweep down the circular
stairs three steps at a time.

Patrick has already dressed J & S, hasn't he, and fed them muesli. He's
looking dour. Poor love. Tina's a drag in the mornings, hmm?

In the back yard, Alice gathers all the kids for school. Polly's tearful
today, doesn't want to go. But if she stays at home, the others will want to.
She's squeezed, complaining, into the Ami. Yes, we drive kids to school at
the moment.

Back in Billiard Room, at 9.15, Tina takes toast and coffee on the run.
Says: 'I'm supposed to be servicing the Ami with Paul, he'll have started
by now.'

Molly comes in, demands a boiled egg, which I make. Lesley and Jay
arrive together - bickering. Then Jonathan, wiping his boots. He's been
gardening for an hour already.

The post arrives. Bookings for 'Connections' are looking up at last! In
the library, I clip £3 deposit cheques together and make out a bank pay-in
slip. And the Peace Pledge Union are due any minute - they've offered to
build library shelves (in my old room). Income is at last about to overtake
expenditure. Yippee!.

At coffee time, Jay is now in his flash white shirt with its red and green
rodeo designs. He's about to do a Dumfries trip - for food, pig meal, chicken
feed, cement, brake parts for the van. He's taking Molly. Tiffany and Tam
want to go too, but Jay says: 'one small child's enough.'

I bite back from saying: 'We always used to take two or three.'

On the front of the house, Alice, Catriona and Lesley are repainting a window frame - protective coats of leftovers in red, yellow and purple. Their denim boilersuits and dungarees will become the height of feminist fashion for some city women two years later.

In the stables, Rich, bare torso and a five-day beard, is finishing a new, transportable pig hut while Kate B. plays with George and Angus.

And in the garden, Carol is picking raspberries, Julia is contemplating her rows of flowers for drying and Jonathan is weeding in amongst the peas. Behind them, on the cottage track, Tim is working on a magnificent new hen-house.

The lunch bell sounds. Tina and Paul stroll hot and oily back from the stables garage.

Lunch, on the lawn, is a collaboration, Bridget bringing bread and cheese from the Aga kitchen and Patrick, yoghourt and a Technicolor salad - vivid nasturtium flowers, wine-tinted beetroot tops, the soft blue of borage, all the green hues from celery to watercress - from Billiard Room

Carol and Dave eat with us. The sun is high, and there's also a blotting-paper moon. Alice reports Polly was fine when she got to school - simply ran into the playground when she saw the Logan kids.

Apart from Jay and Molly, still shopping, the Group is all together - which is rare. On occasions like this, I love The Group. I forget my thoughts of leaving for - ooh, hours.

In the Diary, Jonathan the CP enquires, quasi - poetically:

"But does it matter that we are never all together/
why look for a moment in time/
if there is a sense in which we are all together/
it is never in one here and now./
But we are held together/
if we delay/
chickweed and groundsel multiply by fifty thousand."

From the outside, we seemed to be a tough, hard-working, cohesive, mature group. A tribe, a collective, a commune. An extended family of sorts, running a market garden, smallholding, children's holiday camp, hotel, restaurant and small garage and at the same time residents of Laurieston and Galloway, social creatures, fully extended, no time, you'd have thought, for anything else.

From the inside, the reality was something else. Most real warmth and closeness existed between lovers - if then - and it was mostly hidden.

'Let's work together today,' or 'Let's have a trip out to Carrick together,' were forgotten Group love-calls.

And as a 'political group' we were inert. We were too exhausted in

Autumn, too cold and pre-occupied in Winter, too manic in Spring to recognise and confront the contradictions of our lives - they'd become established. Just matters for sly digs.

For Example:

Manure for the organic garden, fetched by diesel-powered Land Rover.

The children going to school, the only place where they can have regular contact with other children - but where they're learning the basics of sexist, authoritarian and prudish attitudes.

Also, being driven to school!

Dozens of discussions of non-consumerism, anti-materialism, voluntary poverty echoing loud in the Accountant's mind as he accumulates monthly totals for bought-in food, tools, books, records, petrol, trips away, booze, shoes, phone calls.

The simplest systems were breaking down: kitty loss was now as much every month as it had been in the whole first year.

And of course, we were split. A Billiard Room Group evening might see us - Tina, Lesley, Jay, Jonathan and Patrick and me, grouped round the Jotul like a firemen's picket.

While the Aga Kitchen would be empty - Julia, Richard, Paul, Alice, Catriona each to their separate tasks, separate dreams. Catriona would sometimes join us in Billiard Room. And Bridget and Tim, snug in their own kitchen.

Or your PO would be off to a gig with his band, 'Ryder', playing Top Twenty covers for a Friday evening social at the Dumfries R.A.O.C. club, alongside four friendly, blithely sexist, Scots blokes, for a fiver in the hand, which is "no bad, ye ken".

'Do you think I should,' I asked you, 'I mean it's another contradiction, isn't it?'

'Sure. Of course. Fine,' you replied. 'It's contact with the locals at least. Be nice if you could play in CD then we could come and watch.'

I once clunked home at 2. a.m. to find Jonathan - this was my first and only 2 a.m. meeting - writing In The BR Diary. Still sans capitals, but.

"billiard room in the middle of the night with music and coffee
becomes suddenly a wide and comfortable private place
enough doors and space between me and the sleepers.

"first project - exploration of time and space. the imminence of natural beauty.
second, acceptance of struggle.
first problem - there is no place for struggle - or time no -

I began by saying I had found a comfortable place for struggle - but time -"

Thank you, Jonathan, I think we'll have to leave it there. What? You'd like some more? OK then, just one last number:

"I must trust other people with the milking
stop blaming and being blamed
at the moment the simple life isn't

"I've worked for long periods with my body and stopped thinking,
always had my back to the sun -
so maybe this is time for my head
to move towards a life of balance

"the goat is in the orchard
the hay is in the rain."

Jonathan copied a poem, 'A Voice,' by Tadeusz Rozewicz into the Diary:

"They mutilate they torment each other
With silences with words
As if they had another life to live."

and so on. Mournful stuff. Jon came to the PA's room, looking for solace, but the PA, precarious himself, wasnae too helpful.

We have a couple of clear, good, business meetings. But then suddenly we are into this summer's sixty-day, whirlwind mystery tour. There'll be some new hopes, new delights - but mainly action replays of the previous two years.

Once again, with many hundreds of visitors, the Rezzies become 'The Androids'. We work eighteen-hour days, emit pre-recorded phrases, pin up notices. It was as if 'The Show Must Go On.' Or, just possibly, 'business is business.'

Hello, nice to see you again. No, pigs don't eat onion skins. Yes, we pool income. Yes, pretty stable, five new members this year and no-one's left for nearly two years. Yes, the children still go to village school. One tea bag makes two cups. Twelve acres, but it's mostly drive and the bits of woodland and lawns around the house. No, we don't usually have tea-bags at all, it's just they're easier when big groups stay. Yes, the way the left ignores eco-issues is outrageous. Look, we're as confused as you about sexual relationships. And please don't bring illegal drugs into this house.

No, not much "turnover" of people. We don't even use that word. In the three years since we came here, three adults have left and eight have joined.

People asking this have pens at the ready. They look confused, and ask: 'That's good, isn't it?'

And we reply: 'Is it?

Women's Week 1975 came first. Of course, we "support the women's movement." But this week, as some visiting women will point out, it's more obvious that "the women's movement supports us." The week was written up by in Peace News and The Scotsman.

Paul and Dave had a working week in Lothlorien - with, I would guess, Polly and Tiff. Tim became invisible. The other men, meanwhile, scattered: how symbolic is that?

Jay took Molly to his Mum's in Devon; Richard, Billy to his brother's in Southampton; Patrick, Joel to Leeds (I wonder who Patrick was after, there?).

Jonathan scooted to Amsterdam, chasing a hopeless, never-going-to-happen romance with Tineke (while the rest of us think: Santa Lucia and Belfast already this year and now Amsterdam!).

The PA himself went to Drumglass to stay with a new neighbour, Doug.

Next were the Belfast teenagers. Dave H., from Oxford, had - brilliantly - raised most of the money. And Tina and Patrick had tapped the local Rotary Club. They were a mixture of Catholics and Protestants - but managed to set their identities aside. They flirted and fancied each other across the divide: danced and were happy.

'This was the first time I've felt free in my whole life,' one of them wrote back later. We felt all the work was worth it just for that. Even though they'd nicked £50 from the kitty and it had taken Mike - it would have to be Mike - to get rather interventionist to get the money back.

But a year later their romances were dead, Tina and Patrick found. Connected by a mile or so of telephone cable, but separated by guns and social pressures as if it were a thousand miles.

Then there were four weeks of 'Connections.' Like the Alt U a year before, only the edited highlights remain.

The first morning, I remember arguing with a visitor who thought the house was too filthy to stay in - but he was more freaked out because I happened to be wearing Lesley's long, multi-layer skirt that morning.

(But no, Dear Reader, before you get excited, that's about it for me and wearing skirts. I found I can't do without the possibility of running. Maybe, running away. Which you can't do, in a skirt.).

And Jonathan's first day of Connections began with a project to offer services to visitors - a piece of carrot? a light for your cigarette?. He'd circulated "Some Information Of Interest To Visitors", which said (nothing like a bit of local colour to cheer up the punters):

"I'm wearing a shirt of Mike's, Kate's white trousers and a bracelet Julia gave me. Jay put my washing in the machine, Tina hung it on the line, I don't know who took it off the line before the thunderstorm. I found it in the dining room at dinner time. Let's freeze some peas I said to Alice, she and I picked them, they were podded in a meeting last week while we picked over our despair and then I lost track of them. I think Alice must have blanched them, put them in plastic bags that Carol bought and stacked them away in the freezer."

The sound background to all this was another young rock band from London using the equipment. in the Top Tower. Loud guitar riffs cut across the garden; but only from 4 p.m. (when they became fully awake) to 8 p.m. (when we told them to shut up). Hard work, rock music!

Connections weeks were, vaguely, themed. But the plan didn't work. The weeks overlapped and coalesced. It's easier to say that every week touched on: 'The Revolution Of Everyday Life;' Communal Living; Children and Childcare; Education; Radical Psych; Utopian Futures; Women's (and Men's, and Children's) Liberation. And every week was a 'music and dance' week. A week with children.

And endless, endless discussions about discussions. About self-organising and what that meant. With small groups to discuss same, no doubt intended to report back to the plenary sessions, which they never did.

John H. read a play he'd written, which centred on a clash between a confused urban lefty and a rural libertarian - John H. vs. Gerry, obviously - which got easy laughs.

Keith C. designed and built a scaffolding tower in the back yard, intended to help us fix the inaccessible gutters at the back of the house, above Billiard Room. Made of silver birch trunks, raising it was a magnificent communal effort (but it stood unused and a year later, nervous of high winds. we took it down. Sorry, Keith.)

A group including Jen L. and Alice B. mused about a utopia where people communicate by colours and music and live on pure water, pure air - oh, and some fish, fruit and veg. Which later discussed sexuality and relationships on the lawn while I sat at my window and Lesley leant naked over me, and pulled me back into bed. Is this the revolution, then?

We produced a weekly magazine on the old Gestetner, twenty or more pages of personal statements and poems: sadly no copies survive with this PO.

There were yoga classes, football matches and daily swims in the loch.

I wrote a piece with Colin A. in which, by stretching definitions of words, we came out, for example, in favour of Free Enterprise (freedom from state capitalism), Competition (struggling together to beat the Man) and against Welfare (against those who bum and scrounge off society, i.e. The Rich). Many of the lefties didn't get the joke and thought we'd turned into fascists.

In Old Kitchen, Jay's Notice For Cooks said: "Now picking - broad beans (tender enough to eat whole), peas, sugar peas, lettuce, carrots, beetroot, potatoes, spring onions, chives, garlic, shallots, turnips, swiss chard, marrows, cabbage, globe artichokes, green peppers, chillies, courgettes, cucumbers, some ripe tomatoes, strawberries, gooseberries."The visitors cooed.

Lesley turned her room, for one berserk evening, into The Spinning Wheel Café - with Patrick at the door as commissionaire, Catriona as a surreal bunny girl, Paul as a gypsy, playing excruciating violin, Tina camping it up as the Owner's Daughter. I was the rude waiter and Lesley the genteel patronne.

Carol built a tree house, with the help of assorted admirers.

And we had a Men's Meeting! At last! In my room! With me, Tim, Dave, Jay and Jon (Paul away: Pat and Rich didn't bother.)

Visitors were bewitched by our wonderful children (of course). We tried to keep to an agreed 8 p.m. bedtime. But of course, if there was a party -or a meeting - they'd stay up.

And if a party: Lesley and I had a little dance routine, didn't we? Which looked and indeed was simple, but only if you knew the secret code. We were pleased with ourselves - we'd dance, others would try to copy us and fail.

'Today Molly pissed on the chair in the Wendy House,' wrote Alice B., a temporary rezzie, of whom more in a minute. 'Every time she smiles she makes me smile and when she looks guilty or whatever it is, that makes me smile too. The other day, Joel called Tina a little bourgeois pig, I can't remember what she called him first.'

Tina and Catriona replaced the Morris gearbox. Come lunch-time, the grease-smeared people wearing overalls - were women. Quite rare, that, thinks the PO.

Visitors did maintenance work for the fun of it! (We had hoped they would.) Roof leaks were patched, wood fetched, walls painted ('Looks like the men from the council have been through here,' Jonathan grumbled when some favourite graffiti were painted out by a team led by Patrick). All this will give rise to future 'Maintenance Weeks.'

Richard, I believe, showed people how to fish.

Ryder and friends played an afternoon gig on the lawn (I remember singing 'I Shall Be Released'). Agnes Murdoch, our local councillor, who lives five miles down the valley, rang up to ask: "Can you please turn your record-player down?"

Finally, in Billiard Room, we had another group of Belfast teens - Killy had leant us their mini-bus to fetch them from Stranraer. While in Old Kitchen, Communes Network had its first ever re-union. Volleyball competitions have continued ever since. It should have been an important weekend for us - but I think we were 'visitored out.'

For some of us, this had been a great, a fantastic Summer. But when it was over, there was the backchat. In Billiard Room:

'Paul's been away all Summer - first, to Jersey with Alice.'

'But then Alice was great, really threw herself into Connections.'

'She's still really unhappy about Paul and Meg.'

'Then Paul was away with Meg to Chamonix, to Lama Chimé's Buddhist summer camp.'

'And Meg paid for that.'

'But Julia's been away the whole summer, too.'

'That's 'cos she's freaked out by not-getting-on with Jon.'

'And now Dave's scooted. Fed up with Carol.'

'But have you heard, Richard wants Isabella to join.' (Rich was briefly enamoured, platonically he says, with this young Italian woman. With neither skills nor money. We say: 'not now.')

We remained chaotic.

28

So Do You Have, Er - Multiple?
Early on, Lesley asked: 'Is this the way it's going to be, then?'
    'You mean me..?'
    'Spending a few nights with me then going off back to Tina.'
    'Well, I suppose so…'

Tina wrote:
    "There's a gnat whining around the candle and a number of objects, facts and feelings whining round my head.
    "My world is maybe a swindle. Endless false bottoms that fall out at a rate of 5 or so a day. And with my coil, less a contraceptive, more a deterrent, the world's falling out of my bottom.
    "I'm lying next to sleeping Michael, whom I love, but he hasn't brought me sleep. Next, bar a wall, to Lesley, Michael's lover whom I know to be lonely and a little mad and whom I like and could love, if there's time. And next, bar another wall, to John H., almost my oldest friend, with whom I can make friendly love and who is in my room with Marie J., whom I hardly know."
    "This afternoon, I learnt, Patrick fucked Carmen S. while I discussed Marx with sickly Tim whilst loading 10cwt. of grain.
    "Patrick's room is on its own - at an hour most appropriate for sleep, or something. So my own, genuine lover is probably doing something, with someone, somewhere else.
    "Jay, Lesley's ex-lover is 3 yards and 2 walls away with perhaps Kate B., Richard's lover or Carol, Dave's lover. Dave is in London. Jon is down the corridor with the dogs belonging to Alice B., my and Michael's and Lesley's lover.
    "Julia, Jon's lover is probably alone. Richard, Julia's husband, is probably alone or with Kate B. Catriona is probably alone and perhaps lonely. Alice who was in tears and terror two mornings ago because the BBC implied that Paul had fallen off Mont Blanc lies, un-widowed, alone. Paul is safe with his lover, Meg, in Chamonix."
    "However meaningful or cataclysmic an item of broadcast news, it is neutralised, or at least impoverished, by the next. So here, it feels, with people, or the events that happen for people."

On a warm twelfth of June, the loch below shimmering, no movement at all in the wide, hilly landscape, except my hand, lifted and lowered by her breathing. We were naked, on a blanket, up in the top field. She passed me the illegals.

In our minds we had: Can anyone see us? Are we getting sunburn? Are the kids all right?

But most of all: Will it maybe work, this time?

We have a long, deep kiss. Tongues teeth lips foreheads noses; toes. The works.

Then we have the stroking and squirming part: the swimming, flying, slippy-sliding. I notice, as lovers do, and as I have before, that like others, she has a slight trough above her collar-bone, a miniature re-entrant above her hip, a slant to her eyebrows akin in rock-climbing terms to a "v.diff." and as for her shoulder: that would be a serious, "hard severe."

She also, astoundingly, has eyes! Which have irises! Containing pupils!.

Plus tiny goosebumps round her nipples, like foothills offering homage to - oh, fuckit.

I don't really want to be here anymore and I am bored stupid. Because we both know that it's a charade, we are playing out here.

Alice B., a shepherd, plus working dog, not to mention several degrees in Peace-related studies and a spiffing boy's haircut - was by now in that undefined zone, as Tony had been: a rezzie if she wanted to be. Her first diary offering was: 'I can't remember clearly anymore, but there was this delicate, beautiful beginning that got lost somewhere…'

Tina echoed: "A web that began to be spun - was smashed, brashed by more emphatic persons, more certain happenings. Early mist, burnt out by a hot day. Lovely weather we've been having. Yes, turned out nice again."

Explanation: Patrick, threatened by (or, anyway, not caring for) Tina's relationship with Alice B., savaged it by sheer physical commandeering of all of Tina's time. And Tina let him.

Mike withdrew hurt and cross and waited for Tina to come and see him.

And waited and waited.

I needed someone to talk with. What do you think, someone, do relationships produce the sexuality and sensuality they deserve, or is it the other way round?

And I don't know about you, someone, but I'm a little confused about Masters and Johnson and the, ha ha, demystified orgasm, all heart rate and blood pressure and contractions of this and that intensity.

And where making love when you're tired fits in, or when you're a bit pissed or stoned, or to music or feeling lonely or depressed.

And about Reich's differentiation between orgasm and, you know, just coming.

And making love with a new lover too near a thin wall - in this anti-erotic house. Or under the stars on a summer night, which I once did but it was a flop. Emotionally, not literally.

And then all this Tantric stuff, I mean orgasm as a great spiritual event, which arrives by not seeking it. And making love as meditation, make anything of that? Or male orgasm without ejaculation?

Or maybe you think orgasm is a phoney target, making fucking like a mountain climb, disappointing if bad weather turns you back?

Or maybe it's the warmth and closeness and the pillow talk that's more important.

And by the way, do you think people can be happy with just one lover? Or a hundred? And should sex be hidden away, couples behind closed doors? Or what do you think of everyone sleeping together, the Long Room notion?

And where does attraction fit in, and....

And why don't we ever talk about all this, I mean when we have theories about childcare and cooking and diet and illness and cars...are you listening, someone?

'Hey,' says Lesley, 'You've been and slept with Alice B.'

'Yeah, well, so did you.'

I was obsessed, that summer, with puzzles of sexuality (it made a change from worrying about the accounts).

Puzzle numero uno was about making love with you.

It would always be late: and we'd always be tired, right? (Lazy morning lie-ins or alfresco afternoon trysts were for other lovers.)

And of course, we'd cuddle, and stuff. Talk a bit about the children. And fall asleep, most times.

But if not, I'd reach to touch you - and you'd be taut. Your hand would shadow mine and stop me and I'd remember how you used to read Donne to me - but couldn't make myself say - "Licence my roving hand." So: No immediate America.

So I'd wait. Until warmth would arrive in you, and you'd draw me over and hold me tight and we'd whisper each other's names again. And the world - kids, the house, the group - would dissolve. And we'd make love and you'd - definitely, if not devastatingly, come. And we'd smile and giggle. And I'd murmur I love you.

(Now, although it's Summer, we seem to be at best in a permafrost. I haven't stopped loving you. Nor wanting you.) (Hence the dozens of letters) (And you say I'm "making a rod for my own back." What does that mean, exactly?)

I tried to talk about the way we made love. Like a fool I started: 'It's great, but...'

And I think all you heard was what came after the but. You got it into your head that I didn't enjoy making love with you anymore, when the opposite was true. And you've not forgiven or forgotten yet.

And I'd picked a bad time. You were upset, jealous about Patrick getting off with a visitor, Rike (I'd warned you, he would). And with others. Writing pages in your private diary beginning: "jealousy feels like a thump in the diaphragm, sudden weakness of arms and legs, sicky around the throat and there's not enough oxygen in a normal lungful of air."

Jealousy, say Freud, Cooper and various Zen and New Age writers is: "A narcissistic wound, compounded of grief."

"Feelings of enmity against a rival."

"The loss of a-b symbiosis when c arrives on the scene."

"Tied up with repressed homosexual desire (Cooper)" (as if jealousy is a solely heterosexual thing!).

"The result of Attachment."

"Fear of freedom."

What a load of nonsense we listen to.

'You really needed someone,' Lesley said, when it sunk in about the triangle, 'I mean, it needn't have been me.'

'Well I'm glad it was you,' I respond, a little hastily. 'And besides, you needed someone...'

'I didn't think to talk to you about me and Mike at first,' Lesley apologised to Tina, 'because I didn't realise your relationship was - well - still going on.'

'Lesley's really sharp,' I tell you, 'it's all a put on, this I-haven't-been-to-university-so-I'm-dim stuff.'

'I do feel a bit jealous,' you said.

'But that's not fair, look at how long you and Patrick have...'

'I do feel plain ordinary jealous too,' I write to Tina, 'Jay being younger and taller and slimmer and good-looking.'

I remember saying hi to Jay on the top corridor in the mornings and getting only a grunt in reply. Ah well, can't win 'em all.

'You never really got close to anyone else' - you actually reproached me, later. Reproached for being faithful! Or anyway, inadequately unfaithful! I suppose this translates as 'if you had, I could have made more of my relationship with Patrick.' Well, fuck you. And it's not true anyway, Lesley and I sort of held it together for a year or so.

Dear Lesley, I remember an evening in your room, listening to your old 78s. A walk over to call on Neill and Rosie, behind Greystone Cottage. A trip to the sea with a Kids Project group. The times we had to hurry out of bed for supper. Hugging in the Billiard Room kitchen. Visits to the Laurie - you looking glamorous, so the locals would nudge and wink. Carry-outs of Carlsberg special. Days when I'd come home at 4 a.m. after a gig, and crawl into your bed and sleepy arms. And a gentle evening by Loch Ken, with some home-made wine. And the strawberries...

Dear Lesley, I remember hard times too. Jay slamming doors. Being sad about me and Tina when I was with you - and feeling guilty for not being able to just be with you. Times when you'd want me to break off from doing the accounts or writing letters to summer visitors and come for a walk.

And I remember the summer solstice when, like assorted loonies, communards, atavistic freaks and primitives up and down the land, we sat round a bonfire all night, watching the sun just dip below the hills - and you cutting me dead, chatting up Doug from Drumglass - and a few days later, popping off to screw him, just like that. And not telling the rest of us, and missing your shift with the Milton kids.

I suppose I'd always known you'd sleep with someone else. And that I would too. And that this would change things. As it did.

Later, you said you'd decided it had better be you, first - you'd feel too put down if it was me. And I think I felt, besides a little hurt and a little angry - relieved, free again.

'You got off with Pauline M. (a visitor),' said Lesley.
    'Yeah, but you shagged Doug.'
    (pause)
    'And by-the-way you fancy Richard, don't you?'
    'Oh, yes,' says Les, quite openly, 'Sure. Of course I do.'

We held a 'Relationships Meeting' in the Aga Kitchen. With jars of wine bubbling slowly, a light fall of children's toys in the corner. Drawings on the walls, mossy twigs, Julia's planting plan.

Suspended overhead, Jonathan's tobacco crop from last autumn, now brittle and dusty, waiting to be cured. Sprigs of blossom on the long table. Fifteen uneasy people round it.

Alice Bridget Carol Catriona Dave Jon Jay Julia Lesley Mike Patrick Paul Richard Tim Tina.

Tim and Bridget with nothing to say. Tim makes it clear: 'Relationships are your problem, not ours.'

Carol and Dave looking grim. They've asked to move back into the house, but neither living group has offered them a welcome, either separately or together.

Paul, with nothing to say about his relationship with Meg, just wants to say he's giving up his job in the Autumn.

Alice with nothing to say ('What does she do all day,' I asked you, 'she's never in the garden, never does the visitor work, yet she reckons she's as busy as Bridget.' 'Dunno,' you replied.)

Richard, Julia, Lesley and Patrick - nothing to say. Jay brings out his formula - that he's against coupledom. Jonathan mumbles something and Tina reminds everyone that I'm now quite deaf and I say 'Look, I'm not that deaf, but if you will mumble' and Jonathan says, 'Well, you mumble yourself.'

Tina says we ought to be able to talk about relationships. Yes dear. Why don't you begin?

Catriona snaps: 'It's all very well if you've got a relationship...'

I was last in the circle. 'Well,' I began, 'I'm feeling good about my relationship with Lesley and...'

I remember people looking shocked: Jay, venomous; Patrick, angry; Lesley, herself, appalled.

Tina again: "It seems we have little alternative but to choose tumult or alienation. Or do I mean disaffection. There's a lot of it about.

"Actually it's not a choice - we are all tumultuous and alienated by turns which may be measured out in split seconds or in months.

"I would like it to be our avowed intention to become conscious of the way we act with each other - and visitors. I fantasise that out of this consciousness might grow a manner of co-being which is neither a shutting-out nor a tumult nor a sterile accommodation to each other.

"I feel, rather than can justify, that it's generally useful work, as well as necessary to us to make life tolerable let alone fruitful.

"I mean of course that we should change as well as notice what we're doing to/ with each other.

"We already understand how overt (broad) social relations fit with advanced capitalist values and accept the need to subvert them. Can we understand how, as it surely must, our intimate behaviour dovetails with the same values? Can we be subversive? Can we describe it, for ourselves and others?

29
Autumn 1975

Julia wrote: "Thursday September 11th 1975. Today we had a Maintenance Meeting and decided to clear the goat yard and walls so that rainwater doesn't overflow. We'd just cleared the gullies and lo and behold, the heavens did open. Lead-shot-sized hail descended on the goat yard, then the storm departed to New Galloway with an up-yours clap of thunder." Julia then went awol again, for a few days.

Perhaps because "Laurieston Week" was upon us. Jay had offered the "It seems to be Permanent Crisis here" argument, not realising we've been there before; but Pat, more successfully, had argued the "Crisis, what Crisis?" line. So this year, it's our *"Not Crisis Week."*

And indeed, when we get together, on the Sunday, Dave having cooked supper in a candle-lit Old Kitchen, it feels almost cosy. Whether people have enjoyed the summer or simply survived it, they seem quite cheerful. We spend the evening in amiable chat, centring on How To Spend The Week. Talks about talks. And structure: some want lots of meetings; others, few; still others, just one-to-one conversations. And style: talking, listening, playing music, going to the beach, eating together. And topics: the usual suspects. Why Are We Here?; Are We Communal?; Work Projects; Carol and Dave coming back to the house.

Also, would everyone kindly shit in the Elsan? Which is our out-door loo. This is Jon's way of collecting our shit for composting. It never took off.

Being Happy Here. Jay Tim and Tina add "The Politics Of Communes." Mike mentions Facing Conflict; Jay agreed and first Carol did then she didn't. Pat wanted us to cover Kids And Schooling. But the big question looms: can Meg join?

We agree: let's meet at eleven. Yoga or meditation beforehand, all welcome, at 10.30.

Next morning, it will have to be the Meg question first.

Immediately, some of us - not just the PO - grumble that we don't know her, she only seems to want to be here to be with Paul, what does she want to do here? And anyway, how are we? It's hard to define what she's joining. And so forth.

Jonathan wonders, in a kindly fashion, 'How will Meg find it here,' meaning he's worried she won't be happy. Bridget, Catriona, Carol and Dave share this anxiety.

But Paul explains: 'I wouldn't want Meg to join if I thought it wouldn't do her good.'

By the by, we collectively get to hear, at last, the full Meg, Nigel, Bridget and Tim background. Back when we were setting up LH, these four were based in the Lake District, looking to live together on a small-holding. But Nigel and Meg had moved to Glasgow, for Nigel to begin his nurse training. And Paul had got together with Meg, from, more or less, day one.

We have a diversion - 'We should really talk about More People generally.'

Tina says she'd like loads more, Tim declaims his support, Pat agrees with Mike that we should have maybe 30 adult members. Catriona says she'd like that - and says that, at the moment, her life feels like working in an office. Embarassed, we ignore her, but jump to another familiar detour - shall we do up the stables, build other accommodation…?

Alice says she really wants just Meg to join, but no more for the moment. (I have given up trying to understand Alice).

And in the end, we of course say yes. It was like when Julia wanted Jonathan to join - how could we say no, to someone's lover?

That was it, for the Monday.

Except that later, Paul and Tim, talking to Jonathan and Mike, admit they are worried by Meg's "over-friendliness." They explain that yes, Meg can appear ecstatic, but is actually, er, let's say already as depressed as anyone here. 'You can see her, happy - but not weeping in her room.'

(So that was it, I thought. Paul had wanted Bridget and Tim - Meg's friends - to join, so that Meg would be more likely to want to come here, too.

'It feels like it was kind of your master plan,' I challenged Paul, much later.

'What do you mean?' he demanded, angrily.

I tried to explain and that's when Paul - the former schoolboy boxer - and six-footer - punched me, cutting my lip. Not good news for a part-time, semi-pro sax player, I can tell you.)

On Tuesday morning, with no agenda set, Tim says he'd like to talk about something 'concrete.' An image Marxists often use, to mean something absolutely, fundamentally solid. Something to build on, obviously.

Which delights the PO, who, as a nuclear physicist, in an earlier life, regards concrete, like everything else, apart from passing black holes, as mostly emptiness, riven with force fields and with here and there some rather small squiggles of mass, boogieing in an utterly fluid dance of energy.

But I don't say any of that. No point in upsetting Tim. (Although it's no bad image for us, empty space plus squiggles.)

Alice (surprising the PA), suggests the big topic: MONEY (Paul, taking minutes, in his beautiful architect's handwriting, chose capital letters.)

She means, as we all instantly know, not what we earn and spend, but the Money In The House, and the leftover Capital In The Bank.

We break for coffee and shortbread in the middle of the garden. (And we feel so lucky, to live here, to be able to do this!)

After which, Paul asks 'Well first, can we outline present arrangements?'

He always does this, doesn't he? Formal Paul. And, fair enough, maybe the new people don't know.

So the Accountant rehearses: 'OK. Tina, Mike, Alice, Paul and Maureen pooled their resources to buy the house. The legal owners are Alice, Tina, Carol and Maureen. Julia chipped in just enough to pay back Maureen back. The unspent balance, the Capital, is just over six thousand quid. Everyone else brought cash to live on - but not capital.'

Accountants are good at fudging, that's their trade. We all realise that 'everyone else' is too sweeping. Quite a few brought no money at all. And we all know that, over the summer, Meg spent all her ready cash - quite a sum - taking Paul on their Chamonix holiday. But we aren't allowed to tut, publicly.

'And Tim and Bridget' - the Accountant pauses - 'have joined, but are still deciding whether or not to pay in their capital.'

There is really only one proposal on the table - that, like the Shakers before us, or the Kibbutzim now, we should hold all our property - money, possessions, whatever - in common. No-one quite puts it that way.

Mike revives proposals to (1) create a Trust or a Housing Association to own the house and (2) agree that the Capital is pooled 'without strings.' Old Hands knew he meant that Paul should not be able to spend 'his own' share of the Capital before first setting up a proper Building Project, with others, and, so to speak, 'bid' for funds as other projects might. A somewhat unrealistic scenario.

Tim says he's doubtful about what he's jumping into (although we thought he'd already jumped). He insists, loudly and again, that 'we do not have a decision-making procedure.' (How come you even got to be here, then? thinks the PO.)

Jonathan, the CP, says to Tim that he should be careful, when pruning the rhododendrons (the PA is not making this up).

Paul writes: L U N C H.

Richard has made the day's soup, rolls and salad. But with his own, delicious variations. (We each have our own: watch out for us in the food guides.)

Paul went missing over lunch. He'd disappeared in order to write his proposed Four Points: a beautiful, illustrated document, which the PO has to hand.

Perhaps still high because we have, so quickly, let Meg join, this is Paul, astoundingly, agreeing that he wants:

(1) Ownership of the house to be made equal, through a Trust.

(2) Anyone leaving to be given what they need.

(3) Everyone's personal capital to be pooled 'without strings attached.'

(4) All possessions to be property of the Trust - but special things remain in specific people's guardianship.

Wowee! This is Paul, the primitive communist, the early Christian, whatever, that I never knew. I'll look after my own knickers and toothbrush, Paul, if that's OK. The rest, you can have.

In the Radical commune, we are hardly likely to go beyond this regarding the physical world. Perhaps we would also formally pool our responsibilities, joys, heartaches?

Had we done this, Marx would still have called us - contemptuously - builders of "Castles In The Air." Fuck you, Karl.

After lunch, with Dave writing nearly illegible minutes, we add the small print.

(1) People who've put money into the house might as well wave it goodbye since realistically we're never going to be able to pay anyone back, unless perhaps new people arrive with 'replacement' capital.

Meg says 'If Nigel and I sell our flat in Glasgow...'

Ownership of LH would be shared between all of us by setting up a Trust or a Housing Association.

What's a Trust, asks Les. A legal entity thing, says Dave, which we'd all be an equal part of.

Or a Housing Association. What's the difference, asks Carol. One member, one vote says Catriona.

Either way, says Mike, writing the pre-amble would be key. 'Yeah, we know,' Rich interrupts, 'crucial.' 'The hard part,' says Mike.

What's a pre-amble anyway, wonders Bridget. The statement that would make it clear what we're about, presumably, says Jools. As if we know, replies Jay. It's all too woolly at the moment, says Alice, adding: 'This should be more a People meeting than Business.'

Shouldn't be a difference anymore, suggests Tina.

'Dialectics' mutters Mike.

I agree with Alice, says Meg.

We shouldn't leave it vague, offers Jonathan (known for his vagueness).

Moral Pressure! Psychological Pressure! says Tim. Pecking order! Some people drink whisky! (What is he on about?)

Tina says she wouldn't use the word moral - but says 'we are committed.' (Meaning, clearly, are Bridget and Tim really with us, or not?)

Jonathan thinks we're not capable of working out anything in detail together right now. And that all this sounds like two years ago. So Mike snaps at him: 'Why don't you propose something new?'

Patrick, Rich say fine. Really good

(2) Giving people who leave what they need would obviously need to be "within the reasonable means of the Trust" - is how Paul puts it.

Patrick, Rich, Catriona say fine. Really good (None of them have anything to lose).

(3) 'I thought the Capital was already pooled, says Carol.' 'It's disgusting that we have Capital,' counters Dave (he may be called on that at some point).

Paul reminds us he wants us all to acknowledge that he needs to set up the Building Project. Rich says all this talk of pooling is odd, when there's so many people saying they don't give a toss - Jon, Patrick and Jay for example. Catriona agrees we should all share the responsibility for the money. Tina says she wants 'everything to be clear.'

The Capital should be a fund, says the PO, to which any Project Group, Building, Garden, Crafts, whatever, could ask for money. It could give out loans, says Catriona, which the projects should repay. Until that happens, says Julia, it should be frozen. Agreement with that does a pass-the-parcel from Julia to Alice to Meg to Paul to Tim.

Indeed, everyone agrees with all the above, except Tim. Alice says we all felt like Tim, at first. (No Alice, we didn't - if we had, we'd never have got here).

But nothing happens. Nothing changes. Months later, you'll hear: 'The Capital? I thought we sorted all that out in Crisis Week?'

After supper, we have a wee surprise. Jay has written a discussion paper about how to manage money!

He suggests that a "pocket money" system (which we don't have and nobody is now proposing) would mean that "rather than resolve differences, or come to see them as reasonable differences, you abolish them."

Bless. We have been round this circuit many times before, but of course there will be ten thousand things newcomers do not know.

But he signs off with a sting. Where before there has been only a whispered possibility, he seriously proposes: the Living Groups should be financially separate.

Wednesday of Not-Crisis Week is occupied with people wanting to meet and talk in small groups. Alice doesn't find it genial to talk here at all, Lesley is not talking in large groups, Tim's anger spills out incoherently again, Catriona feels a total despair, Jonathan wants to go to a football match, Meg thinks we should only say good things about each other as bad things don't get worked out.

Thursday somehow evaporates but on the Friday evening, we have supper together and Tina presents a funny but seriously firm proposal to start our own free school. "in a year's time" and do things meanwhile to improve relations the village school. We all agree (we are briefly back in a relatively friendly collective mood).

Which must have seemed like as propitious a time as any for Meg, Paul, and the rest of Aga Kitchen people to reveal to Billiard Room that Meg is two months or so pregnant. They hadn't told us prior to the Meg decision because 'we didn't want to put pressure on you.'

The Billiard Room people think: 'How very considerate' and other less generous thoughts.

That Autumn we have a shuffle rhythm of chop, a backbeat of change. And Mike's new rock band, Taloola (Ryder having split up, as bands do), rehearsing here on a weekly basis.

Dave, having been away for a month over the summer, had returned and got together with Alice - not really such a surprise, we reflect. He starts describing (Alice's) Balcony Room as 'our room,' walks around beaming, joins the Aga Crew. Carol, after another Guernsey (parents) trip, moved with Tiff and Tam back into the house and joined us in Billiard Room.

Alice B. wrote: "Looking back through the diary, I came to Tina's description of me as her, Mike's and Lesley's lover - and here I am now, a few weeks later, as Jon's lover - something that got past a beginning - it was weird to find somebody who liked TS Eliot and maps and dogs. It's all been a bit much, what with smashing my cosy lesbian identity."

"But really I'm a shepherd and tomorrow I start my new job gathering the sheep up at Grobdale of Balmaghie and on Thursday Alice and I are going to Lancaster to pick up all my possessions and then I can move up there, wonky generator and all, and be on my own, like I think I want, except…"

(Your PO had wanted to chauffeur Alice B. on that trip, with the excuse of visiting the P&CRP, but also to snatch a few moments to talk about another beginning that wasn't. But Alice - Lady Alice - absolutely refused to speak, let alone negotiate. She won, hands down. There's power for you.)

And, Patrick was, I think he said, 'in love' with Linda E., a summer visitor, who lived up in the wilds. From whom he'd picked up another STD. I was furious because he didn't tell me or Tina, nipped to the Dumfries clap clinic, didn't offer to share his antibiotics. Leaving us (Tina, me, Les) to pass the dreaded STD baton, follow on and have even later dates by which we are clear. Bastard.

We are in that balmy time - before AIDS.

And you were furiously jealous, as in Hell Hath Nothing Like. An STD on top of being laid low, three weeks out of four, with your coil, and the protracted bleeding this and your periods gave you.

Excavating our collective memory, I've just found that you wrote: "I can't see why I am so distant from Michael, why I piled all my aggressions/ anger at him. S'pose 'cos Mike is passionate, says it, feels it and no hiding. So he has an opinion of me, so I have to have an opinion of him, or I might as well forget his existence. Which is, in way, what has happened."

You forgot my existence!

But in spite or perhaps because of that, suddenly you and I get our first ever holiday alone together. Pat would have looked after J & S. We went to Lowrush Cottage, Wearhead - I can't now remember who lent us it. I of course took the typewriter and we kept up a correspondence.

You were obsessing - in conversation, in type - about (a) Thomas Helliker, a luddite martyr in the late C18th and (b) Spanish militants recently shot in the street. And the contrast with (c) last night of the Proms, attended by 7000, with its echoes of nationalism and implicit fascism. Feeling shame for the state of our nation.

I think - are we ever going to talk about us?

We are interrupted by a drop-in potential co-visitor who tells us with very little prompting about the woods needed to make a guitar. I am, actually, fascinated. Brazilian redwood is best for the back and sides. Though some favour Indian rosewood. Spanish cedar for the top: or else Swiss pine or German spruce (which are in fact the same). Then for the neck any light wood which won't warp. Example, quarter-sawn Honduras mahogany. It must be a boy thing.

But we were here first: our visitor should please leave. He does.

Then you and I do talk together. We run through - and write up - if not the Laurieston universe, then at least the Pers-Pol/ Happiness/ Fulfillment spectra.

I don't recall that we talked at all about - y'know - other lovers. But I imagine we could still make love enthusiastically at this point, coil permitting.

When we got home I pinned up our meanderings. People said 'how typical of M & T.' No-one responded at all.

That was also our last-ever holiday.

The triangle clunked on. Tina, Pat, Mike (& Les) - keeping the non-couple option alive. Richard still waiting patiently

On 5th October - her 5th birthday - Sophie went into hospital for an op on her kidneys. She was there for 26 days - needing a lot of parental and other communal to-and-fro as it's a 55-mile round trip. If it's working, we'll take the Ami; if not, we'll hitch.

Hitching from the end of the drive to Dumfries - and back - is usually pretty quick, effective and of course, cheap. And you get into interesting conversations. Hitching up/ down the M6 is a different matter (the PO does a lot of that, however).

In November, Jon's Dad died and he went off to his Mum and family for a while. During which time, there was a party, when Alice B. got off with Jay. ("I was the last one on our floor," says Jay, later.)

When Jon returns, he moves - sad, upset - up into the Tower, where Richard had once lived. Access to it is only via the Tower circular stairs, which begin opposite the Old Kitchen door. He installs a "Jonathan is In/Out" slider.

So for a short while, Jay and Alice B. are quite the new-couple-on-the-block. They go on holiday.

And so do Lesley and I. Extraordinary things happened as we hitched north. Do you remember, ducks? The car that braked but didn't stop - and which had overturned by the time we passed it, ten minutes later? The ride in a hearse? The quarry lorry that dropped us smack dab in the middle of nowhere (except mountains?). Fetching up in Inverary, where we found a B&B?

Next day, we hitched to Lochgilpead, then walked to our borrowed holiday cottage, where we found ourselves alone. And uncomfortable with each other - without all that LH background.

It didn't help that we had nothing to do, bar strolling two hundred yards down the beach and back. Or sculling precariously, a half-mile across the estuary, around the high tide, to the inn, which was our only other human contact. We neither knew about nor were equipped for serious walking, which might have made a difference. I thought you would want to know everything about LH history - so vibrant for me. But you didn't.

I had, first time for a long time, a really good conversation with Dave, mostly about him and Carol.

It turns out she has been sleeping with other guys for a while - for example during Comtek - with Dave only finding out months later. So whether because of this or not, he'd spent weeks away, first in London, then Lothlorien, then back to London.

In the circs, I managed to say nothing about how he'd ducked working on Connections (as had Paul, Meg and Julia). Nor about how he'd put together the Communes Network visit, then evaporated from it. He'd dropped out because of a big row with Carol, when he said he wasn't going back to the cottage. I'd had to run it (actually, I'd enjoyed that).

In Laurieston Week, he'd cooked the first meal - causing Carol to say, as she had many times before, the he "cared more for the group than for her." Another big argument.

This was when Carol sort of camped in the house, at first eating with Aga Kitchen, but then, after a long trip to Guernsey to her parents, went to a Potlatch with Alice at Wick Court, then in the end fled briefly to Dumb Toms. And had a hypothetical abortion (i.e. planned but ultimately not needed).

I felt much closer to Dave after this, but not close enough to own up to my own short encounter with Carol. Which I hoped to repeat.

Meg went into hospital with a threatened miscarriage.

So Paul (and others) took over the hospital commuting. But with the little Land Rover out of action, the Ami iffy, Paul hired a car! No hitching for Paul! And of course, he's extremely worried, we all understand that. But there are some intakes of breath here, some mutterings of "Tina and Mike hitched to see Sophie."

There is simply no room to make the obvious comment to Paul. We are trying to be some kind of revolutionary, low-eco, sustainable collective. Hiring a (flash, new) car does not quite fit in? He is never going to get it.

Meg came home, her pregnancy happily intact, two weeks later.

Julia, absorbed with meditation, was building her own, separate life. She was now lovers with Arthur - who was splitting with Liz. Leading to loads of dramatic freakouts and confrontations - Liz shrieking, Arthur catatonic. One night, Liz paints herself bright blue, smashes some cottage windows and ran around yelling and it fell to Tina to talk her down. Later, Tina writes "there have always been more anger and tears than belly-laughs and peak experiences."

Carol meanwhile turned her attentions to Roger L, who has just moved to an idyllic cottage near Gatehouse.

With Dave back in the house and Carol elsewhere, we had an empty cottage. Neill and Rosie wanted it, as they were being bounced out of Bellymack by Farmer H. Jay thought we have to help the homeless.

The PO predictably comes up with a prioritised list of what the cottages should be used for. Residents with special needs, blah blah. But he makes a trip to Lancaster. Meanwhile, Neill and Rosie (and their kids, Ben and Emma) get the cottage.

30

The Aga Kitchen lot came together for meals, but little else. So if people wanted to chat after supper, they came to Billiard Room.

But the Billiard Room crew weren't doing much better. If we had a kids group, we'd be together, but as co-workers. Ditto when we had a big group - say, Manchester Free School - to look after in the Old Kitchen. Otherwise, in the evenings, desultory groups of two or three souls would huddle round the Jotul.

I couldn't stand it. So I made up a new game.

I created a sitting room, of sorts, in Sunny Room. And established a kitchen in Sunny Room's attached, walk-through scullery or linen room, using bits and pieces retrieved from the junk cellar - the electric ring cooker that Dave had bought for 'Carol's Kitchen;' a Camping-Gaz stove; and assorted, pots, pans and crockery.

I named this, 'Mix Café'. (Others immediately misspelt it, 'Mick's Caff.') ('Mixcaff,' however, is acceptable.) I wanted it to be the home of an 'Imaginary Living Group.'

A place where:

"You can be comfortable. With an open wood-fire next door, in a warm, south-facing room with a view.

"You can be other than yourself.

"When cooking - without random visitors, garden customers, phone calls, people making snacks to deal with - you can just cook. (But we will also do snacks.)

"Children are never 'in the way.'

"We research what we consume."

On its opening night, I served dinner to Tina, Patrick, Lesley and Jonathan. Veg curry and rice, naturellement. We discuss the politics/ ecology of eating rice. And conclude that rice - indeed all imported food - should be eaten very infrequently indeed.

Tina passed round a list of 25 "agreements" she wanted Billiard Room Group to make. It's Tina-style: funny and provocative at the same time. She's proposing that "This Collective Agrees To:

"Produce a new joke, or a story, each week

"Produce £60 a week income on average

"Spend 26 days a year on house maintenance

"Be conscientious about visitors

"Make parenting a collective responsibility

"Serve lunch on time, at 1 o/c. Ditto, supper, at 6 o/c."

(And I was thrilled, that you were again in full flow about our lives.)

(Later, in Billiard Room, folks write YES to almost all these suggestions. But nothing much changes.)

The evening ends:

Teen: 'I feel a bit dead.'

Les: 'I feel a bit dead.'

Teen: 'I just said that.'

Les: 'Oh I thought you said deaf.'

Jon: 'What?'

Pat: 'I deff thought you said.'

Jon: 'What?'

Mix Café was also to be, in my mind, an extension of the P&CRP. Somewhere where I would discuss this thesis project with everyone (and in the end, everyone came - except Jay).

And it was fun to write the flyers.

"Crazy Mick's Tup Café. Politically OK eco-fine cheap tasty food. Only six hours via Prestwick from New York. Appalling service, erratic opening. Payment accepted in chanterelles. (A 'tup', Dear Reader, is a ram, a male sheep. And 'tupping' is what he does.)

"Chez Michel. Booking essential. Entrance by examination only.

"Mix Grill. Egg n' chips, 4/6d. Fresh coffee, 6d. Instant coffee, £3. Filthy. No booking.

"Norman Normal's Normality Restaurant. Delightful food and service, friendly staff. Very Nice." (Norman, Mix Café's stores clerk, was to keep meticulous records of all food and other materials consumed.)

(Writing this two years later, the PO is in fact momentarily back in Mixcaff, cooking onion soup and wondering who's coming to lunch.)

And How Do You Earn Your Living?

Freefall sputtered on, in a subdued way, with Patrick and Tina in some confusion with each other. We hosted the Tongs, Mearns, John Simnet. And it was still such fun to do - being paid to take kids to the beach. More driftwood fires, sausage fry-ups, chats with the Groans. Plus we handed out contraceptives. It occurs to the Accountant that we should have sought NHS help with financing that.

211

Julia was again back working at Lybro's ("Running to and fro, hard working at the mill"). And teaching the CD yoga class.

Meanwhile Richard, Tim and maybe others spent a few days mussel-picking on Heston Island - camping nearby - and delivered almost a ton of mussels to the processor in Kirkcudbright. But received only silly money (it was too early in the season: mussels too small). They'll maybe try again in the New Year.

Paul was doing yet more designs and planning permissions for Lothlorien.

Plus this is when your PO starts as a student in Lancaster, passes go, collects grant cheque. There is murmuring that I have not paid this in. Well no, I say, I will have to spend time in Lancaster and it costs, so I'll pay in what's left. Which I do. This doesn't stop the murmurs.

Dear Tom C. I stayed at yours - Dumb Tom's - and got hitches into Lancaster. And then out to the Uni, from that place where hundreds of students hitch from. I loved my library card and did light-years of work. I had reading lists - from Amish via Kibbutzim to Zedd Collective, I read the damn books. Contemporary communes or communities, historical, you name it, I read it. I wrote - and still have - I would say about 2000 pages of notes. Any chance of a degree given by weight? Only kidding.

So: I did try. But none of what I read spoke to me (except, maybe, the Situationists and For Ourselves). Nothing seemed relevant to Laurieston and my life there.

We have a meeting in Mix Caff. I try to explain that anyone could take part. We could split up the grant - £850 a year, no less - into a rate per hour, for whatever people wanted to write. 'The money is for almost anything connected with Laurieston, as long as I can put it into a thesis.' Jonathan and Catriona offer their diaries, but in the end, nothing comes of this.

Plus, the PO announces, I did pay in all the money from playing with the band last year. All £20 of it.

Catriona worked on Freefall, but spent time mostly alone in her Craft Room (aka Tony's Old Room), making stuff to sell. And Richard took down a piece of leaky guttering from above Morning Room - planning to cast a glass fibre replacement. Sometime.

We were thinking a lot about Work. And we were busy with it: if not money-making, then at least money-saving.

Patrick revived the Dalek and cleaned the chimneys. Tim started building a super-duper new chicken house.

Paul, when home, manically did maintenance - besides building for himself, Meg (and, fingers crossed, the new baby) a self-contained sort of bed-sitter in what, at this point, becomes Platform Room. I rarely see him (this is perhaps good group-working).

Paul again calls a Building and Design Group meeting. Not much happened.

A "Small-Holders Group" met! Ta-da, ta-da! This was Richard (pigs), Tim (chickens), Julia and Jay (garden), Jon and Pat (goats, all purpose). This was a first! They mainly agreed to think through all the economics and work-time spent, 'so as to shut Mike up.' Good Plan!

Other matters were: The potatoes have blight. Trying to sort out that strawberry bed is going to drive me insane. Flora and Emma have got meningitis. Pig breached the electric fence. Again found later with her snout sticking out of a nest of bracken, piglets popping from her. Is there something about us pigs don't like, when about to give birth?

Two sacks of dried broad beans were left in the rain, and are spoiled. Mike has been shifting manure, pretending to be a labourer. What a wanker.

Thinking about 'Doing Useful Work' - (Aim No. 97) - The PO wrote yet another list, setting out criteria for the kind of work we should choose to do (he no longer remembers why). This would be work which "is creative, stimulating, joyful, playful and instructive, uses and helps us share our skills, derives from and feeds back to our lifestyle (especially, that it fits with our children's needs), is collective rather than individual, is, obviously, open equally to women and men and is ecologically sustainable (e.g. local materials, blah blah.) It should make (or clearly save) some money. We should feel physically and spiritually better for it. And if can offer work to local people, via a cooperative, great."

When Tina, Patrick, Michael, Lesley and Alice have a "Community Café In CD" project meeting, Michael brandishes the above bit of paper. I can't imagine why he thought that would be helpful.

'How can we ever get started if you're going to bring all that up?' cries Alice, rushing off in tears.

You were right to object, Alice, to such a tedious statement of the bleeding obvious.

(Of course, if I were to raise the matter with you directly, you'd say something like: 'If you have to ask, I can't possibly explain.' And you've written that, 'Apart from Bridget, I am the hardest-working person here.' Which you maybe are, dear. But I have no idea what it is you do. Nor what Bridget does.)

Later, without Alice, we try again. And cover questionnaires, adverts, reaching out to kids with no place to go, hosting claimants union meetings, self-help, childcare, must talk with local social workers. Meeting ends (project never re-surfaces).

I suddenly remember why I wrote that list of criteria. It was to show up just how poor our present work choices were. Because, we were, in the main, a bunch of intellectuals. Paul's teaching will have given him some stimulation - and this Lancaster thing studentship at least pays me to think.

Whereas most of our work - gardening, Kids Project, catering, cleaning etc. - was in fact dull and repetitious, tolerable only by having different people to chat to and or as a sort of yoga practice ('washing-up as meditation.'). Much of it was physically demanding. I would say we were slow to learn from mistakes, slow to share skills. (Plus if you learned a new skill, you'd only be called on to use it immediately, wouldn'tcha?)

And we also had to offer emotional or counselling type support to freaked-out visitors ranging from the upset to the downright mentally unwell. For which we had neither training nor experience. We did what we could. Alice, I have mentioned, was particularly put-upon.

And You Keep Goats, Right?

Jonathan writes in Mixcaff diary:

"5th November. This afternoon I stepped knee deep into an obscure ditch, which I knew was there. I mean, I knew where the ditch was, but not where I was. Molly was sitting on my shoulders and didn't fall off.

"Now after changing my socks and trousers, instead of 1. writing a nice letter to Florence (ed: that's Alice B.), 2. moving my room again, 3. sitting knitting watching unknown flightless objects grumble through my skull or 4. talking to goats, here's a list of things goats like to eat in November:

"Hogweed, wild raspberry, fallen elm leaves, hazel leaves, brambles, the fern very common in the woods whose name I don't know, sow thistle, heather, conkers, grass (it has to be Henty's grass, I'm afraid), ash keys, sycamore helicopters, plaintain, kale, runner bean haulm, beetroot, broom, ash and sycamore bark, hay, that foreign plant which grows in the orchard with the fat hollow stems and big pointed leaves and spindly flowers, yellowing leaves on the brassicas, nettles occasionally, ivy, holly, wood sage, elderberries."

The PA thinks this deserves to be the basis for a: "Short Breaks For Goats - Scotland-In-Autumn" brochure.

And How Do You Make Decisions?

Because of course Tim is asking. We presume he wants to see rules, committees, quorums, voting, majorities…stuff which he is never going to get.

And we try once again to explain. 'We keep talking until we agree. We all have a veto.' (This rather ignores the rights of people who are away at the time, etc.)

'And autonomous decisions,' the PO points out 'like, Meg getting pregnant - will always have a huge impact on our lives.'

We have a meeting in Aga Kitchen. Everyone wants to stop children looping, on bikes, from the front door, round the back, then through the Hall. Except Richard, and his veto wins. Until George rides into me carrying cups of hot tea, hurts me, gets himself scalded - and the kids stop anyway.

Another issue is that the children are watching too much TV (I think it was just since this summer, that we have allowed TV back into our lives.) They are getting too much commercialism/ sexism. On the other hand, they probably do need to be aware of what other children are watching. We want to move the TV from Morning Room to Shelves Room. Except Richard, who likes the set where it is. So it stays. That's consensus?

To me it's Richard, obstinately preventing change. But you can't be cross with Richard. That's the system.

The children pass around impetigo, which all kids are more or less bound to do. Someone bought a brand-new cash-box. Tut tut. There are more trips away. Julia to Throssel again, Richard to somewhere I've forgotten, Catriona to somewhere she doesn't like. Jon and Mike to Cambridge, getting paid a tiny sum to give a lecture on Communal Living to some social science students. Alice, accompanied by Dave, to Glasgow to teach people how to run a playgroup (some of us think that's quite funny).

Mixcaff Diary, 14th November: The Billiard Room Transport Collective sub-group agreed that the only realistic solution to the problem of the broken Land Rover is World Peace - this is all quite logical, really - abandonment of all weaponry; the house shrinking; more land; recycling all waste; everyone shitting in the Elsan; telepathic communication; friendship if possible, otherwise at least tolerance of our past and current lovers' lovers.

The PO pins up a quote he must have thought was apt:

"There are a few nearly universal signs that a house is going through a low period:
"The house is unusually messy, breakfast dishes stay piled in the sink.
"Note-writing replaces personal communication
"People spend more time in their rooms
"Sometimes no-one signs up to cook
"When there are guests, some people feel like strangers in their own house

"Sub-groups mean others start to feel left out

"People privately think of leaving and may tell outside friends not to mention this."

(Adapted from "Changes In The City," Communities Magazine #5).

The Billiard Room gang finally returned to the Old Kitchen.

Mixcaff Diary records: November 29. Believeitornot, I think we are now, suddenly, worse off than last Winter - when we had the hep.

We have no communal focus whatever. Billiard Room - so firmly supported by everybody as the place to be - stays empty, the Jotul unlit except for visitors. We are in disarray. Jay bickers with Les (but is happy with Alice B.) Les is holding up, just. Jonathan's unhappy about Alice B. Patrick projects 'happy-go-lucky;' actually, he's uptight as anything. Tina agrees with everyone. Carol is not wanting be with us in any positive way - just wants to stay away from Dave.

The Old Kitchen is uneconomic, unworkable, horrible. The Aga Kitchen is hardly a social centre. Nurses' Dining Room - how quaint that name sounds now - is deserted. Catriona's room is full of beautiful things but is not best placed to be a centre.

Meanwhile MixCaff is frequented by assorted derelicts in search of warmth.

The sunsets are formidable.

31
Winter 1975/76

On December 3rd - Tina's 34th birthday - we talked about More People Joining. 'Organic growth,' some people say they'd accept. Meaning, slow, but unpredictable.The PO objects to this usage. 'Organic,' he points out,' 'can mean speedy, like the population of lemmings, or white blood cells in my father's bone marrow.' (Mike's Dad has leukaemia).

'Alternatively, entirely regulated. Like the way, an acorn becomes an oak. Influenced OK by sun, moon, wind, rain, soil and so forth - but essentially accordingly to plan.'

So 'organic growth,' the PO sums up, regarding LH membership, 'is not necessarily a friendly image. In our case, I'd rather have lemmings.'

(This new phrase 'organic gardening', meaning no use of chemicals, was something else.)

I find I have no memory of Christmas 1975. (Strange, that, how memory works better the farther back you go). But it was, my notes say, another Laurieston-only family do, with a turkey, raised by Bridget, and the works. Plus avocados, cashews and other luxuries. Still in Billiard room. And I do recall ten huge Xmas trees, standing in tea chests, in the hall, courtesy of Jonathan.

There is, at least, a wonderful (if incomplete) group photo.

We would then have done the necessary. Family trips. Everyone away to parents.

We still had another flood of friends and visitors, including another band to use the drums and amps.

And on Hogmanay I played with Taloola at The Cosmo Ballroom, Carlisle. With (and here, Reader, is my brush with the seriously famous) Billy J. Kramer headlining. Actually he was too old, and we were more popular. (It was a similar deal when Ryder had played opposite Desmond Dekker in the Drill Hall, Dumfries.)

Very much later that night, I was dancing 8-some reels at Kilquhanity. I don't know how I got there or who drove. But then, I'm a rockstar, big in Carlisle. Can't keep up with everything.

But I do know I was sober enough to scribble, before falling asleep at about 8 a.m.: "I'm Frightened. Lonely. Ignored. Isolated."

'You bring these things on yourself, Michael.' You said. This is the sort of, supposedly comforting, bullshit you have started to say.

Despite icy gales, no more beeches fall in the drive. But they brought down the ash in the "new field"- which is what the would-be cow-people are now calling the big lawn between the stables and the pond - now being fenced off. Jay having found strong oak corner posts from the forestry.

And the big sycamore was felled. (Well, OK, actually, I helped do that. As I'd been taught. You make a preliminary V-cut on the side you want the tree to fall. Then you cut into the opposite side, slightly above. The tree's own weight does the rest.) (Mick Reid, trees felled, call +44)

We occasionally glimpse deer, tip-toeing down from the forest, hungry for grass. Buzzards watch us saw up the ash and the sycamore. Golden eagles overfly Grobdale: the PA saw one, just the once. A big bird, indeed.

It is surely cold. "Bitter, rock hard weather," writes Jonathan.

Julia describes her days off from Lybro's: "Late to rise. Loathe to face this dash from bed to last night's clothes, the rushed, shivery dressing. Then Land Rovering to fetch wood; cutting logs for communal fires; making smaller pieces and snapping kindling for my own fire. Playing with children, maybe cooking. Afternoons, any of several varieties of coping. After supper, looking for meaning in erratic woodfire flames and smoke."

"Several varieties of coping." Maybe we are all going barmy?

Jonathan in Mixcaff diary writes: "January. It's hardly worth calling this a 'new' year, now that each year resembles the one before."

Days of drizzle and sub-daylight: barn owl days.

Mixcaff Diary, January 2nd. A day late, Mike posted some Resolutions (in Old Kitchen, where else?):

"(1) I'm quitting Billiard Room Living Group (which doesn't even seem to exist anymore.)

"(2) I'm going to be based in Mix Café.

"(3) In fact, I'm leaving Laurieston Hall Group. I'll still be living here, but I'm aiming to:

    (i) Take my name off the bank account (be like Lesley and Jay)

    (ii) Withdraw my capital - pro-rata to what's left - (be like Tim and Bridget)

    (iii) Lose the hassle of endless meetings (be like Liz n' Arthur, Neill n' Rosie, long-stay visitors like Jim R., Linda and Flick A.).

    (iv) Get some agreements clear about earning a living.

"(4) Crazy Mick's Imaginary Living Group is open to new members. Potentially, everyone. Book, or just drop in.

"(5) I'd like to talk with any/ all of you about this."

"PLEASE REACT."

In fact, I don't do any of these things (except cook in Mix Café, sporadically). This writing was meant to be a seriously good joke - leave the group, but start another, only do it right.

The PA, while now clearly mad, was in fact quite cheerful. But any Samaritan would have seen this as 'a cry for help.'

Others might have seen it as Mike crying wolf. Perhaps everyone had their own, painful pre-occupations, and were hardly in a state to pay attention to the PA at this point, spewing out, as he was, failure this, disaster that, start all over here, let's all move somewhere else there.

Only Catriona came to talk. The PA was becoming quite fond of Catriona. Tina, the well-known, sought-after, feminist poet, says of her: 'she's actually got a much better figure than Lesley.'

This was, obviously, Ideological Purist Mike, reluctant to be in the same income sharing group as Bourgeois, Individualist, Middle Class Consumer, Paul.

Or, perhaps better: it was Isolated, Depressive Mike, lacking support, who couldn't tolerate a Living Group which called this 'your argument with Paul' rather than 'our' argument.

Or a group lacking rules (or at least budgets) about spending money. So that we bickered endlessly about what was OK and what was not. But on a new scale. Paul's brand-new engine for the Ami - not £250, but £400, I ask you. When, about this time, Dave bought a perfectly fine, fully working, car - OK, OK, a Moskvitch, what's the problem? for £50. But Paul the Architect has to have his Ami.

A group which also, without a murmur, lets Paul buy a radial-arm saw, 'vital for the Building Project' - for £317. What Building Project, wonders the PO. (Also, what is a 'radial arm saw?') (And why is it still unused, boxed in its original packing, 18 months later?).

Or a group which had clocked up a breathtaking £990 of kitty loss (making a farce out of trying to keep accounts). (Although Catriona had now taken on managing the cash box and would fiercely nag people to fill in the cash book.)

A group which made three car trips to CD today and one to Kirkcudbright. We'd have thought four trips a week excessive at first. I'd like not to feel so bad like this, so often.

And a group which doesn't make its living, given that Paul, and fair enough, has stopped working in Glasgow. So that the bank manager is upset because we have an un-authorised overdraft.

And this despite Freefall hosting more Mearns, Milton Tongs and

219

Craigmillars and the erstwhile Billiard Room lot saying 'at least we're earning something.' (Yeah, thinks the Accountant. That's 3 groups x 8 kids x 2 days @ £2.20/ day is £106. Less, say 40% costs - food, petrol, overheads and so forth - leaves £63. For 7 people, each claiming 6 days' work. Do the sums!)

And even though Tim, Richard and Catriona go mussel-picking again (but realise the money they make hardly pays for the petrol. End of project.)

And even with Catriona joining Julia at Lybro's. Which she soon stops, realising it's not worth the candle. (Julia perhaps likes the chat.)

And while the Smallholders, apparently, meet repeatedly, but without ever once talking about income, expenses or budgets. (Let alone 'protein accounting,' another matter raised by the PO. Example, is feeding grain to poultry, to boost egg-laying, a good use of protein?).

Or a group in which Bridget and Tim (their own capital still intact) ask for (a) £360 for Bridget to set up a pottery and (b) £200 to buy a cow.

The Accountant thinks (a) 'How much return will they produce?' and (b) Are you fucking joking?

Bridget anyway spends her own money and starts building a kiln in the stables.

'I'm defeated by the power of Bridget's cheque book,' wrote Jay. 'Of all the knives I lie on, the sharpest is Tim and Bridget.' (So the PO is not entirely a lone dissenting voice.)

"Lying on knives": one of several varieties of not coping.

Our faces have the worn look of hosts waiting for the last visitor to leave the party. Except, we all live here. We are the party.

"The truth is not the truth unless it is alive," writes another long-stay visitor, Mike S. Dramatically, but not helpfully. We are plainly alive (he had recently burst in on me in bed with Les and Alice B.). Does he simply mean, we don't have the truth? We know that, thank you. Silly fucker, we conclude. Wrongly, because there was a true emotional note, there.

And Katrina G., staying with us for a month, printing fabrics in Craft Room, says: "I wish very much that you could find some way to love and get in tune with each other because otherwise you are just suffocating each other and it is very sad to watch."

Or a group which, when Trev H., an energetic and inspiring man, crucial to the formation of People In Common, dies tragically in a motorcycle accident, dares not say to Dave and Alice, who are to go to the funeral, look. You know we've agreed that long distance car trips are only for those taking kids.

Because of course, they wanted the Ami. So the Accountant objects.

Predictably, Alice demands: 'How can you say that at a time like this?'

Which confirms my view: hard as nails, that woman. It's a class thing. But it seems the group agrees, or at least does not demur: 'One simply cannot hitch to a funeral.'

In retrospect, I wonder if Lady Alice, Alice Palace, ever hitched anywhere? (It would be completely mind-blowing, Alice, dear heart, if you were to suddenly hitch here.)

A group which continues to ignore Tina's best advice: writing the weekly collective poem. Which is just not happening...

In fact, Mixcaff bookings flow in. For a little while, people seem to enjoy the notion of a new kitchen/ new company. Maybe I've hit a marketing nerve? Certainly I wasn't cut off.

Monday 5th Jan '76: Tina and Julia - lunch. Later, referring to herself, and suddenly strong, Julia wrote "Who was the pedantic fool who came to eat with you today? Delicious lunch though. Time that woman joined a commune in S.W.Scotland and stopped thinking about how not to think! And talking about how not to talk!"

But soon after this, she retreated totally, again. Was seen at snatched meals in Aga Kitchen or tending the propagation beds. 'It's important the plants are looked after.' (No, Jools, it's important the people are looked after.)

Tuesday 6th, Rich, Kate B., Bridget, Tim. (We argued, without getting anywhere.)

Wednesday 7th, Joel will cook Kids Tea. (Dave brought Tiff and Tam - and he'd obligingly soldered up a lead to connect an old cassette player to my antique amp. We had music for tea!)

Friday 9th, Jon, Pat, Catriona.

Sunday 11th, Pete M., Tina. (Pete. M., a potential joiner, had brought a kids group, then come back on his own, then sent his wife, Avis M., and now was back on his own account again.)

We talked abstractly about the state of play. So many fires burning round the house.

'If we ever make the Radical Commune here at LH,' the PA mutters, 'then in January there will of course be only one communal evening blaze. Winter vegetable stew will predominate. Plus winter salad, pickles, chutneys, served with whole wheat. I still think Sunny Room would be favourite. Dry wood, dry wine. Scrabble. Old photographs. Crocheting home-spun wool (which I sometimes do).'

In February, Norman announces:

"Dear Folks, we've spent as much on coal in the last six months as we spent in the whole of last year. So I thought I'd let the Hydresse out for 36 hours, to see how we cope without constant hot water.

"You can subvert this plan by (a) stoking the Hydresse yourself or (b) rushing to take a bath this p.m. or when it comes back on; that's up to you.

"Love, Norman Normal (stores clerk and official bore, Mix Café)."

Now you are seriously depressed. So I have to be the one, although we are hardly speaking, who looks after you through your flu, coil, migraine, boyfriend problems, co-communard problems (and later, girlfriend problems). Spells you when you are just too tired to take on the kids. Whereas you…never mind.

So this time, as I'm feeling down, you vapourise for a couple of weeks, I have no idea where to. But you were writing, writing (to and about Pat):

"Jealousy is absolutely wanting something that you absolutely can't get by yourself for yourself.

"It is a sudden swift seeing-for-the-first-time that intangible things to do with another person are necessary to your (well-)being.

"And the simultaneous seeing that those things may not be there anymore."

Jonathan is busy with turf heaps. Richard and Les, with pigs, house maintenance. Patrick and Jay, gardening. Bridget and Tim, goats. Dave, Jay and Pat, fencing the new field (we have not yet agreed to buy a cow, but a fenced field will make that decision easier, n'est-ce pas?) Also, the fencing costs plenty, no-one has agreed this, but then, who gives a shit anymore, the Accountant wonders. Aloud, but talking to himself.

Carol hides out up at Grobdale. I have forgotten what's her problem. Children visit from Greenock and Craigmillar.

Then Patrick and Tina are ill. And Jay, Rich and Julia are away. Then Meg and Jon are ill.

Then, the diary notes 'Flick A. has gone.'

'It is damp, misty, mild,' Jon notes, gloomily.

Nigel visits a lot. Reader - he's Meg's husband, remember? Do try to keep up. He's working as a nurse in A&E at a hospital in Glasgow. I love this story:

There's a throwback Sister who wants to address him as 'Nurse Potter,' rather than 'Nigel.'

'Excuse me, Sister,' says Nigel, 'if we're being formal, that should be Nurse Doctor Potter.' Because he has a Ph.D.

And she can't bring herself to call him that. So he gets called, Nigel: setting a precedent, changing the culture.

A good-looking fellow, is Nigel. Sometimes wears the kilt.

Jonathan would sit himself squarely on the bentwood chair in Mixcaff: tired, muddy boots planted on the floor, baggy trousers. Jon the rustic. Yet sometimes with the schoolboy grin, hair falling over his face. Exhausted a lot.

(Alternatively, once, bursting in to interrupt a Mixcaff supper with: 'Latest News from the Eurovision song contest! Oom bah-bah, bah-bah! Oom bah-bah, bah-bah! Oom shana nah-nah - woop woop!')

He was preoccupied with the "Laurieston Wild Flower Guide," which I understood was to be a saga of the horticulture, agriculture, silviculture and communard culture of S.W. Scotland and somehow involving our visitors; versus the Multinationals, their pesticides and Farmer Henty. I might have not got that quite right. A new marriage, at least, of magic and science. At the moment, we are very short on both.

"Coltsfoot in flower," he noted, "nettles 2 inches, comfrey 3. First yellow catkins, Feb 29th."

And I would ponder an image of LH as its own solar system. The house itself - the sun - some explosive but unapproachable idea. The rest of us zooming around it in elliptical orbits, now close to one person, now to another - but all of us flung into deep, dark, cold space on a regular basis.

Dave planned to hold another 'Land' conference at Easter and put out newsletters and - new idea - included his mailing list with it, which helped networking. Enthusiastic bookings flowed in.

Tim finished his really substantial chicken house, behind the garden, beneath the biggest Wellingtonia. But then - to draw attention to issues he's not happy with - our lack of decision-making processes - he says: "I intend to withdraw my labour." A masterstroke! Does he imagine we are his employers? Presumably this means we are just simply expected to feed him for nothing? Which, of course, being hippie-idiots, we actually do, for many, many months.

Alice pins up what she calls her 'political philosophy.' Bless.

"I feel more drawn towards us managing to work through our differences, towards living more harmoniously, productively and out-goingly, than I do towards working towards any particular political philosophy.

"I would like us to listen to each other more, accept each other more - then possibly decisions would arise by group consensus."

The PA is inclined to invite you, Reader, to imagine the PO's response. You might begin with:

"Mike hopes we will never work though our differences, as he wants to live in permanent animosity, hating everyone, producing nothing and being completely introverted."

And to think of the time Tina and I and others (well, Jay and maybe Jon, a bit) have put into trying to explain: Listen! Argue! Fun! Spark! Chew the fat! Discuss! Help us all find the truth!

Alice just never got it. Never worked through a difference I can remember.

"I don't think it's productive to push my views or listen to anyone else pushing theirs."

Yes dear. This is Alice in a strange space, a sort of goddess-feminist thing - oh enough, already. I can't be arsed. Alice, you'll have to write your own book.

Alice blathers on, but three things spring out, as Alice reviews the last, sorry year:

"We've decided to postpone charging for Lothlorien." 'Who are We,' demands the Accountant? 'Do you mean, Paul is working for nothing?'

(Yes she did, and he was.)

"We've had Mike deciding to leave the group." Well sort of, Alice - you can't even be bothered to read what I'm saying.

"And we've had Meg in hospital and Sophie in Hospital." Tina scribbled "she noticed!" on this, just in time to prevent me from hallucinating.

Tim and Bridget finished building their own kitchen on the top floor of West Wing. And Paul was frantically finishing Platform Room. Which is a good, creative use of space, is has to be said. After all, he is an architect. Just not an anarchitect.

I spent the end of March - for the first time in my life - seriously ill. I had two weeks of flu (all this time, I never knew why those lazy fuckers didn't just get out of bed, get on with it.)

Then my right testicle swelled up: more scary than actually painful. Western allopathic medicine sorted it fast, I'm once again happy to acknowledge.

Meanwhile it was back to Plan A. We all live together in Old Kitchen having, for the moment, come full circle.

32

The Capital.
We were skint. And a couple of visitor groups had cancelled - losing us the income. The only money left was the Capital, which was consequently under some pressure.

Dave wrote four pages of "Proposals" for the Capital.

None of it should be spent on living (including stuff like cars, house maintenance). We should give away 10% of it per year. And also set aside money for known projects like first stage of the stables; major house repairs; Small-Holding; Kids and Craft projects; costs of setting up as a housing association. So, no building project then, Dave? An oversight, obviously…

The PA agrees with most of this. But notes, again, that it's none of Dave's money.

The collective fails to meet, let alone discuss stuff,

And Alice offers two close-typed pages which really boil down to one idea - divvying up the capital and giving it to specific individuals to look after. For example to Mike (no specific project) and Paul (Building Project and/or stables)

(Mike's view is still that it could all be for any purpose - but that projects should bid for amounts which - because they've thought it through - they can show they can repay. Perhaps Mike was a banker in a previous existence?.)

And You Have Multiple?
Alan C., passing through, sees "a lot of that old Couple Project thing here." But Jay, returning from a holiday with Alice B., let it be known that they were now 'like brother and sister.' Now where have I heard that before?

It turns out - says Radio Gossip - that, before joining us, Meg had demanded Paul full-time for three months. None of that sharing with Alice. So that, apparently, was finally the end of Paul and Alice. Leaving Alice at a loose end.

Radio Gossip also relayed apparent crushes. Richard for Bridget, Jay for Bridget, Tim for Lesley, Tim for Alice, Mike for Carol, Julia for Pete. M., Catriona for Rich. The PO has no idea where these suggestions originated.

Tina was, I think you might call it, wrestling with Patrick. She won. Pat finished his relationship with Linda G - who then needed a lift to Dumfries. Tina drove her there. It could only happen at Laurieston.

(Actually you wrote a very funny, if acerbic, open letter to Linda G. Saying Patrick is quite scrupulous in his follow-up. But has a rather heavy case-load. You mention Mary, Rika, Carmen. I think: gosh, is that all he's managed? Because he leers scratchily - and surely, attractively - at every passable visiting woman.)

And the PA could hardly expect Lesley to be a permanent lover, since he was still sleeping with his wife. On and off. More off than on. Unless he split with the wife? He intermittently considered that. But of course the reason he wasn't available was that, perhaps foolishly, he was still hoping that Patrick would fuck off and die - or at least, just have a major heart attack. Leaving the PA free to talk with Tina about their future together. To, er, become a couple again. Get us all out of this mess.

How Do You Get On With The Locals?
We are often still accused, I think that's the word, of "not having much interaction with the locals."

This will always be from a townie, often an academic, who does not, in fact, even know his/her own neighbours. And by now, we have understood. All visitors ask themselves: could I live like these people - maybe join them? And when they think, No way! - they will need to find fault. As if we'd have, them, anyway.

So we just say, 'how true.'

Because, fair enough, all we do is use the local shops, garages, cash n' carries and the local fleapit. Drink in the village pub. Go first-footing in the village. Give talks to the Women's Rural, the WI. Send the children to school (though maybe not for much longer). Run the Youth Club. Sell garden produce. Chat to the local police.

Then Richard is in the sea-fishing club. Carol Paul and Jay do local design work. We have extensive contacts with Lothlorien, Kilquhanity, Woodfoot while it lasted, Ed & Val, the Dumfries Social Work Department, George Thompson MP, the Anti-Tritium Action Campaign (ATAC), the Scots Campaign to be Rid of the Nuclear Menace (SCRAM), Dumfries Youth Centre, the Rotary in CD (who raised money for the Belfast children to visit), the CD Health Centre,

Dumfries R.I. and a Dumfries band called Taloola.

No, that's right, really, very little to do with the local area.

You're Not Self-Sufficient?
We have a new deal with the Forestry Commission: we are free to roam the

Laurieston forest and extract dead wood. The assumption here is that eco-costs of the petrol and the Land Rover are more than covered by the wood fuel gained. The Accountant would be interested to see the detailed calculations. But details are there none.

And Multiple, Er, Do You Have?

On a north-wind, freezing night, Richard and Lesley went together to Dougie's leaving party at Ullioch. Mike, playing with Taloola in Glasgow, came home to find Lesley, who had always welcomed him into her bed even at three or four in the morning - not there.

Rich had always referred to Lesley, in his extensive ramblings in Mixcaff diary, as "your girlfriend." Mike had always sniffed a somewhat salacious aroma in the way he said that.

And so, all-of-a-sudden, Rich was calling her "my new girlfriend." Or simply "Les." Nothing if not upfront, Richard. And Lesley took up feeding the pigs.

Actually, Rich, you checked it out with me, didn'tcha? And I would have said, fine. Because it was always going to happen (Lesley knew that even though you maybe didn't). I didn't 'mind' (in the English sense). It was easy to see Lesley as your lover.

It made a change to the Molly situation. Before, when Moll woke in the night, crying fit to bust, it would often be me - because Jay and Les were rowing (point-scoring) - who would go and comfort her, put her back to bed. Or, if that didn't work, bring her into my bed, with Lesley - or without. (Call the lawyers!)

But suddenly Jay, still fighting, and now perceiving Lesley as "hiding behind Richard" (instead of behind me) will always be on the alert. When Moll cries, he'll snatch her up and dump her over into Richard's room, Teapot, whenever Les was sleeping with Rich. (Molly. Pawn. Chess Game. Not good.)

33
Spring 1976

April 1st was cold. "Now in April it is still Winter," Jonathan noted. I'd slept alone for about the millionth time, Tina being with Pat and Lesley with Richard. Next morning, without a word to anyone, I packed a rucksack, picked up the sax and left, finally, for the first time. I hitched down to Dumb Toms, fully intending to stay there.

This is when you turned up, talked me down, fetched me home and promised we'd leave together, just us and J&S, in the Autumn.

I do realise now, that would all have come from heavying you about kids, responsibilities - I can easily make you feel guilty, hmm? When what I should have been doing, was not nagging, but wooing you.

What a complete fucking idiot I was. If I'd just once said, 'I love you!'

Back at the ranch - Spring was noisy and energetic, if chaotic. Bright, cold Spring days, with a percussive sound-track of hammers, bow-saws, spades, pots and pans. Mike's typewriter clatter in Mix Café. Electric guitar from the top of the tower. Bird calls. Heated discussion in Big Front Room - for example, workers from BIT in London having their own 'crisis conference.' Kids playing on the inflatable. Pigs squealing to be fed. Shouts, wailing and car doors slamming as Meg, who had fallen and, it turns out, broken her wrist, is driven off to the Infirmary. That woman has no luck at all.

We host Land Week, another Dave spectacular and it's quite productive: visitors finish chain-sawing the fallen sycamore, trim the ash. Neighbour Davey Mair, with his tractor, drags the tree stumps clear of the new field, then chain-harrows it (apart from the oats, sprouting in its sunny corner.)
Freefall ran more-or-less continuously. We had the usual suspects (Milton, Craigmillar, Mearns, Weavers' Field) plus young adult males from the Sir John Hunt school.

And the PeopleCentre - in Old Kitchen - had a Gingerbread group, and several women-with-kids groups, for example from Maryhill in Glasgow, and Calderbank and Rochdale from North Lancs. The Rochdale women painted a fine mural.

All this activity was enough to re-establish, pro tem, the Billiard Room Group, now including Catriona and Carol, as the renamed 'East End.' While the 'West End' retreated back to the Aga kitchen. Richard, one of its members, says "I hear we are called by some the Bourgeois Capitalist Pigs and sometimes it feels like it."

Trips away - mostly, un-announced - were by now ubiquitous. Your PO is included here - commuting to Lancaster Uni and Dumb Tom's. And wanting Lesley to come stay and impress the snotty undergraduates - she never did.

Alice and Dave had a long honeymoon trip, I think we might call it, away to London. Partly to attend a "non-political" conference about Land. (How can that be?) Returning, Alice says she will work in London in the Autumn, temp-secretary-ing (but this never happens).

Tim and Bridget went on a possibly goat-related trip to Wales, was it? The Accountant simply remembers that the Land Rover failed on them on their way back and we had to rescue both it and them at a cost of hundreds.

Carol fled away again, possibly staying with Keith C., maybe doing yoga, somewhere near Dumb Tom's. Julia flew, once more, to Throssel Hole Priory.

Richard and Kate B. went on holiday to Portugal. Lesley, natch, will briefly return to Mike to show two can play at that game. In fact, she'll complain: 'It's really nice being with Richard, but it isn't very sexual.'

And Mike will say, 'That's a shame.' While thinking, if thoughts can have triple-f: 'She's complaining! To me! About sex!'

In my occasional Diary, I wrote: May 2nd: Mixcaff:

Woke with Les. She went to see to Molly.

Sophie came, said Joel wanted me. Thought Joel's mumps troubling him, but he just wanted to ask about his dream.

Chatted w. J & S for a while about cosmos, planets, moon. Also, how do plants work, exactly? Magic time.

Jonathan has finished curing tobacco crop.

Still eating swede salad, swede stew, swede pudding. Last of the dried broad beans.

Julian G. rang to talk about Anti Tritium Action Campaign (ATAC). Tritium heavy isotope of hydrogen, needed for H-bomb. Proposed plant, Chapelcross, near Annan. Chapelcross, made-up name. Cynical powers-that-be.

Catriona: Kitty loss is £50/week.

Joel OK. Late birthday party. Alice gave him Sonya's fishing rod. Girls don't fish, boys don't crochet. But Joel happy.

Fucked w. Tina, p.m.

First day, Galloway Food Co-op. About 10 callers.

Edinburgh Theatre Group still here.

Meeting about Work. Tim shouted.

10.40 p.m. Rain, gloom, nothing happening. Drinking home-made, smoking last of dope, writing this.

Then Jon called in. Tina turned up looking for tobacco. Carol, too. Mini social scene.

1.30 a.m. Must write to Sue C.

In May, I felt better. We had Spring, at last. Other people were doing the summer bookings (for Women's week, Communes Network, A.S.Neill, Alt. Socialists, Gingerbread, Rochdale Women).

And do we multiply? Robbie, Meg and Paul's son, was born. Toot toot tarah.

In leafy June, Jon wrote: "The people are lonely. No blame."

Mike wrote - Diary again:

PeopleCentre Group - dead.

Alice quarrelled w. Dave. "Shouldn't have a Work Collectives conference until we have our own Work Collective."

Too right, we shouldn't. But Conference now fixed for December.

Communal parenting not happening.

Dave bought a hydraulic jack. £76. Says 'It works really well.' I bet it does. I predict we will use it about four hours a year. What the hell, thinks the Accountant. We are in the black.

Patchily but unmistakeably the Group finds new energy. Students and staff visit from Bradford's School of Peace Studies; and more kids from Weavers' Field. We make hay for Farmer Gordon and Farmer Henty. There are trips to Annan to support ATAC. Robin Cook, no less, makes a stirring speech. 'You're happy now, aren't you?' says Lesley, seeing me being a political activist. I think: you don't understand at all.

34

So Do You Have Meetings, To Sort Things Out?
I wrote:
"The situation is that Meetings have broken down completely.

They are sporadic. Not everyone comes - always some are ill, some away, some unable to face meetings as they have been, some just not bothered. It's rare we start on time. People come late. And we never finish - we simply fade out. Usually, late in the evening, when we're too tired to think straight.

"Meetings are held in rooms which have no relation to anyone's daily lives - in particular, lacking all the information (letters, accounts, books) we might want to call on.

"Most times we sit so that there are those 'in the circle' and those outside it. People bring sewing or knitting, to hide behind.

"We do not know how to start a meeting properly. In particular all the bad vibes between people get suppressed only to resurface later when we 'really get going,' thus wasting everyone's time. The general feeling of meetings is a quicksand of apathy, boredom, depression or hysteria. Sometimes people walk out in a rage. Sometimes they amble out as if they have come to the wrong room in the first place.

"Although we could meet every day for years and talk about really important things (feelings, money, children, projects, relationships, politics…) we fill up the agenda with trivia.

"The level and pattern of discussion are variously chaotic, childish, irresponsible, repetitious.

"We lack a way of structuring discussion so that, very often, the 'conch', as they say, is up for grabs. Sometimes we degenerate into classic, dogmatic, male-chauvinist-pig ways - and I don't just mean the men. Interruptions are frequent. The last meeting I was at, four out of five contributions - I counted - were interruptions. In other words, despite all the rhetoric about being open, trusting, caring, responsive: we are simply not very good at listening. Then there are those who rarely speak. The tyranny of structurelessness applies.

"Increasingly, people play the game of 'where's the manager?' Rather than call a meeting themselves, people talk as though their lives were run by some separate bureaucracy. Thus, 'shall we have a meeting' becomes 'have you heard anything about a meeting?'

("He's a laugh a minute, is Mike," was one comment.)

But Doesn't Your Being A PO Impact On The Community?
Aha. Hmm. OK then.

"Mike sits in Mixcaff," Patrick wrote, "throwing out pages of wonderful ideas, but people feel - how can he know what's going on?"

I wrote and I wrote. Partly, because it was my job. My student grant meant I was being paid to promote World Peace by, er, living my life here. I did also think I would reach and pull heartstrings, change minds, make a difference (but I was going about it the wrong way.)

So: I re-wrote The Aims.

Proposed that we make an all-out effort to transform ourselves.

Proposed asking outside friends to come and help us out of our stuckness.

Analysed money, income and capital in depth.

Suggested MIRACLE (Mixcaff Relationships Analyser and Communal Living Evaluator) - a sort of structured game to help sort out Living Groups.

Put forward ideas on How To Have A Meeting.

Laid out an overall structure for Project Groups. Advocated quite specific Mission, responsibilities, and time and money constraints for - deep breath here - the Building Project, Garden/ Smallholding, Freefall, PeopleCentre/ Events, General Visitors, Pottery and Crafts, House and Grounds, Vehicles, Stores and Purchasing, Finance and Accounts, Children and The Committee Of The Revolution Of The 24th May. Phew.

Oh, and I sneaked in some essays: "Taking The Kids Out Of School", "Dear Cow Meeting", "Becoming A Place Of Learning", "Improving Our Links With The Local Area" and "Adults And Children".

Not to mention several pages of stoned rambling about Living Groups/ Lifestyles. (Which I still think are slightly funny.)

And, lastly, I did a Situation Report for the P&CRP, to nail next year's grant.

Let's say I typed about 250 pages. With just one carbon copy. (Young Readers - ask your grand-dad.)

Looking back, I realise I was also reverting to my old job. Though self-appointed, I was doing consultancy. Especially, I was not particularly promoting my own ideas. Although I put in my own two-penn'orth, I was mainly structuring and sorting out everyone else's thoughts.

There was very little feedback to all of this - just some scribbled-on comments.

Forlorn wads of words. But people did read the stuff. Secretively. Took it to their rooms. Snuck it back on the hook. Some of it dribbled into our lives.

And How Do You Make A Living?

I wrote that people going out to work had always provided the main income. Paul, in particular. The PeopleCentre and Freefall had provided most of the rest. And we had relied on 'funny money' - cottage rents, bits of state benefit, money people earned before they joined.

But we had 'lived on capital' in the sense we had not really maintained the house, cars, machines, etc. We had made no provision for 'depreciation.'

"Surely it was obvious to everyone," the Accountant continued, "that with five extra adults, two extra children, and without Paul's Glasgow income we would be running into trouble."

And it was indeed obvious to everyone. But then, everyone had unshakeable excuses why they personally could not do anything different, certainly nothing more. The gardeners claimed the garden; others, illness or depression.

But as Spring went on, we remained just about solvent.

So Do You Ever?

Tina proposed a "Meeting About Work, but with no hassles - just general principles."

That Tina, what a sense of humour!

We begin late, but at least all sixteen of us are here. Straight away, Alice says this is too many and she wants to split into smaller groups, to have a quieter, more supportive atmosphere. Carol and Catriona agree. But lethargy wins. We stay as one big meeting, apart from Catriona, who leaves, in tears.

The PO, of course, again offers his stuff about work criteria and the various Project Groups. So we yawn for half an hour. Keeping pigs, for example. Did this 'blur the distinction between work and play?' Or 'Offer scope for creativity? Meet group needs? Help us relate better to each other?'

But then, Julia. It was said she was keeping all the propagation work to herself and otherwise doing nothing, spending the rest of her time alone or with Arthur, avoiding contact with other gardeners. We livelied up ourselves (as Bob Marley recommended).

Later, Jay talked a lot about individual as opposed to collective working. Mike runs with this for a bit and suddenly there is Tim, yelling at him: 'That's what makes me so mad.' Meeting ends (just as it's getting really interesting).

But over the next few evenings, Richard taped some interviews. (Yes! I know! Richard!.) So that the PO can unpick some threads:

"We always take so long to start" - Bridget, Lesley, Rich.

"Shame that Catriona left early" - Jon, Mike, Rich.

"The subject of the meeting was too big" - Rich.

"Good to talk down Mike's list of criteria" - Bridget, Lesley, Rich, Tina.

"It was good the thing about Julia and the propagation house came out" - Lesley, Rich.

"Some people are trying to force ideas down other people's throats" - Julia.

"There is a Garden Collective, if we see it. I don't want to be in a powerful position" - Julia.

"Communal work projects should be a group responsibility" - Lesley

"What was Jay on about?" - Jon

. "The meeting was typical, pretty horrific. My life here is becoming one of enormous lengths of silence punctuated by incoherent rage. What I don't like is that what is going on is not what is in the words. There is something else going on, behind the words. The words are levers or tools for that thing. It just produces rage in me" - Tim.

"I was totally unprepared for Tim's anger and frustration" - Bridget (Jay, Jon, Mike said something similar).

"It was a good meeting and I felt speedy and positive after it" - Lesley.

"I'd like another meeting" - Julia.

"We need to work out how people can express themselves without it devastating other people" - Jon.

"The field is sitting out there, waiting." - Jon

So Do You Ever?

Suddenly we have a flurry of meetings. Spring energy. Down to business. We confirmed that Pete M. could join. And that Julian, who we are seeing a lot of, with all the ATAC meetings, could return to the stables, in his famous caravan and convert a corner into living space.

Catriona's friends Jamie and Liz can visit. Lee C. can come and stay again. Linda is OK to stay indefinitely, spending half her time 'being here' and half 'working outside,' paying £1.75 a day.

And in an Education meeting, following Tina's clear proposal last Autumn - we agreed, seriously, we would de-school the children. That is, not send them back to the village school this autumn. See what the authorities throw at us.

What's more, we talked about each of our children's specific situation and needs. Like communal parents should. Bill, George, Joel, Molly, Polly, Sonya, Sophie, Tam, Tiffany.

Angus, Bridget and Tim made it clear, would still be going to the village school. Such a weird choice we made, in inviting them to join.

Robbie, at one month, was bouncing along.

Julia chose this rather powerful moment to announce she'll be leaving, with Arthur, early in August, to live up at Lothlorien. We must have looked appalled.

'But, no,' she says, 'It won't affect the de-school idea. This'll still be Bill and George's home.'

We can be charitable and imagine she meant this. But it wasn't going to happen.

The Capital - Endgame.

We eventually agreed, regarding the capital, that part should be set aside as an emergency fund, for unexpected big bills or to help people leaving. Some could be spent on more land. Or, as Tim put it, 'on anything with no social cost, which we should all have fair shares of.' He means, "after the revolution."

The rest could be loaned to projects provided they have a worked-out way of repaying the loan and it's clear who the people involved are. In each 'Project Collective.' Dave proposed an ingenious inflation-related repayment scheme.

Bridget and Tim still didn't pay their money in.

Then on April 11th, seven people - Dave, Jay, Alice, Julia, Catriona, Lesley and Jon - less than half the group - met and decided to take £1500 from the Capital to cover various project expenses and to set aside £1000 for the Building Project. The Accountant thinks: 'Excuse me?'

No plans, no repayments were envisaged. The money would, in part, cover setting up the Housing Association framework: "Dave will ask David Sainty" - our local solicitor - "to register Laurieston Hall Housing Co-operative." But what will our 'rules' say?

But instead, almost immediately, and for the first time, money is drawn from the Capital account for us to live on. This was to be seen as loan to Lothlorien to enable them to pay us Paul's and Dave's wages. The Accountant, apoplectic, disbelieving - did however countersign the cheque. He was cross, but not enough to ignore the will of the Group.

Then in May, Jonathan paid an inherited £500 into the Capital. The Smallholders immediately buy a new and bigger Versatiller 'out of Jon's money.' Mike is speechless.

And in the end, Julia, preparing to leave, wants her capital out.

'But you were always clearest,' we rebuked her, 'yours was pooled?'

'Well it was, while I was here. But since we haven't used it and like Paul says, not everyone has paid theirs in and I need it.' Quite so, Julia.

So finally the Accountant works out everyone's share of the unspent Capital and - although this will take some time to happen - it is paid out, to Alice, Paul, Mike, Tina and Catriona. End of story.

Julia spends her share on a caravan. She'll have to wait for her share of money-in-the-house. There is again talk of setting up a "Maxi-Co-op" which will own ours and other communal properties and be big enough to act like an alternative building society. This never happens.

And Do You Ever?
There were a couple of Smallholders meetings - these had continued all Winter - which made new efforts to clarify what they were doing. Unsuccessfully, thinks the PO. They never talk about Time. Costs. Income. Paul, Dave and Richard reconvened the Building project and Dave wrote a long set of minutes about their proposed Aims and Objects. Brilliant. But it just doesn't happen.

We had 11 meetings of the PeopleCentre Collective in May and June - usually, brief, business-like meetings, held straight after lunch. Tina and Patrick wrote about Integrating The Kids Project With Our Lives. Dave wrote a PeopleCentre Newsletter. Patrick, a long and thoughtful piece about our directions and activities. Your PO, thoughts about continuing the Anti-University. Apparently he wants to be Professor of Rock and Roll.

Rich, always late, joins these meetings. Says nothing, but is somehow licenced not to do so.

So, Do You Ever?
We had one of the best People meetings we ever had. The invitation said IDLE group meeting. Come if you are Idle, Depressed, Lonely, or Exhausted.

The Agenda was: Some Problems:
1. A lot of people thinking a lot of others have a cushy number round here.
2. The tensions between childcare and work; high- and low-earning projects; money-earning and maintenance work; office workers and gardeners/ smallholders; the idle depressed and the neurotically active.
3. The entirely unresolved aspects of avoiding sex-role typing.
4. People feeling they can never take time off.
5. Our insufficient income.
We gabbled into the night.

And Multiple?
I wrote to John H: "I am getting on fine with Tina., but am a bit distant from Lesley, who is carrying on with Richard who, however, has been on holiday with Kate B. in Portugal just now.

The PA is deceiving himself, there. Though sleeping sporadically - what fun that is - with both Les and Tina, the PA actually doesn't have a future with either, but doesn't see this.

And Do You Have Multiple?

You will say that instead of wooing you - offering you something you might actually like to come back to - all I did was threaten - I don't know what - pain, probably for you, me and the children.

I know I should never have spoken of rights, duties, promises - but I expect I managed to make you feel guilty for still screwing with Patrick. Perhaps, all the time.

On the other hand - if you had any feelings for me, they were surely hidden.

Now in September, 1977 - with writing about the past sort of catching up on me - I am still crying myself to sleep. I am still terrified of living without you. Although that is obviously going to be the situation. You being with Jay.

We will meet, talk about the kids, and maybe sleep uncomfortably in the same bed, with a fuck out of the question.

And Multiple?

There was just you, Catriona, and me. In the caff.

You told me you'd seen someone really hurt by an affair when you were fourteen and how that had left you frightened of getting into a relationship. So you didn't want our friendship to 'go sexual.'.

Then you went to bed while I sat up, getting drunk and feeling sorry for myself (again).

You'd been a friend for months and suddenly it seemed silly that I couldn't come and cuddle up to you. So I carried a candle into your room, which woke you up. And I asked to sleep with you: you said OK. We hugged and stroked each other.

And so - ignoring what you'd said earlier, and by now feeling amorous - I reached to touch you. But you froze. So I stopped. I did stop. (I am a bit ashamed of myself here.)

Later, you wrote that I was completely tactless, hinting that you should get a coil, or the pill. Sorry about that.

But then you did indeed get the pill. And we became lovers.

And Self-Sufficient?

The smallholders again propose to buy a cow. The Accountant, of course, points out that using the figures they've produced for time, costs and milk yield, it's a loser. Plus what if we get sold a dud cow?

But Jay reworks the figures and makes a cow appear abundantly worthwhile. The Accountant doesn't believe it, but has other things on his mind.

We buy Hega, a Jersey Cow.

35
Summer 1976

Laurieston Hall is a down-at-heel, but comfy hostel, catering mainly for white middle-class English people having a good time while agonising over whether this is politically OK, plus a few white working-class Scots who remain understandably wary of us.

Taking an upbeat view, you might say we were, at least, a successful hotel business. Not that we use the H words (Hotel, Hostel, public House). Nor were we a B & B. Much less, a Café. Nor a Restaurant.

No! We are a PeopleCentre! We, er, well, like, we have groups of people to stay, and we cook for them, right? (The PA remembers a time when we thought there would be dozens of PeopleCentres.)

And so, this summer, we host another series of PeopleCentre weeks (most of them not organised by me). We do the business. Actually, we are good at this. Hundreds more people swoosh through, earning some of us our minimal living. Enabling us to keep the drones (as my inner voice calls them).

First of all was another Women's Week, during which all the men again de-camped. I went back to Drumglass, this time having it to myself. This was me, living alone, for the first time ever. I could scream and shout undisturbed. Play sax at 3 am. So I did. I pondered on my dependence on my co-communards - and contrasted this with how hard I found it to bear their actual company.

Actually I wasn't completely alone. The house cat brought in and, working steadily, ate a baby rabbit, leaving only the fur, stomach and guts. I was transfixed.

Next up was another Communes Network week - an event open to anyone with an interest in communal living (as opposed to the first ever Communes Gathering, which Birchwood were scheduled to host in September, for 'real' co-communards only.)

A wild, party-type week. During which you told me, with a theatrical sigh, as if it had been a chore, that you'd slept with Jay. And indeed, you've presented it that way ever since. Jay as your unfortunate, but inevitable fate.

Poor you. (Actually, I am sorry for you. At this point, I might have rather lost touch with my sanity, but you, I think, were emotionally dishonest and untruthful.)

A four-minute warning sounded in my head. I ran to my bed, cried, then slept for 18 hours. Patrick hit you, when you told him. I still find it hard to believe, Mrs. Feminist Poet, that you actually scolded me for never hitting you. But you did.

Nightmare ever since, really.

However, there was the A.S.Neill Trust weekend to cook for - having them here felt like quite an accolade - they exist to support Summerhill School (and free-schooling generally). For me this was cooking as therapy.

Then we hosted our own 'Free School' Week. Since we were still planning to make our own free school - that is, withdraw our kids from the village school - this should have been an important week for us. We held a rather staged meeting with the children themselves - a rare event. Surprise, surprise, they all said they'd like to leave school. So we drifted, in fact, into confirming our earlier decision. We'll do our own free school.

It is only later that I understand you thought, because I was so enthusiastic about de-schooling, that I'd forgotten about leaving with you this Autumn. Whereas I was thinking - this will be so good for LH. Even though you me, and J&S, will only be part of it for a short while...

Suddenly, Alice and I have a lot to do with each other, writing letters to the Education Authority. We summarise our proposed (fictional) syllabus and our (really extraordinary) range of academic qualifications. I still wondered if Alice might have twenty minutes, but I keep this thought to myself.

'Fish Week' was Tim's production and saw him coming briefly out of his isolation. His idea was to turn the pond into a productive fish farm. So the pond was drained, the existing trout being caught and kept in a small retaining pool. The major task would have been to clear out the accumulated sludge - but having seen just how much there was, it was decided this was too big a job. Too late, unfortunately, to stop herons eating all the trout.

Fish Week had about a dozen visitors (when we needed 40 plus to make a profit). So. negative inputs there, fish- and money-wise, comrade.

Alternative Socialism was the first national gathering meeting to discuss Keith P.'s paper - and this was my week to organise. It was a talking-late-into-the- night event. But some partying too. Mix Café was open a lot, because it seemed like a good idea to offer visitors the option, and because it was a last echo of the idea of an interaction between Living Group and Conference, the 'Place Of Learning' and the Home. The list of visitors defined a group which would expand and run - have several national gatherings - before fading (but could perhaps be seen as the basis of the Green Party).

Collectively, after Women's Week, no-one knew where to be. The East and West Ends re-dissolved. We mostly cooked in the Old Kitchen, ate in the front dining room - as if we were visitors ourselves (apart from Paul and Meg in Platform and Bridget and Tim on their own). It was suggested that we try and make the front dining room, all 600 cubic metres of it, cosy for winter and have it as our one communal home. I liked this suggestion

In August, in Mix Café, I presented my latest crazy idea for healing the commune/ having a good time - Making a film.

Which would start at dawn, from the top of the Meikle Dornell. The landscape, looking east, would be in silhouette, but begin to blaze. Beautiful Galloway. It is going to be a perfect Spring day. No sound so far - cinematic cliché.

As dawn breaks, the camera pans west to the CD by-pass. Picks up a westbound, huge, Volvo artic, rumbling to a stop. (This is the kind of truck which makes you feel, if you should float in one down the M6 from Shap Top, miles above the titchy cars, like a minor deity.) Next shot is at the roadside, with a hitcher bound (we soon find out) for LH. Sound is on. She thanks lorry-driver, slams the big door (a great, crunchy sound). The camera pulls back and pans clockwise, over Laurieston Village, and reaches the Hall itself. Zooms in on the WOW sign. I'll write a fanfare.

And first, there is an idyllic scene, in the big downstairs front living room. Which is transformed. Platforms have been built, so there is even more space. Everything is neat and in its place. A couple of people are laying out breakfast and making tea for the milking crew and other early risers.

'Well, you get the idea,' - I explain to the people in Mix Café - I think it was Alice, Jonathan, Tina, Patrick, and Catriona - 'it's everything we're not, it's our collective dream, if we can make one up…'

Then, I continue, the camera pulls back into the Hall and there's us, as our real selves, arguing. Surrounded by mess. And the film crew, and actors…The idea, I stumble to explain, is that actors play us. We each brief our own actor, then they improvise. And making the sets might be what we want to do anyway. Cinéma Verité or what? So we'd be filming our own, real attempts to grow and change. It's a documentary and a film-within-a-film. It might be fun, might bring out conflicts in a safe way, might give us some control, since real film and TV companies do often bang on our door?

What do you think?

But people were 'tired.' And went to bed.

You are not, I think to myself, half as fucking tired as me.

Michael: Banging, head, wall, which part of this do you not understand?

"Laurieston Hall is a community of 16 adults and 10 children. Summer '76 will be our fourth summer here. We support ourselves by working from here, including gardening and tending animals (Smallholding Project), looking after children from cities (Freefall Kids Project), organising conferences or providing space and facilities for others to organise their own (PeopleCentre Project), designing and building farm buildings and housing for local people (Building and Design Project) and selling what we make ourselves (Craft Project, Garden Sales.)". (Alice's blurb for this summer's visitors.)

And the people are:

Alice and Dave, who have remained a couple.

Alice has taken to declaring 'this place exploits me as a woman.' None of the other women have the faintest idea what she is on about. As if she wasn't in charge!

Meanwhile Dave, did, after all this time, just before Women's Week, call a Men's Meeting!

Carol, sporadically. She took Tam and Tiff over to Gatehouse for a week, to live with Roger L., initially for a trial period. But from then on, she was essentially doing a long-drawn-out move.

Jonathan, who wrote "My story with Julia ended in speechlessness. From empty phrases to no phrases at all. Maybe now I could respond to her if our lives weren't tied together through living in the same community. As it is, I see only her indifference to "the place," her contempt for what shelters and supports her."

Suddenly, Jonathan has an attack of activism. He writes: "We must now be energetically concerned with:

1. Living together (support warmth understanding personal criticism consumption)
2. Working together or co-operatively and Division Of Labour. This year's magic word is synthesis.
3. Earning Our Living.
4. Self-Sufficiency.
5. Political work, people work."

And he adds: "How can we live together in a way which strengthens us in times of crisis?" But then he writes, "the powers of reason always speak ironically, or doodle at the typewriter, putting inverted commas round every difficult word, for most words have continued to lose meaning." Yes dear, I'm sure they have.

Not Julia. As pre-announced, Julia left with Arthur, moved to Lothlorien - and took George and Bill with her, which she'd promised not to do. Her plan was to school Bill at Lothlorien - fit him into their tutor system - while George would go to Corsock Primary. So our own planned de-school was shrinking fast.

Everybody was shocked. Nobody knew what to say, except of course your PA, who obliged with an angry, abusive and of course unproductive tirade. Which Julia refused to listen to. The PA has a word for Julia at this point.

The Accountant (still me, despite what Alice says earlier) who in Alt. Socialism week spends a couple of days providing Keith P. with a three-page analysis to explain just why it was fair for us to charge £2.50 a day for full board as standard, £1.75 concessions, £1.25 for kids. To support us living on an average of £12.50 per week, per person.

(I know, makes you think of your grand-dad, or perhaps his grand-dad, doesn't it? Back when wages were £10 a year but then, you could buy a 6-bed detached house in Hampstead for £150?)

Tim And Bridget. Who now, it seems, are to move into far cottage - Liz having moved up to Grobdale with Alice B. - pay no rent, and have practically nothing to do with us. While Bridget is developing her own, independent pottery business in the stables. And Angus will still go to Laurieston school, and not be part of our Free School. An Alice-in-wonderland situation.

Lesley and Richard. While the PO has been penning, but not sending, absurdly apologetic farewell notes to Lesley - about how his relationship with her isn't, um, really working - he is the last to realise that in fact, Rich and Lesley have become the new, beautiful couple on the block. They are still together as I write this in 2008. You can't argue with that.

Paul and Meg. Once again, Paul has drawn up yet another list of 'absolutely vital' house maintenance work. You have to admire his tenacity, which is similar to mine for precision and Jonathan's for vagueness.

And his latest idea, taken from Lothlorien, is that we should hold hands in a circle before we eat. I think, silly fucker. He does not realise just how far away I am from holding hands in any circle involving him. (But of course, Paul was right: we could have held hands, and maybe felt better. Now that it is too late, I am sorry.)

Meanwhile, we all begin to notice that Meg is - well, depressed is probably an under-statement. And the PA and others often find themselves consoling Robbie and nappy changing him.

Catriona, with whom the PO likes to spend time. But as she rightly says, 'we were never in love, because you weren't there.'

Tina, Mike, Patrick, Jay and Georgina V. Perhaps it was all the 'too polite to refuse' syndrome, but it seems to me you get some kind of prize here, being the first person to have three ongoing heterosexual relationships, while also trying to nurture a new lesbian fling.

In fact, I think you were rather apologetic with Georgina V., explaining - as you worked together later, doing serious car mechanics - that you shouldn't have led her on, given that your life was rather full already, relationship-wise. You had quite a case-load.

Patrick, of course, would simply have insisted you were his lover. You would have had to duck and dive to see Jay at all. Or me. Or Georgina V.

Even so, people were already beginning to bracket the two of you together. 'Jay and Tina', they say, have gone shopping for a cow. Fencing. Dairy equipment.

So 'Jay and Tina' enters the lexicon.

Nigel. Who is certainly a fixture by now. The PO is not clear when and if he stops being a long-stay-visitor and becomes a member. He comes to meetings. Ditto Linda. It is all a bit like Tony's osmotic joining process.

And while *Flick A.* and *Keith C.* are also omnipresent, they never in fact ask to join. And they fade away separately…

July. A nationwide drought - pictures of dried-up reservoirs, their underlying clay split into mosaics. Suburban lawns - my Mum and Dad's included - turned brown. Suddenly used bathwater is termed 'grey water' and is dolloped nationwide onto tomatoes.

We however are still blessed with burn water. Farmer Gordon's sons again call in for water for their cattle.

The Building Project advertised for work in the Galloway News. No-one replied. I did say it shouldn't have said, 'LH Building Collective,' it should have been 'Simpson & Daughter.'

I had begun to take a childish, stupid pleasure in being proved right, when things went wrong. I radiated huge sarcasm and cynicism.

August and September rushed by. We were busy with Freefall - more Craigmillars, more women-with-kids groups from Glasgow and Rochdale, more Gingerbreads. Everyone shells broad beans. And we had another Garden Party for all our local friends. As part of the entertainment, the PA taught himself to fire-breathe. That is, to spit paraffin onto a lit torch, making a jet of flame. It's mildly impressive. How does paraffin taste? Horrible, let me tell you.

36

> *"Laurieston Hall is a filthy, neglected satellite spinning in*
> *permanent, earth-static orbit miles above Kirkcudbrightshire. A*
> *sixty-five room space slum, groaning with hopelessness, leaking*
> *misery." (Mixcaff Diary.)*

And Multiple Relations?
I try and talk with you about your promise to leave, but you simply say 'It wasn't like that.' You sidestep, saying you're too worried about the children and the Free School.

For some reason, we go together to the Laurie Arms - we never have before, just the two of us - and sit in its posh, newly-built lounge bar, to talk this through.

'The children will be fine, either way,' is my opinion. 'So could we talk about us? I'm wondering what I can rely on from you?'

'It would be better if we did not have expectations of each other.' Is what you said.

'What?'

'It's probably better not to have any expectations at all.'

It was a while before I could speak. I was thinking 'After sixteen years, I'm not allowed to have expectations?'

'So I should stop talking about us leaving together?'

'I think that would be good for a while.'

Actually, Mrs., I think this was you, very clearly and conclusively, ending our marriage. This is about a year ago now (I am catching myself up quite fast, here).

Of course, we will struggle on for a while. Ditto, you and Patrick (until you ultimately commit to paper that you really, really need to be apart from him).

So this leaves you and Jay. He is doing the decent thing - also the easy thing - hanging back, waiting for you to sort yourself out.

I Thought You'd Split Into Two Living Groups?
'Laurieston Lists' wrote Jonathan, 'is a very freaky thing to be doing.'

Which is odd, because of course we have been here before - proposing dividing up the 14 adults - Tim and Bridget weren't included - and sometimes the long stay visitors, too - into Living Groups. Amazingly, nearly everyone had a go at this. The process drags on into the Autumn. In the meantime an ad-hoc 'Sunny Room Group' flickers into existence.

37
Autumn 1976

Later that Autumn, I wake up in Catriona's bed. In her top-floor corner room, which used to be Lesley's. And which now has its ceiling lowered with catenaries of colourful cloth and its walls packed with weavings, tapestries, dried flowers, sketches, 'seed pictures,' postcards and photographs. Every surface is covered - with books, stones, carvings, tools, balls of wool. Her guitar rests on the chaise-longue which belonged to my grandparents. On the floor is a rug, patiently plaited from jumble-sale scraps. It's beautiful, Alternative Technology. She's a recycler, is Catriona.

We're lovers, but I can't become a couple with her.

Partly because I don't want to give Tina the comeback - if I tackle her about Jay - 'Well what about you and Catriona?'

Partly because she'll soon transform from the warm, slender, sexy being she is now, next to me, into Loud Woman, stomping about, slamming doors, wearing serious glasses and the trousers with the nineteen patches. The formidable antithesis of conventional glamour. Someone whom I'm not used to, yet.

And partly because I think - she doesn't want that, either.

Outside, gorse is still flowering, there are black seed pods on the broom. Soft, white clusters of hazel nuts are blown to the ground. New kinds of fungi are brought home - we have experts to identify the tasty ones. Splotches of autumn colour appear on the beeches and the horse-chestnut, as if sprayed by giant aerosols.

Still no-one knows where to live, but this situation continues to be masked by the constant wash of visitors.

Somerstown returned after a long gap, with Sue C. (who's by now friend rather than lover). We had Special Needs kids from Beormund School in London. Glasgow I.S., a couple more times. A.S.Neill for another weekend - and it's such a long journey for them for just two nights. An adult group from Craigmillar. More Mackintoshes.

Visitors helped out. The garden is cleared of pea and broad bean haulm. In the house, there is much freezing and drying of vegetables and herbs;

salting of bacon; cold-storing of potatoes. And crumbling of blackberry and apple, syruping of rose-hips and winemaking.

On clear nights, people lie on tables on the lawn, gawping up at the universe - because our patch of sky is indeed star-filled and mind-blowing.

The 'Laurieston Lists' process - deciding who wants to live with whom - continued. The PO could devote an entire thesis to just this one episode and still have more to say.

Jay typed, rather formally: "I think all variations on the two ends system are doomed to failure without a Great Leap Forward (GLF) in who we are and what we are capable of. I have been thinking of small close contented living groups as being the springboard for this GLF. But it won't come out of space. Nine o'clock meetings won't suddenly just work one day, however we go on trying it again and pouring our energies into it. Best not to rush into anything on the usual 'Well, I'll give it a try, I don't think it'll work, but it would be great if it did.' basis. This is how 90% of our energy for creating communal organisation goes straight down the drain. Thus despair remains all powerful."

Thanks, comrade, for that really helpful contribution. No seriously

Nigel scribbled that he wanted whatever group he was in to work on an 'encounter style' level. Reading his handwriting is seriously slow, hard work, like translating from a foreign language you don't know too well. But he does say - he won't live with Meg, but would be OK with Paul. Very worthy, I thought.

Richard says 'There seem to be some bad vibes about Bridget and Tim.' (Well spotted, Richard! We are approaching the same planet.)

Alice writes 'In the past I've tried to suggest solutions for other people - now I'm going to say what I want, for a change'. I am grateful to Alice here for the sudden realisation as to what is meant by 'hollow' laughter.

But of course, Alice reveals little of herself. Except that she wouldn't want to live with Rich, after he quit the Aga group, calling it 'too bourgeois.'

Tina wrote that her priorities were to live with "(a) Michael (b) people with attitudes close to mine and (c) people who are even-tempered/ easy-going" - while acknowledging these three criteria may be incompatible.

Let me tell you, darling, if you want (a) you are not going about it the right way.

For a while, nothing much happened.

Patrick imagined Alice and Dave "tucked up with their hot water bottles."

Mike noted that Meg and Paul, in their luxury flat, sorry - Platform Room - had both a brand-new, private woodstove and gleaming, made-in-Sweden steel axe.

The Accountant presumes this is Meg spending her remaining private money, rather than pooling it. Ah, well. It's all too late.

Jay spots that Tim and Bridget have the "Wine-of-the-month-club wine in their larder." "And they lie down," Tina speculated, "with their long limbs plaited together for extra strength."

Lesley canoodled publicly with Richard. Sits on his knee, as they play - like children - This is the way the lady rides. Her tits bouncing. Jonathan and Jay were shut off round Jay's fire.

But a new pattern emerges quite suddenly.

Carol, earning her first money as a yoga teacher in CD, promptly takes it with her - and moves in with Roger L. over at Syllodioch.

Tim and Bridget, having simply squatted the far cottage (with little positive approval - in fact, despite some quite vocal opposition), demanded 'financial independence.' The Accountant notes this is a difficult request to refuse ('No, we don't accept that, kindly sign over all your current cash and future income'). He notes also there is no offer to pay rent. On the other hand, the PO feels it's probably for the best. All things considered (as the usual exaggeration flies). Besides, as an anarchist himself, the PA understands he is always free to act. Both now, or in the future.

Michael, Catriona, Tina, Patrick, Alice and Jonathan hold a 'group most likely to' meeting - and stay on in Sunny Room/ Mix Café.

But then Jonathan defected, moving instead, with Jay, Lesley, Richard, Dave and Linda, into Tim and Bridget's former kitchen, now renamed The Squat. Actually, Jon, that was a slap in the face. I really wanted and needed your company, and had hoped you needed mine.

So there is a new round of room-swaps.

And the children were distributed: Polly, Sonya, Sophie and Joel in Sunny Room; Molly in The Squat; Angus down at the cottage (and still attending school, 'because he likes it'). And Tam and Tiffany joining George and Bill as commuters.

For whatever reason, I can't now remember what kicked this off, I left finally - for the second time. That you were again off with Patrick, was definitely involved.

I stayed up all night and hitched off the end of the drive at 6 a.m., in a moon-lit mist, aiming first at Lancaster. This time, it's a bit obvious I'm play-acting. The P&CRP are scheduled to visit in a month's time and I can hardly not be home. On the other hand I'm not actually living at LH. I've taken one of Alice B.'s spare rooms up at Grobdale. With its wide, soft colours.

I join with a P&CRP meeting. Listened to arguments over lunch between the P&CRP's Politicos and Alternatives.

Politicos: Capital is in crisis. Fascism is rising. Essential not to 'opt out of the struggle.'

Alternatives: The alternative is working. SUMA is shifting hundreds of tons of wholefood every week. Others, magazines, crafts. The Grauniad now has an Alternatives ads section (woodstoves, Korean ginseng, saunas). Politicos achieve nothing, merely perpetuate conflict.

It seems neither group can really hear the other. How like home. Except, I no longer know whether I'm a world political or an alternative geezer. Or at home, a clown or a madman.

And of course they all ask, first, 'How is Laurieston?' - which leaves me gasping - rather than 'How are you?' Which I might cope with better.

I was aware the P&CRP was thought by Lancaster Uni establishment to be too lively and chaotic - they wanted rid of it. But, embarrassingly for them, the P&CRP was always World Famous in the eyes of US and Canadian academics. That afternoon, there was to be a Review, by the Chancellor, the Lord High Factotum, the Subfuscs and Daleks.

Stafford Beer, the famous systems guru, was the independent on the Review Team. Everyone queued up to meet him - so all and sundry were gob-smacked when he and I have a big hug and loud hello (we'd been drinking mates in past lives.) The P&CRP lives on. I do hope I'd helped.

Before I left them, I confirmed that everyone - both staff and students - would be welcome to come and visit Laurieston in November and let us have their thoughts...

I can't remember how I got to Leeds, but vaguely recollect getting pished on Pete Somebody's homebrew, singing songs with him and some other blokes playing piano and guitars, and sleeping the sleep of the drunk alongside Bridget R. Then hitching south to Sheffield, working a volunteer shift in the Brick Rabbit 'alternative' caff, staying with Shirley L. and hearing her voice in the morning coming out of the radio at 5.45 a.m. Momentary panic until I remember, she works for Radio Sheffield.

Spinning a coin by Sheffield's M1 viaducts. Choosing between South (London) or North (vaguely, homewards). Comes up, North. My first lift was to Barnsley. So then I aimed at Townhead, the home of Lifespan. And by 11 a.m. I am shifting barrow-loads of topsoil for a herb patch and after lunch collapsing into bed with Lindsey X., a previous one-night stand, who had, by chance, arrived to stay the day before.

Some kind of constructive serendipity there, then.

And the next morning, utter confusion until I remember where I am. And sleeping next to, er, Pat T., it turns out. After which, I came home.

And you don't like all this, do you? Because you really want me to fall for someone else, make a real new relationship. So you can sort yourself out with Pat. No, cancel that. With Jay, of course.

Incredibly, the commune holds together. There was a little money in the bank. Dave and Richard did an outside building job, with Paul as self-appointed (and resented) supervisor.

And on Sunday 17th October 1976, in Sunny Room, we hosted a 'Yes, We Have No Collective' social evening. Everybody came. Alice showed the early slides (for the children, this was for the first time). We had an 'odd-sock swap.' It was a friendly, companionable evening.

Then everyone bar Paul and Meg coalesced in Sunny Room. Mix Café's limited cooking facilities struggled to cope.

Dave built an excellent metal and concrete fireplace which aproned into Sunny Room and warmed the group as it lurched towards Christmas.

By the end of October, the free school experiment was failing fast.
Except I had a super day with Sophie, visiting Glasgow, to do I don't remember what. But just to have a full day, with the long drive each way, and to chat away was magic. And it was such a focus.

I mean, how do you tell your children about the Big Bang? Galaxies? The Origins Of Life? Amoebae? Bacteria? Stuff like that? (Let alone evolution.)

And Soph was inquisitive, sharp, sceptical, all the way. As we stopped for tea, periodically, I had to draw diagrams.

But more usually, day after day, either nothing would happen or various combinations of parents would sit glumly with children trying to figure out what to do.

It's all very well to assume children will learn by doing - when adults have something to do. But we were in limbo.

Meanwhile Meg announced she was "...going to Glasgow for a short while - with Polly, Robbie and Paul. I can't really explain why I'm going but I s'pose it's to smoke dope, eat greasy fish suppers and talk to people who actually enjoy my company. Instead of here, where 'Paul and Meg' are such a problem. We're taking the Ami, which allows you all the luxury of not being dependent on motor vehicles."

I think: Yes, Ma'am! Lord and Lady Muck! Take whatever you need!

And then we had the much-heralded, partly exciting, partly feared, visit from the P&CRP people. I feel my course title has switched to Applied Schizophrenia. Because I want the Programme people to admire this LH Commune - although it is clearly a shambles - and to love me - the red-eyed wreck over there in the corner.

38

And Have You Stopped Beating Your Wife?
We hitched to Birchwood Hall, didn't we? Where we'd stayed, five years before, with Paul and Alice - and kicked this whole thing off. This time, it was with Alice and Dave. And the first ever Communes conference. So we made, or renewed links with Glaneirw, Towy, East, Dragon, Buckingham Road, Old Hall, St. Julian's, Crabapple, Lifespan, Wheatstone.

But none between you and me. We didn't fuck once.

Moving into October, although it was less than a year ago now, I can't remember which came first.

Maybe you'd told Patrick you were finishing with him and he went away, saying he'd be gone for three months - but he came back after only two weeks, didn't he, old fuckface, and you jumped into bed with him, with your usual 'You don't mind, do you, love, his first night back.?'

Well, yes I do. How long does this story have to go on?

And then you went off with him on a 'working holiday' to Ireland - drumming up Freefall business.

Alternatively, it was Ireland first (and I'm a brave single parent, in the midst of living group chaos), then his foreshortened trip away. Either way, you finish up in bed with Patrick. And like a fool I am pre-occupied with this. I quite forget that the crocodile waiting smugly in the shallows is Jay.

Later, you wrote of an 'accelerating distance' from me. I think you got sympathy for that. But it was your foot on the pedal.

How Do you Make A Living?
The Accountant writes his annual 12-page report. Which boils down, for 1975/ 76 - Year 4 - to: Total expenses, £10712. Income, £9550. Net Loss, £1162. No-one pays much attention.

And Beating Your Wife?
We had a recap.

'If I leave properly, will you be able to cope OK?' I would have meant, with being a single parent.

'Yes,' you replied, 'I suppose so.'

'And you still think we should have no expectations of each other?'
'Yes.'

How Did The Rooms Get Their Names?
Nah, how sweet. That one again, amidst the chaos. From the P&CRP students. The earlier names are in a guide-book-type handout. Some copies remain. More recently we have: Teapot - some kids painted a big teapot. Library - was once our library. Bean - we dried broad beans there. Sewing, Ali's Old, The Squat - guess. Mix café - was Mike's idea. Bit boring, really.

And Do You All Sleep With Each Other?
(By now, Crabapple, bravely, have indeed tried this out. But with a 'non-sexual' clause written in there.)

I reply, 'Not anymore,' implying we are now wise beyond comprehension. As you do. The inquirer's face is a picture.

And Are You Self-Sufficient?
From the garden, I believe we have globe and Jerusalem artichokes and sweetcorn.

The goats have gone, except for Quest, another billy, who became our third goat suicide - strangled himself on his tether cord a few months later.

And The Wife?
At least, you did split with Pat. The Diary sees him writing 'This Is Not A Crisis' and waffling about his defence mechanisms. Specifically: "I feel the gap between understanding that Jay and Tina being loving with each other is a good thing, and the fact that Jay is simply a next-door neighbour, not someone whose feelings I can share or appreciate."

We have got the poor lad talking bollocks. And, incidentally, writing poetry - 'The Gordian Slip-Knot' - but I will save his blushes and your patience, Dear Reader.

39
Winter 1976/77

In December I floated down from Grobdale on the first day of Dave's Work Collectives week, to do a cooking day - I'm still hanging on to membership-by-participation. Jonathan wonders why, and I explain (a) I do like to cook and (b) I want to see who's here. Indeed, the house is bustling and the delegate list reads like a mini-directory of the working alternative movement. And (c) to see Catriona. Also (d) my kids live here, remember?

Catriona: I just hope I wasn't a complete shit.

I think I said, 'I'm sorry our relationship is a bit funny.' Actually I was frightened of losing you.

(Writing this, nine months later. You have taken up with Pete D. Who has joined in the interim, and who wrote of a Maxi-Coop meeting, "Jolly interesting to hear about all that theory and stuff." No comment.)

But we still are, tender, caring, sympathetic, yes? Sexual, but not blouse-rippingly-passionate?)

Tina: we had an almighty row about Christmas, remember?

I was hoping, absurdly it now seems, that being away with you and the children would in some way repair us. You know, us and the kids, together...

I think I was being so heavy about it, you said maybe it would be better if we didn't go. Then I freaked, got hysterical. So we went.

Of course, it was useless. At my parents, then at your Mum's, we turned in more-or-less competent performances of happy family. There are so many times I'm not proud of.

New Year's Eve: Picture Sunny room. Records playing, failing to hide the thick silence.

The children subdued. I'm holding Catriona's hand and rubbing her neck a bit as she cries softly but openly. Paul comes in and offers me his hand, but his face looks tense and I don't dare take it. Don't want to catch his disease.

The PO pinned up:
"They all looked drugged or half-asleep... in their fouled and disgusting streets full of ordure and bits of refuse... as if they were

253

somewhere else... they walked and moved and went about their
lives in a condition of sleepwalking... essentially isolated, shut in,
enclosed... inside a net of wants and needs that made it impossible
for them to think of anything else." (Doris Lessing, The Four-
Gated City.)

I have mentioned 'depression' quite often. And you have often charged me, so to speak, with being depressed. As if you are saying 'after all the love I gave you.'

As though it was my fault, my choice. And before Laurieston too. You will hark back to the Obidos trip, when we lived in Cascais - a day when I was worried sick about work, listless, pissed-off with the kids.

And it was true, the prospect of being father-provider and mortgage-payer for another thirty-five years often wiped the smile off.

But I saw myself as the joker, the entertainer, the happy-go-lucky. When the pressure got heavy, I could laugh at my place, part of this five-billion species, marooned on an obscure planet, a mere molecule of a cell in the bloodstream of the mysterious elephant of the universe, nothing to be afraid of.

Your actual, guaranteed genuine, rock-solid depression, which makes a walking disaster area out of everyone it touches, only arrived about now.

New Year's Day was when it became clear that you and Jay, gone away separately, were in fact together. Right, that's me then. Leaving finally for the third and last time. Taking the Ami. Sax and LPs in the boot. Dumb Toms, here we come. Depression didn't last.

40
September 1977

And Have You Stopped Meeting Your Wife?
Foolishly I left my heart in your pocket. Could I have it back, please?

You write, "I wove myself into you and you into me. It was a fault which ran the length of our fabrics"

Another time, "Your sobs shake me more than my own. The times I've lain hurting for you."

Of course by now, I have realised this is you as the Writer. Giving your character, 'Tina,' feelings you would like her to have.

Why Did You Leave?
The PO is not going to attempt a review of 1977. He's described bits and pieces.

"Mike is still bombarding us with his writings from Dumb Tom's."

The main event in September was that - as predicted - Tina, Jay, Jonathan (and Joel, and Sophie) moved back to London, to set up Kollontai collective, together with Sheila E. (and Sarah and Emma).

And the PO, the PA, me, Michael - leaves Dumb Tom's and follows them, to be near J & S. I moved in temporarily with John and Wisty H.

You and I saw each other hardly at all. But we did the last run of the Christmas farce. Some odd building your brother G. was inhabiting was the last place, the last time, we fucked. So it goes.

And Self-Sufficiency
You can't beat a good list. Bridget, still down at the cottage, just wrote, before going on holiday:

1. Make sure chickens always have water.
2. Silkies - soft fruit. One small plastic bucket (in 1st bin) of laying mix (3rd bin). In the morning, collect eggs and put in grain store. Turn all eggs in grain store daily.
3. By garden wall: check food (layer's mash) and collect eggs. If one goes broody put it in a box quietly by itself with some food and water until I get back.
4. Keep all the feed hoppers topped up (we need a sack of soya meal and 1 cwt of mixed grains, or wheat if unavailable, from CD) .

5. Ducks get one pressure cooker full of cooked stock-feed tatties mixed round with small plastic bucketful of cracked wheat. One duck usually lays under window in Hega's stall. Otherwise just keep a look out for eggs (alternatively give one coffee tin full of cracked wheat.)
6. Geese get ¾ small bucketful of cracked wheat. You may have to give the gander a good kick to stop him from attacking you. Keep ducks and geese separate when feeding.

So: Why Did You Leave?

I've been focussed on last Christmas and New Year. Remembering again the cup of cold coffee Lesley threw. It's felt weird, climbing up the ladder of the past in a desperate attempt to meet myself.

But suddenly, I've caught myself up.

Here I am.

Spring 2008

I made the notes for this epic while still a student of the P&CRP, during 1976-77. Then I spent a couple of years trying to wrestle this stuff into a book. I couldn't do it. Time moved on. The notes sat in boxes. I met Sue B. (now my wife of 25 years), had other interests. Thirty years zipped by.

Laurieston Hall is no longer an income-sharing commune. However it is home to a thriving community, within a housing association framework. There is still a high degree of co-operation regarding shared chores (maintenance, wood-collecting) and work projects (running conferences and events, gardening, livestock).

I am looking at photos from Spring 2003, when Sophie commandeered the house for her Bollywood-style wedding. And here we have: Jay and Tina - Tina with a fabric pot-plant for a hat, which keeps pricking the side of my face as we eat. Jonathan is there. Alice, Patrick, Richard and Lesley are still rezzies. Carol, Julia, Linda and Paul - all living locally - pop by. Of the other Groans referred to here, Bridget, Tim, Catriona, Dave, Meg, Stuart, and Nigel are alive and mostly well. Sadly, Nicky Walton died in 1989.